The English Novel
in the Nineteenth Century

The English Novel
in the Nineteenth Century

ESSAYS ON THE LITERARY MEDIATION

OF HUMAN VALUES

edited by George Goodin

ILLINOIS STUDIES IN
LANGUAGE AND LITERATURE
63

University of Illinois Press

URBANA CHICAGO LONDON

© 1972 by The Board of Trustees of the University of Illinois
Manufactured in the United States of America
Library of Congress Catalog Card No. 71-186344
ISBN 0-252-00288-1

In gratitude to
ROYAL A. GETTMANN
from some of his students
for all of his students

Contents

Preface

Although the following essays were written to celebrate the man to whom this volume is dedicated, they also celebrate the idea which has informed the work of Royal Gettmann — that the most important contribution of literature to our knowledge of human values can be revealed only by a study which is itself distinctively literary. His classroom sessions usually ended with tentative suggestions connecting the work at hand with permanent human concerns, but they always started with questions about specific literary details. Indeed, he thought the subject of "Asking the First Question" so crucial that he devoted an essay to it, and there he explained the method that so many of his students have felt with wonder. "But however important the Author and the Reader may be, my first question should be focused upon the Work. An inquiry about the first two may carry the discussion into psychology, sociology, anthropology, or even current problems, regions where I am a grotesque amateur. But the Work is peculiarly and distinctly my province, by training and by preference. . . . Before I have done with *Madame Bovary* I may touch upon Flaubert's 'World View,' but I had better begin with a question, say, about the description of Charles's hat" (*College English,* XXVIII [1966], 592). Such a method implies that the growth of a person and of his knowledge about human values depends on reading life *out of,* not *into,* a literary work. Paradoxically, the contrary procedure of beginning with large views about life itself is more apt in the end to produce merely literary knowledge.

The idea of a distinctly literary approach to literature is, of course, widespread today, largely because of Coleridge, who attributed it partly to his own schoolmaster, the Reverend James Bowyer. In one of the handsomest tributes a student ever made to his teacher, he wrote, "I learnt from him that poetry, even that of the loftiest and, seemingly, that of the wildest odes, had a logic of its own as severe as that of science; and more difficult, because more subtle, more complex, and dependent on more, and more fugitive, causes. In the truly great poets, he would say, there is a reason assignable, not only for every word, but for the position of every word." The poet frees himself from the logic of science by his intention of giving pleasure rather than truth, but the by-product of this intention and the end of poetry itself is knowledge, a knowledge that is accessible only through the attention to details that a search for poetic logic requires. Just as, for Carlyle, happiness can arise only from the pursuit of something else, so the truths of most concern to literary criticism arise indirectly — mediated through the rhetorical choices with which the poet attempted to give pleasure.

For this reason, two of the most desirable qualities in the student of literature are discipline and a concern for the human. Not many years ago the second of these was often neglected in the hope that literary scholarship and criticism could be a science; a concern for values was considered a threat to the desired objectivity of literary study. At present we may be facing the opposite danger of excessive subjectivity. In both cases there is a presumption that values in literature are too evanescent for discussion. They are indeed evanescent, and for this reason are more satisfactorily studied in the give and take of teaching. There the framework of assumptions that constitutes a discipline can be continually challenged, the questions that we ask can be refined, more proof can be demanded, the tangential can receive its due, and the irrelevant can be exposed.

These essays cannot possess that advantage, but the ideal they hold up is the same — to argue from questions of literary technique to conclusions about human values, to argue, for example, from Charles Bovary's hat to Flaubert's world view.

ONE

The Hostile Universe: A Developing Pattern in Nineteenth-Century Fiction

BY LEE T. LEMON

If the purpose of serious literature is to help man make sense of his experience, the special province of literary narrative is to expand our awareness of the forces that determine our fates. Very generally, every narrative shows man in relation to the world about him. More specifically, though, because the irreducible nature of narrative involves a protagonist and an antagonist in some kind of conflict, the picture shown is not a still life but an action shot of forces in opposition — of man wanting, and of man being temporarily or permanently frustrated. Despite the ingenuity of novelists in varying the elementary pattern — from multiple protagonists and antagonists at one extreme to the protagonist whose desires are mutually incompatible and who is therefore his own antagonist at the other — the basic concern of serious fiction is the individual against the forces that determine his destiny. Allowing for such windage factors as tone and point of view, a goodly part of our analysis of fiction consists of abstracting the elements involved in the conflict and estimating the strength of the tensions generated so that we may understand the value system implicit in the narrative.

In the remainder of this essay I shall survey a number of classic nineteenth-century novels and glance at a few earlier works in order to characterize the forces against which the authors pitted their heroes. The pattern that will emerge as we move from the early to the late years of the nineteenth century will be one of increasing complexity, of the growing complication of those fate-determining forces. It would be tempting to relate that increasing complexity to broadly cultural developments — views of the beneficence of nature before and after Darwin, of the social order during the political turmoil of the period, of religion during the theological and ethical controversies raging then, and so on. Such a study would, I believe, be quite valuable, but this is a comparatively brief essay, and so shall limit itself merely to outlining that increasingly complex pattern within the fiction.

First, however, a few disclaimers. There are exceptions to the pattern I shall describe. Scott's *Heart of Midlothian* and Hogg's *Confessions of a Justified Sinner,* despite their dated manners, are exceptionally complex in their presentation of the elements that determine human fate; in that respect neither novel is typical of its period. Second, I do not mean to imply that because, for example, Hardy's view of human destiny in *Jude the Obscure* is more complex than Austen's in *Pride and Prejudice,* the former is the better novel. Other things being equal — as they are not in this instance — I should want to make that argument, but that is another argument. Third, I shall not attempt to establish radically new interpretations of the novels I examine; to do so, even if it were necessary, would require considerably more detailed analysis than there is space for here. The contribution of this study lies not in its original analyses of individual works but in the pattern it attempts to clarify.

If we ask why Elizabeth Bennet and Darcy meet the fates they do — not only their presumably happy marriage but also the delays to that eventual bliss — we find that the answer Jane Austen suggests in *Pride and Prejudice* sounds curiously old-fashioned and simple. The things that happen to Elizabeth and Darcy, and to the other characters in the novel, happen to them because they are the kinds of persons they are — but not in any Freudian sense, for Austen's characters are much the same on the outside as they are on the inside.

A large part of the machinery of *Pride and Prejudice* is, in fact, devoted to describing just what kinds of characters the *dramatis personae* are. Perhaps I can make this point and another by citing some of the important areas of human concern that are omitted from *Pride and Prejudice.* External nature does not exist in the novel, except to give Jane a slight cold so that Elizabeth, in order to nurse her, may visit the Bingleys and attract the attention of Darcy. There is no concern with either organized or natural religion, nor with politics and social reform, nor with psychological complexity. The characters are delineated solely by their social relationships with each other, and the nature of those relationships is defined by what and who the characters are.

This singleness of purpose in *Pride and Prejudice* might be most quickly recalled by noting the manner in which the irony of the opening sentence doubles back upon itself. When Jane Austen tells us, "It is a truth universally acknowledged, that a single man in possession of a good fortune, must be in want of a wife," our natural skepticism about such universal truths is aroused. The skepticism is quickly reinforced when we learn that the vacuous Mrs. Bennet lives by that belief and the more intelligent characters seem to reject it. Thus far, we have the split vision typical of irony — in this case, the split between the "universal truth" and the way things really are. But by the time the novel is completed, we learn that each "single man in the possession of a good fortune" who appears in the novel is indeed in search of a wife; Bingley and Darcy, the men of good fortune, do in fact pursue and marry their women. (Jane Austen also suggests a corollary: that single young men not in possession of good fortunes do not seek matrimony, as the examples of Reverend Collins and Wickham show.) Even though Darcy is temporarily blinded by his pride and Elizabeth by her prejudice, the irony of the opening sentence of the novel turns out to be only apparently irony. It takes, I believe, a writer supremely assured of her purpose and of the harmony of her world to play such complex games with a "universal truth."

Although there is temporary blindness in the world of *Pride and Prejudice* (and foolishness in the characters of Mrs. Bennet and Reverend Collins), there are no irreconcilable difficulties. Even when characters are misjudged — as Darcy and Wickham are misjudged by Elizabeth — Jane Austen shows the source of the error to be in the subject rather than in the object. Darcy and Wickham are misjudged not because they are complex and certainly not because there is any fundamentally confusing depth in their characters; they are misjudged, rather, because of a defect in Elizabeth's otherwise fine character — her prejudice against Darcy. And because her character is basically sound, the disharmony between the world as she sees it and as it is, is only temporary.

I am perhaps oversimplifying somewhat. Elizabeth's prejudice against Darcy is in part justified; his pride is equally justified because he is the most attractive and capable man in the novel, and because the thought of Mrs. Bennet for a mother-in-law is sufficient to give any reasonable man pause. But the essential point is that in Jane Austen's world characters may change — not radically, but their imperfections may be smoothed away — as they become aware of the world around them. Life is sufficiently orderly that one has only to grow up enough to perceive it intelligently, to act accordingly, and to accept the appropriate reward.

It is important to note that the perception of life is limited almost exclusively to its social aspects. Perhaps the crucial action in the novel in this respect is the Wickham-Lydia elopement. What is surprising in the action is, largely, the attitudes that are not present. Wickham is not a moral monster (in the manner of, say, Richardson's Lovelace); he is not a schemer (like Dickens's Uriah Heep), nor a coldly calculating seducer of young virgins (like Dickens's Steerforth), nor a star-crossed, demonic lover (like Emily Brontë's Heathcliff), nor a fated, economically deprived figure (like Hardy's Jude). When the elopement is discovered, there is no significant outcry about ruined maids or the loss of virtue. It is a social blunder, not a moral evil, and Wickham is proved to be what the reader knew him to be all along — not an evil man but a rather shallow cad.

I should add quickly that I am not accusing Jane Austen of moral insensitivity. The discriminations she makes among her characters are too precise for that. The point is, rather, that the issues that plague later novelists do not infect her world. It is curious, for example, how little we are told of Darcy apart from his character as a social being. Yet, perhaps, we could confidently guess much about him — if guessing about the life of a fictional character were not a cardinal sin of criticism. We confidently assume that Darcy has all of the religious, moral, and economic opinions appropriate to one in his social position, and that when he is not on scene in the novel, he is doing nothing that would surprise us. From start to finish Darcy is a gentleman; although he is a bit rude at times, he is completely defined by that essentially social term. His reasons for interfering with Bingley's marriage are those of a gentleman, as are his reasons for approving it later. He has only to learn, to adjust his perception of the world, not to change himself radically.

It is as if Jane Austen considered Darcy to be so clearly defined by his social position that she felt no need to explore his motivation, his beliefs, and so on — just as, apparently, she assumed (unlike Emily Brontë) that there was no need to dwell upon the cruelty of nature when Jane caught cold.

What we are considering, then, is actually a matter of focus. This is not to suggest that Jane Austen's view of the world is simple — far from it. She presents a fundamental set of human relationships very exquisitely. Nevertheless, the focus is entirely upon one level of human awareness. That that level is on the surface, on exterior human behavior, gives *Pride and Prejudice* its oft-noted limitations. But that same narrowness of focus permits the elegantly precise detail that helps make *Pride and Prejudice* rewarding fiction.

This notion of levels of explanation of human fate may be made more apparent as we consider *Wuthering Heights*. The concern with character and social relationships that forms the exclusive focus of *Pride and Prejudice* is still very much built into *Wuthering Heights*, but the basis of both character and social relationships has shifted as additional factors have been added to account for the fates of the characters. Like Jane Austen, Emily Brontë understood that relationships of privilege and position are important in the determination of human destiny. On one level, that is, Heathcliff is the abused former servant suddenly in a position of power over his former tormentors. Nor does Emily Brontë neglect to remind us that Heathcliff's revenge consists in large part of depriving the Earnshaws of their social status — hence the material about Heathcliff's mysterious acquisition of wealth and good grammar, the marriage of Heathcliff and Isabella, and that of Cathy and Linton. Hence also the constant master-servant relationships that recur throughout the novel. Emily Brontë's world, almost as much as Jane Austen's, is a world of money and privilege.

But it is a world of much else. In fact, one of the frustrations in reading *Wuthering Heights* — and in this respect it is a very modern novel — is the difficulty of determining precisely what controls the destinies of the characters. In Jane Austen's world money and position define character; in Emily Brontë's they are merely materials to be used in the realization of character. A way of making the same point with a significant variation is to note that the emphasis in Austen's fiction is primarily on saying, "This is the way people are"; Brontë seems to want to suggest to the reader how they got that way. It is not enough for the later novelist to describe character; she must search for its causes because she cannot take them for granted.

Earlier I referred to the scene in which Jane Bennet catches cold; in it, nature is treated with complete and common-sense objectivity — if a person goes out in a certain kind of weather, even with the best of intentions, a cold is the natural result. Jane Austen would have felt the question of whether nature is malignant or beneficent rather foolish. Emily Brontë, on the other hand, works diligently to establish parallels between the rugged ferocity of the landscape of Wuthering Heights and the rugged ferocity of the people it has shaped.

To detour for just a moment, perhaps the most mysterious figure in the novel, and certainly one given very little critical attention, is Hindley. Hindley Earnshaw is in many ways what textbooks call the inciting force. It is his arbitrary cruelty to the young Heathcliff that creates in Heathcliff the need for revenge that comprises the major cause of the tragedy. What motivates Hindley? Emily Brontë never quite tells us. We see Hindley's jealousy of Heathcliff, but that does not account adequately for the excessiveness of Heathcliff's anger. It is here, I believe, that we see the kind of concern with and uncertainty about fundamental human matters which is so foreign to Jane Austen. The hints we are given simply do not add up, but somehow, by the time we become acquainted with the young Hindley, we are ready for the possibility of a moral monster. With that affective logic that the best writers make such good use of, Emily Brontë establishes the illusion that in some mysterious way the same malignant nature that shaped Wuthering Heights has shaped the soul of young Hindley. We are told that "wuthering" is "a significant provincial adjective, descriptive of the atmospheric tumult to which its [Wuthering Heights'] station is exposed in stormy weather . . . one may guess the power of the north wind, blowing over the edge, by the excessive slant of a few stunted firs at the end of the house; and by a range of gaunt thorns all stretching their limbs one way, as if craving alms from the sun." After finishing *Wuthering Heights,* it is difficult not to apply this description to the morally stunted characters — to Hindley, like the north wind, bending others to his will, and to the gaunt Heathcliff, craving alms from Catherine. And, of course, the name Heathcliff links the man with nature in its more rugged and primitive aspects.

The part that nature plays in shaping the destinies of Heathcliff and Catherine merges with the part played by the demonic. Catherine's twisted longing for Heathcliff, we are led to believe, is stronger than death. There are at least two senses of the demonic present in the novel. There are first of all, the demonic wills of both Catherine and Heathcliff. Again the comparison with Elizabeth and Darcy, also very willful characters, is instructive. Darcy in his masculine and active way, and Elizabeth in her more feminine and passive way, both bend the world to their wills. When Darcy does not want Bingley to marry Elizabeth's sister, he acts as arrogantly and as willfully as Heathcliff. But, unlike Heathcliff, Darcy is in control of his will — another way of saying that there is no apparent disharmony between what Darcy is on the surface and what he is in the recesses of his soul. Heathcliff's will, though, is literally beyond his conscious control; he is obsessed, driven by his desire for revenge and his love for Catherine. And Catherine, who seems to control Heathcliff's destiny, is ultimately as driven by forces beyond her control as is either Heathcliff or Hindley.

The second sense of the demonic present in *Wuthering Heights* introduces an entirely new level of reality — the supernatural. We can explain away the ghost of Catherine, and Emily Brontë certainly gives us material to do so. We are told that the peasants believe in ghosts but that they are ignorant and superstitious; we know that Heathcliff constantly senses the presence of Catherine, but he is a man obsessed; and we know that Lockwood sees the ghost of Catherine, but in a nightmare brought on by fatigue, Heathcliff's abuse, and his reading of Catherine's journal. Each possible supernatural manifestation is explained, and each explanation by itself is credible. But the ghost of Catherine does brood over Wuthering Heights, and our rationalistic explanations are less convincing than her presence.

This tendency to posit and then to retract or cloud possible explanations for the fates of the characters is, in part, what makes *Wuthering Heights* such a frustrating and yet such a powerful novel — frustrating not only in the driving force of the characters but also in Emily Brontë's absolute refusal to let her readers rest with a simple explanation. We know fully why Elizabeth Bennet refuses Darcy and why Darcy acts in the Lydia-Wickham elopement. More accurately, Jane Austen satisfies us that we know everything of importance. We never fully understand why Hindley is so cruel to the young Heathcliff, or the source of Heathcliff's and Catherine's passion.

If we can take *Wuthering Heights* as a symptom of its time, we can say that the best mid-nineteenth-century English fiction was beginning to reflect the multi-dimensioned complexity of the factors involved in human destiny. Although this is a large generalization, it is, I believe, largely true. At the risk of oversimplifying, happiness for Richardson seems to consist primarily of being wedded and bedded — in that order. Despite Fielding's greater vitality, happiness for his heroes consists in discovering a relationship with a well-established and relatively prosperous family. Both assume a reasonably good heart and a reasonably good head, and they posit a world in which it is possible and profitable to heed the dictates of both. The step from Richardson's or Fielding's world to Austen's is much smaller than the step from Austen's to Brontë's. Despite important differences among them, Richardson, Fielding, and Austen create worlds in which values are known, in which the values are primarily social, and in which the great good is to enter into conventionally satisfying relationships with one's fellows.

Perhaps the increase in ethical uncertainty and the consequent increase in fictional complexity can best be shown by another mid-nineteenth-century novel, one more overtly and extensively drawn in English social life than is *Wuthering Heights*. Critics have often noted, accurately enough, that *Vanity Fair* is a novel in the tradition established by Fielding and carried on by Jane Austen. The critics are, I suspect, referring to the crisp irony of the style, the level of society depicted, and the concern with exterior social relationships. But unlike the earlier novelists, Thackeray is less interested in the external relationships themselves than in the tension among them and in something he believes to be both deep and universal in human nature.

If we are to take the title of the novel seriously, as well as its final paragraph — "Vanitas Vanitatum! which of us is happy in this world? Which of us has his desire? or, having it, is satisfied? . . ." — we must recognize that Thackeray is saying that precisely the same force driving Becky drives Amelia. It is not necessary to argue for Becky's vanity; we see her constantly scheming to improve her lot in life, constantly trying to display her looks and her talents to their best advantage. The interesting characters in this respect are Amelia and Dobbin, both of whom seem superficially to lack vanity. On the surface, Amelia is almost the ideal Victorian woman — chaste, patient, maternal, fragile. Dobbin is equally the ideal Victorian male — chaste, patient, protective, strong. Yet Amelia, as many critics have pointed out, makes as much mileage as possible out of her roles of suffering wife and mother, just as Dobbin virtually makes a career of being the sympathetic, long-suffering lover. Thackeray takes care to inform us that Amelia may not be worth Dobbin's durable protectiveness and that Dobbin's love for Amelia may be misdirected. The vanity of Amelia and Dobbin in their unsatisfying roles is as complete as that of Becky in hers.

It is interesting to contrast Fielding's conception of vanity (and its cousin, affectation) with Thackeray's. For Fielding, vanity and affectation are essentially illusions; the former is an illusion about one's own worth, the latter the attempt to create such an illusion in others. The Thackeray of *Vanity Fair* would probably accept the definitions and the distinction. For Fielding, however, vanity and affectation are essentially deviations from a norm that is both recognizable and attainable. To exaggerate just a bit, in Fielding's world one has to work at being vain or affected — Lady Booby, Mrs. Slipslop, and the other laughable characters in *Joseph Andrews* expend a large share of their energies in pursuit of their various follies. Much of the fun in the novel depends upon the realization that the ridiculous characters are working so hard for such poor effect, and that it would be not only more profitable but easier for them to live according to the human norm. In Fielding's world, after all, Joseph and Fanny merely do what comes naturally, and so their reward comes naturally.

For Thackeray, however, vanity is not a deviation from the norm — it is the norm. And, more important, in *Vanity Fair* the only happiness attainable is a temporary and illusive happiness based upon a fundamental misunderstanding of the role one is playing in the world. Becky's happiest moments are those in which she imagines that she can indeed become the great lady; Amelia's best moments are those in which she imagines that she is loved and when she later deludes herself into thinking that her overprotectiveness benefits her son. Unhappiness in *Vanity Fair,* unlike that in *Joseph Andrews,* is not the result of the embarrassment that comes when one's vanity is exposed. It is the result of the fact that even a meager happiness must be based upon an illusion, and that because it is based upon an illusion, it is short-lived. In Fielding's and Austen's works there is no necessary gap between the dream and the reality for those who know themselves (or for the innocent) ; in *Vanity Fair* that gap is the only source of man's brief and frail happiness.

One symptom of the kind of unity of man and the world assumed in the earlier novels and denied in the later is the harmony that prevails between social class and character — at least in the morally healthy characters. Neither Joseph Andrews nor Tom Jones has to learn how to handle his position in life; Fielding assumes that such knowledge comes naturally with maturity if the character is morally sound. In fact, in both Richardson's and Fielding's worlds the possibility of a Lord B's or Mr. Wilson's transformation from cad to gentleman needs little or no explanation. Both novelists and their readers were ready to assume that when the time is right, when one is ready to marry the right person, the gentleman will out. The ex-profligate will have the inclination and the ability to assume his new responsibilities. Not to do so in Richardson's world is to be a monster, like Lovelace; not to do so in Fielding's world is to be ridiculous. And in Jane Austen's world (as in Richardson's *Pamela*) each marriageable young lady seems providentially manipulated into a marriage into the precise social group best suited for her abilities. What is significant here is that except for some general maturation and, in the case of the men, some miscellaneous sowing of wild oats, one does not have either to earn or to learn his role in life.

We could make the appropriate contrast with Becky Sharp, but it might be more appropriate to do so with Dickens's David Copperfield. Thanks to Dickens's optimism, his belief in the eventual triumph of the good heart, poetic justice triumphs as completely as it does in the earlier novels we have considered. But the triumph is also a triumph of character, in a way that it definitely is not in Fielding's works, nor even in Jane Austen's. Joseph Andrews and Elizabeth Bennet have only to be discovered. David Copperfield has to fall into poverty not once but twice, and both times he must earn his way back into his social class. Although in the first fall he is rescued by Aunt Betsey Trotwood, the rescue can happen only because David makes the courageous but necessary decision to escape from the Murdstone establishment. And because of the way Dickens handles the development of the character, the reader is led to believe that the psychological abuses heaped upon the young boy by the Murdstones and by Creakle have been necessary preparatory exercises for responding to the practical love he receives from Aunt Betsey.

An earlier novelist might have been well content to end the story with David's re-establishment in his father's family; the abandonment by or expulsion from the family and the return form, after all, a familiar enough pattern. But Dickens seems to want to impress upon his readers that David still has not earned his right to the position he finally attains. Just as things seem to be at their best for David, when he is progressing toward his profession and the economic security that might make marriage to his beloved Dora practical, he is again thrown on his own resources. Dickens will not permit David to enjoy the Victorian version of the good life until he has proved his ability to earn his way into it both by his labor and by his maturation through a bad marriage.

The contrast with the kind of world view represented in, say, Fielding's work is even more striking when one considers *Great Expectations*. We know that Joseph Andrews's problems are over when he finds his real father, who can provide him with what he believes he wants in life; Pip's problems begin when a surrogate father attempts to provide him with what he believes he wants. Pip has to earn his right to be a gentleman, and again that means living through a series of misfortunes. With a kind of long-delayed reverse logic, the early adventures with Estella and Miss Havisham help Pip learn the gentility that is an essential part of Dickens's gentleman — although part of the same experience, like his formal education, temporarily misguides him. Pip's maturation by the end of the novel is due not to the fact that he is rewarded with everything due him — in the manner of a typical Fielding or Austen ending — but, rather, that he is deprived of those things that are not due him.

To summarize so far, in the work of the earlier writers there seems to be no general disparity between what a normally good person desires and what his world — in the broadest sense — will let him have. There is an assumption that character and fate are, ultimately at least, in complete harmony. The same is true in the work of Dickens, but with the important reservation that the protagonist has to earn his character; he can achieve his destined place only after learning to cope with economic and emotional deprivation. But in the worlds of Thackeray and Emily Brontë the harmony is ultimately impossible. Economic forces, society, exterior nature, and internal conflict create an impassable barrier between the dream and the reality.

It is not until near the end of the century, however, that a single novel presents explicitly and in detail an overview of all the various determinants of man's doom. *Jude the Obscure* is, quite literally, a catalog of the causes of human woe. I noted earlier that one of the vexations of *Wuthering Heights* is the impossibility of deciding precisely what controls the destiny of the characters. Yet the vexation results from an analytic judgment made after living through the novel and while attempting to make sense of all its parts. The initial impression *Wuthering Heights* makes, and its strongest impression, is that Heathcliff and Cathy suffer because of their overriding passions and that perhaps it is somehow more noble, more fully human, to suffer so than it is to live passively. *Jude the Obscure* offers no such distracting nobility; in reading *Jude* we cannot escape the relentless exposure of the many traps designed to snare man.

Despite the fact that the whole of *Jude the Obscure* is a systematic display of the reasons for Jude's suffering, we cannot ever say precisely why Jude suffers — not because the reasons are not implicit in the novel but because they are so numerous and so different. We could, for example, read *Jude the Obscure* as a social-reform novel in the manner of the lesser known works of Wilkie Collins or Charles Reade. That is, we could blame Jude's fate on the English educational system, which provided no opportunity for an intellectually ambitious but unsophisticated and impoverished youth. At one point Hardy suggests that Jude's tragedy could have been averted if England had had a good scholarship system. Or we could blame the divorce laws, which made it difficult for an innocent youth tricked into a bad marriage to start afresh — or we could blame the marriage customs and the sexual attitudes, which warped the emotional development of the potentially superior Sue Bridehead. But if we could answer so simply the question of why Jude suffers, *Jude the Obscure* would be no more significant than hosts of other now forgotten social-reform novels.

Or we could accuse that deep, romantic chasm that separates man's most idealistic dreams from his lusts, and so read *Jude* as another novel of a man torn between flesh and spirit. Hardy also provides material for this reading of *Jude*. The rivalry between the physical Arabella and the all-too-*spirituel* Sue dramatizes the division within Jude. But again, we cannot read *Jude the Obscure* entirely this way, for although Jude has immense potential for victimization by women like Arabella and Sue, both of the women work diligently to victimize him. There is most certainly a weakness in Jude's character, but Hardy has shaped a world calculated to prey on weakness.

Or, of course, we could blame cosmic forces. As in *Wuthering Heights,* a peasant chorus is present to remind us that man's fate may be in the hands of the Doomsters. The constant and prophetic warnings against marriage that Jude receives suggest that any love he finds is fated to end in misery. The fact that the children of Jude and Sue are murdered by a character Hardy chooses to nickname "Father Time" may be Hardy's way of reminding his readers that there is no defense against time. We all live with Father Time, and at any moment we may meet his companion, Death.

Obviously none of these ways of reading *Jude* is complete, and certainly I would not seriously urge one reading over another — each single version requires that too much of significance be discounted or ignored. But isn't that why *Jude the Obscure* is one of the most profoundly bleak novels ever written? It is as if Hardy is saying, "If society doesn't get you, your own nature will; if they fail, the predators with whom you live will surely devour you. And if you escape them, Fate and Time assure man that he is doomed to a losing game."

To return to the kind of terms used at the beginning of this study, in *Jude the Obscure* man's conflict is not against a single antagonist but against every possible force an indifferent or hostile universe can summon up. It is a long way from the early novelistic assumption that the only threat to man's happiness is his failure to find his place in society as a member of a prosperous and proper family. In order to dramatize the many determinants of man's fate, Hardy both included and went beyond his predecessors. He created a world in which the passions are as strong as those in the world of *Wuthering Heights,* in which the economic deprivation is as strongly felt as in any of the novels we have considered, and in which human vanity is both pervasive and incurable, except by death. But in *Jude the Obscure* there is no nobility in the passions nor any demonic source of strength; economic deprivation is not to be relieved by honest hard work; and vanity, the illusion that one might live well or love well, does not provide even temporary relief.

Perhaps from this perspective *Jude the Obscure* is the last great classic novel; it completes the pattern with a kind of awful finality. It was left for the next generations of serious novelists — Conrad, Joyce, Faulkner, Barth — to tell the story of how man can prevail in a universe in which all of the forces that shape human destiny are antagonistic.

TWO

Walter Scott
and the Tradition
of the Political Novel

BY GEORGE GOODIN

In *Politics and the Novel* Irving Howe has pointed out the paradox that "the political novel turns characteristically to an apolitical temptation."[1] It deals with the impact of political problems on individuals and with the political ideas that are possible solutions to those problems, but any solutions finally suggested are moral, not political. As a result, the political consciousness of the reader is developed, but not his political hope, because his attitude toward politics itself becomes more and more skeptical. If there is a bias, then, in the political novel, it is in favor of the "passive conservatism" that Trotsky found characteristic of all art, a conservatism which is hardly political at all.[2]

One can account for this tendency in many ways. It is partly caused by the fact that men who are strongly committed to politics usually spend their time working at politics rather than at novels. It is partly caused by the fact that literary criticism has been too formalistic to see much value in those novels that are strongly committed. It is partly caused by the nature of fiction, which resists the expression of commitment. There is, however, another cause that I wish to treat here — the literary tradition of the political novel. It consists of a group of recurrent motifs and plot structures, most of them appropriated from literature that was not designed to develop the political commitment of the reader. Those who have contributed to it — such as Dostoyevsky, Turgenev, James, Conrad, and Silone — are among the major forces in modern literature. It is true that many novelists — Zola, Malraux,

[1] Irving Howe, *Politics and the Novel* (New York, 1957), p. 23.
[2] Leon Trotsky, *Literature and Revolution* (Ann Arbor, Mich., 1960), p. 70.

and Sholokov — have tried with varying success to emancipate themselves from this tradition, but their task has not been easy, partly because the tradition itself has not been defined.

We can see some of the elements in this tradition and at the same
time indicate its continuing vitality by looking briefly at the protests
that recently greeted William Styron's *The Confessions of Nat Turner*.
The novel deals with an 1831 slave rebellion in Virginia, and from the
features objected to by black intellectuals, we can make a fairly comprehensive list of motifs that have proven durable in the political novel:
the hero is represented as a weak man afflicted by self-doubt and in-
decision, he is without strong family ties and is thus a creature of the
very culture he is rebelling against, he is romantically attracted by a
woman of that culture, his political action is motivated in part by the
frustration of his love for her, the religious motivation and enthusiasm
in the historical accounts is obscured, the hero seems to hate those on
his side more than he does his enemies, the cruelties under which the
rebels suffer are not fully shown, the reader is called on to see the
oppressors' motives with sympathetic understanding, psychological ab-
normalities are too prominent among the rebels, and the revolt fails
largely as a result of the inadequacies of the rebels themselves. In short,
the novel offers a political event, but in its treatment of the causes of
that event it deals almost entirely with personal motives, and in its
treatment of the consequences of that event it is limited to what is
either nonpolitical or disastrous. Its implication for the present day is
that current ghetto uprisings are also futile and stupid.[3]

If we look for the origin of this tradition, we will find it, I think, in
the work of Walter Scott, and the one novel that best illustrates it is
Old Mortality. Although I don't mean to revive Mark Twain's claim
that Scott was responsible for the injustices of the antebellum South,
it is nevertheless true that *Old Mortality* contains almost every feature
objected to in *The Confessions of Nat Turner*. Many of these objections
were in fact made against it in 1817 by the Reverend Thomas McCrie.
Considering Scott's treatment of the uprising of Scots Presbyterians,
McCrie charged that the hero was so weak and indecisive as to be
hardly capable of political or religious motivation, that among the Presbyterians in the novel there was not a single character who was rational,
that the uprising itself had been presented as politically futile, and that

---

[3] John Henrik Clarke, ed., *William Styron's Nat Turner: Ten Black Writers
Respond* (Boston, 1968).

the novel could be used to justify the political repressions of the post-Waterloo period.[4]

In his answer to McCrie in the *Quarterly Review* Scott argued on literary rather than political grounds. *Old Mortality* is not a history, he said, but a romance. For this reason it is freer than history from the claims of factuality, freer than the novel from the claims of probability, and freer than either history or the novel from the claims of narrative. Instead there is a "dramatic principle upon which the author frames his plots," placing the reader "in some measure, in the situation of the audience at a theatre, who are compelled to gather the meaning of the scene from what the *dramatis personae* say to each other, and not from any explanation addressed immediately to themselves."[5] This principle was extremely important, not only to Scott but also to many of the novelists who followed, and it helps to explain why the political novel took the direction it did. Before Scott wrote, two of the major types of political novels were novels of ideas, such as Robert Bage's *Hermsprong,* and "victim of society" novels, such as William Godwin's *Caleb Williams.*[6] But the consequences that Scott drew from the dramatic principle — together with the force of his own example — did not encourage the writing of either.

The novel of ideas is alien to Scott's principle because he thought of drama as visual and ironic. Therefore, the amount of space that can be given to abstract ideas is small, and the authoritative statement of ideas is impossible. The dramatic form, Scott tells us, serves to "compel the reader to think of the personages of the novel and not of the writer" (p. 239), and we do not think of the writer because, like the dramatist, he has managed his point of view so as to remove himself from his work. Ideas thus proceed not from the author but from a character or narrator, and they are almost always addressed to another character rather than directly to the reader. Like the description in the novels, they are used in what Scott calls a "reflective" manner: they reflect the character of the speaker and the auditor(s), and the

[4] Thomas McCrie, Review of *Tales of My Landlord* in *Edinburgh Christian Instructor* (Jan.-Mar. 1817), pp. 41-73, 100-140, 170-201.

[5] Ioan Williams, ed., *Sir Walter Scott on Novelists and Fiction* (London, 1968), pp. 240, 239. Further citations to this article are incorporated in the text.

[6] For a comprehensive treatment of political novels before Scott, see Allene Gregory, *The French Revolution and the English Novel* (Port Washington, N.Y., 1965).

first criterion for judging them is not their truth but their appropriateness. Insofar as ideas are directed at the reader, they are addressed to his judgment rather than to his assent, and he must apply all that he knows of the characters and action of the novel in order to appraise their validity. The novel itself may not be inherently critical of ideas, but the dramatic novel is; like drama, it is an ironic web.

In the victim-of-society novel the hero is confronted with what is basically one antagonistic force, and we are led to sympathize with him through a much fuller presentation of his character than is accorded to the agents of his oppression. From the dramatic principle, however, Scott derives the weak hero whose fate is "uniformly determined by the agency of the subordinate persons" (p. 240), and they are pulling him in opposite directions. What Scott is interested in, and seems to find more dramatic, is the strong contrasts he can develop among the minor characters. Writing to Lady Louisa Stuart about *Old Mortality*, he notes that "there are noble subjects for narrative during that period full of the strongest light & shadow, all human passions stirr'd up & stimulated by the most powerful motives, & the contending parties as distinctly contrasted in manners & in modes of thinking as in political principles."[7] In order to develop this contrast, Scott had to show both political sides, which "could hardly be done without representing the principal character either as inconsistent or flexible in his principles" (p. 240). What results is that the hero is relatively uncommitted, yet it is through him that we see those who are strongly committed. The dramatic principle has encouraged not only irony but impartiality, and the didactic, often one-sided, political novel of the eighteenth century is no longer the dominant form.

Turning now to the plots and motifs that Scott did use, we can see that the first type of plot — the only plot one might cautiously suggest that Scott invented — follows fairly immediately from the dramatic principle as he understood it. Basically, what happens is that the hero suffers at the hands of established political power and as a result commits himself to those who are opposing it, after which he suffers at their hands also. Henry Morton is almost executed, first by Claverhouse, then by Mucklewrath and his associates, and this is only part of the suffering caused him by both sides.

[7] *The Letters of Sir Walter Scott,* ed. H. J. C. Grierson, IV (London, 1933), 293.

This figure in Scott's fiction has often been referred to as "the man in between" because he is caught between opposed political forces, but since he seems to have developed from the victim-of-society novel, I prefer to call him a "double victim." The victim-of-society novel had substituted for the antagonistic fate of the tragic hero an antagonistic social or political establishment, and it had tried to suggest, not always successfully, that something could be done about that system to prevent suffering such as the hero endured. The double-victim plot, however, criticizes not only the established power but also its opposition. It creates a dialectic that makes us look toward the hero for a possible synthesis, but if the character of the hero is weak, the synthesis is likely to be implicit and negatively defined — as it is in Henry Morton. We know that he is opposed both to the theocratic principles of Burley and to the aristocratic principles of Claverhouse, but the positive content of his beliefs is largely moral. Yet as I suggested before, we are basically sympathetic toward him, and a wide variety of readers can feel themselves essentially in agreement with him.

The double-victim plot criticizes the established power and its opposition together as well as separately, so that its theme is usually the hazards of political polarization. Both parties oppose private life on the ground that whoever is not with them is against them, and their monopoly on power lends some substance to their claim. Both endanger what Scott called the "bonds of society,"[8] because both are extremist parties emphasizing the differences that separate them from others. Between them they isolate the hero politically and threaten him personally; yet he is a much better representative of the people because of his yearning for social harmony and the joys of private life. He represents their desire for political moderation — and the moderation of their desire for politics.

Another plot Scott uses is what Northrop Frye calls the "New Comedy"— the plot in which a young man loves a young woman but is impeded from marrying her by a "blocking character" who is subsequently removed in order to allow their union. According to Frye, the blocking character receives the brunt of the intellectual criticism,[9] and in *Old Mortality* there are several. One is Lady Margaret Bellenden, who objects to Henry Morton on the ground that his family is Whiggish. Morton understands the impersonal and political nature of

[8] Williams, ed., *Scott on Novelists and Fiction*, p. 257.
[9] Northrop Frye, *Anatomy of Criticism* (Princeton, N.J., 1957), p. 165.

the opposition to him and goes to some length to generalize upon it in speaking of Lord Evandale, another blocking character who is his rival in both love and politics:

> "And to what do I owe it," he said, "that I cannot stand up like a man, and plead my interest in her ere I am thus cheated out of it? — to what, but to the all-pervading and accursed tyranny, which afflicts at once our bodies, souls, estates, and affections! And is it to one of the pensioned cut-throats of this oppressive government that I must yield my pretensions to Edith Bellenden?"[10]

In these blocking characters, obviously, there is a criticism of the established power, but there are other blocking characters too. One is Burley, who accuses Morton of wishing "to sacrifice this holy cause to . . . thy lust for a Moabitish woman" (p. 257). Another is Basil Oliphant, a political trimmer who combines with Burley to defraud Edith of her inheritance. Thus the entire political spectrum is represented in the figures opposed to the union of Henry and Edith, who are free to marry only after the last scene of the novel has left most of the blocking characters dead.

Scott has often been criticized for using this type of plot on the same ground that he objected to its use by so many others: because it tends to suggest that human activities other than love are not very important. Since it became so common, it is not surprising that it has figured strongly in political novels and that, as a result, the relationship between love and politics has become an important part of their subject matter. The novels most favorable to political change show both lovers as rebels who are impeded by the political status quo and the need to work against it. But politics is still placed in conflict with love, which tends to elicit an automatically sympathetic response, and it is not easy to avoid the conclusion that love is a political nuisance or that politics is a romantic one. If the two lovers are on opposite political sides, moreover, the latter of these conclusions is almost inescapable, and this situation is pretty much characteristic of Scott's novels and many later ones.

The plot of New Comedy is much easier to define than the plot of comedy itself, which would seem to be best suited for fulfilling the dictum of Mr. Bayes, so vigorously seconded by Scott, that a plot ought to be something to hang good things on. Since it is fairly generally con-

---

[10] For convenience, I cite the Everyman edition, ed. W. M. Parker (London, 1960), p. 142. Further citations are incorporated in the text.

ceded that comedy favors Tories, I will only state briefly here that most comic theories of the past two hundred years have been "relief" theories, attributing laughter to the perception that something is wrong, followed by the judgment that nothing need be done about it.[11] There is an intellectual criticism of an act, followed by a detached acceptance of it. As a result, comedy can identify misrule, but its solution is usually for us to tend our own gardens.

We can also see the skepticism of comedy as the result of its dealing so much with the disproportion of means to ends. If the application of any power is problematic, the efficacy of political authority is brought into question. In *Old Mortality* this skepticism is not only stated openly but presented through a motif that goes back at least to the wily servants of Roman comedy. Not only do servants rule their masters, but wives rule their husbands, tenants their landlords, junior officers their seniors, and horses their riders. The real king is Feedback, and Scott is his jester.

Such a mood is established at the very outset of the novel when Scott describes Guse-Gibbie: "This urchin being sent for from the stubble-field, was hastily muffled in the buff coat, and girded rather *to* than *with* the sword of a full-grown man, his little legs plunged into jack-boots, and a steel cap put upon his head, which seemed, from its size, as if it had been intended to extinguish him" (p. 27). If this can be taken as a visual presentation of the Scottish citizen over whom English authority is exercised, the symbol of that authority is clearly the enormous and clumsy carriage of the lord-lieutenant, "a thing covered with tarnished gilding and sculpture, in shape like the vulgar picture of Noah's ark" (p. 25). The wappenschaw is ending when Gibbie's equipment stages a rebellion against the power that it was intended to protect. His jackboots, which he cannot steady, spur his horse to run away with him. His casque falls over his face so that he cannot see. His pike escapes its sling so that he has to support it as a level lance. And "his horse, as if in league with the disaffected, ran full tilt towards the solemn equipage of the Duke, which the projecting lance threatened to perforate from window to window" (p. 35). This scene fairly well prefigures the action of the whole novel — a rebellion caused by the overuse of political authority and controlled by little authority of its own.

If the double-victim plot, the New Comedy plot, and the comic plot

---

[11] Arthur Koestler, *Insight and Outlook* (New York, 1949), pp. 57f.

offer substantial difficulties to the expression of political commitment, the *Bildungsroman* or initiation plot would seem to offer more possibilities. In Scott's novels the hero does mature as the result of his transition from "private life" to being "an actor in public life." But in the end he seems intent on returning to private life, and this note of fatigue with public life is often sounded in later political novels. Near the end of *Old Mortality* Scott uses the Wordsworthian motif of revisitation, in which the mature man returns to a place associated in his mind with the time before he had matured. There he cultivates a nostalgia for his youth and a doubt about the value of maturity. Wordsworth argues for an acceptance of a maturity that is much more socially conscious, incorporating the "still, sad music of humanity" into his very individualistic apprehension of nature. In *Old Mortality*, on the other hand, the tone of regret predominates, and the places at which this nostalgia comes over Henry Morton — Niel Blane's Howff and the crossroad at which he decided to shelter Burley — are associated with his entry into politics.

The last type of plot I wish to discuss, the romance, is usually positive rather than critical, celebrating an event in the past achieved by a hero who embodies the ideals common to his own age and that of the author. The political implications of this form have frequently been commented on, and I think that Northrop Frye is basically correct when he finds in the romance a commitment that, insofar as it is political, is on the side of the status quo: "In every age the ruling social or intellectual class tends to project its ideals in some form of romance, where the virtuous heroes and beautiful heroines represent the ideals and the villains the threats to their ascendancy. This is the general character of chivalric romance in the Middle Ages, aristocratic romance in the Renaissance, bourgeois romance since the eighteenth century, and revolutionary romance in contemporary Russia."[12] What *Old Mortality* celebrates is the Glorious Revolution. Scott often refers to the period before 1688 as "those unhappy times," and when he writes of the period afterward, we can feel the relief from violence and politics: "Agriculture began to revive; and men, whose minds had been disturbed by the violent political concussions, and the general change of government in church and state, had begun to recover their ordinary temper, and to give the usual attention to their own private affairs in lieu of discussing those of the public" (p. 352).

[12] Frye, *Anatomy of Criticism*, p. 186.

Scott's rhetorical problem is a familiar one by now — how to celebrate a past revolution without encouraging the political left of his
own day — and his solution is also familiar: to present the revolution
as a historical fatality. In his answer to McCrie he wrote that the
Stuart government "fell a victim to its own follies and crimes,"[13] and
in the novel he avoids all direct presentation of the revolution and all
mention of its positive causes. We must surmise that Stuart misrule of
the type shown in the novel finally generated enough opposition to
overthrow it and that the agents of this overthrow were instruments
of a historical process. Whether we wish to attribute Scott's method to
his Toryism or to his sense of history, it is interesting to note that it
can be paralleled in many other political novels. Instead of seeing the
overthrow of governments, we hear of their downfall, a downfall that
is somehow connected with the opposition whose fortunes we have
been following, but often very loosely connected. It is interesting, too,
that so many writers on revolution — among them Karl Marx, Crane
Brinton, and Hannah Arendt — have a similar view of what causes
revolutions. But if we think that political science has influenced fiction,
we might consider also that fiction may have influenced political
science.

Before closing, I would like to qualify what I have said in two ways.
First, I may have made it appear that the political implications of
Old Mortality are simply an unconscious result of Scott's literary principles, forms, and motifs. Such an error is no worse than its opposite
— the belief that a novelist simply incarnates a political vision that
exists previously — but it is an error, despite Scott's encouragement of
it. In *Old Mortality* the criticism of politics is fairly conscious, as we
can see from the well-known description of Claverhouse:

> The same gentleness and gaiety of expression which reigned in his fea-
> tures seemed to inspire his actions and gestures; and, on the whole, he
> was generally esteemed, at first sight, rather qualified to be the votary
> of pleasure than of ambition. But under this soft exterior was hidden a
> spirit unbounded in daring and in aspiring, yet cautious and prudent as
> that of Machiavel himself. Profound in politics, and embued, of course,
> with that disregard for individual rights which its intrigues usually gen-
> erate, this leader was cool and collected in danger, fierce and ardent in
> pursuing success, careless of facing death himself, and ruthless in in-

[13] Williams, ed., *Scott on Novelists and Fiction*, p. 258.

flicting it upon others. Such are the characters formed in times of civil discord, when the highest qualities, perverted by party spirit, and inflamed by habitual opposition, are too often combined with vices and excesses which deprive them at once of their merit and of their lustre. [Pp. 127-28]

Clearly what is bad in Claverhouse is the result of politics — an assertion that further outraged McCrie. Although Scott's rhetoric resists paraphrase, "politics" means pretty much the same as "party spirit" here, and it is a threat to the private life and character not only of its victims but also of its agents.

The other qualification I wish to make is that *Old Mortality* is not antipolitical but, rather, is concerned with the limits of politics. We can see this most readily in the fact that it also criticizes political neutrality. What old Milnwood, Basil Oliphant, and Niel Blane have in common, in addition to their neutrality, is their concern with money. Milnwood is an "old man, who never meddles with politics, and loves his money-bags and bonds better than any thing in the world" (p. 55). Basil Oliphant is even worse because his neutrality is merely tactical. He withholds his support from either side until he can decide which will provide the spoils of victory, and when he makes a mistake, he changes sides. Niel Blane is much more sympathetically presented. His neutrality consists not of withholding support from either side but of giving it to both sides — sending provisions to both Tillietudlem and Drumclog. Yet his retaining the best provisions for himself is entirely in keeping with his character.

If neutrality is closely connected with self-interest, the entry into politics can develop one's character toward disinterestedness, which is what happens to Henry Morton. At the beginning of the novel he makes exaggeratedly rhetorical speeches in which the tone of immature self-pity is evident. After engaging in public affairs, however, "all that had formerly interested him was obliterated from his memory, excepting only his attachment to Edith; and even his love seemed to have assumed a character more manly and disinterested, as it had become mingled and contrasted with other duties and feelings" (p. 266). In the latter part of the novel Morton's disinterestedness reaches almost incredible heights. He watches Edith protesting against marrying Evandale and tries to slip away unnoticed, so as not to interfere. He is tempted to declare himself to Edith, but because of his gratitude to Evandale, "he repressed forcibly these selfish emotions" (p. 381).

This value of politics seems to be personal, despite the obvious political possibilities of disinterestedness, so that one may still ask whether such novels as *Old Mortality* find any political hope in political action. In novels that deal with an attempt to bring about political change, there are three basic types of resolution, each of which suggests a different answer to this question: the established power can be defeated, the rebels can be defeated, or both can be defeated. What happens in *Old Mortality* and in many later novels is the third resolution. Its appeal is obvious enough if we consider the matter negatively, for it avoids the cheap optimism or pessimism that the other resolutions make possible. But avoiding undesirable alternatives is not all such a resolution does. It carries with it an idea about politics that is quite helpful, I think, and this idea serves to make *Old Mortality* a very perceptive novel. Briefly stated, it is that political activity can be justified, not by its direct accomplishments but by its indirect ones. In *Old Mortality* the Covenanters are defeated, but their effort was by no means futile because it is connected, albeit loosely, with the fall of the Stuarts.

What is involved here is an application to politics of the antiself-consciousness principle that Mill found in Carlyle: "Those only are happy . . . who have their minds fixed on some object other than their own happiness."[14] Just as personal happiness can be only a by-product of personal activity, political happiness can be only a by-product of political activity. There is a disjunction between ends and means or an untidy relation between cause and effect. But actions do have consequences, and disinterested devotion to a public cause will, at the very least, exercise a continuous criticism on behalf of commonly held, even if vague, ideals. Political novels often show the difficulty of bringing intellect to bear on action, because the intellect is critical. But if one can accept indirect and admittedly unforeseeable results as a justification for action, he can harmonize political skepticism and political activism.

[14] John Stuart Mill, *Autobiography*, ed. Harold J. Laski (Oxford, 1955), p. 120.

THREE

Feeling and Control:
A Study of the Proposal Scenes
in Jane Austen's Major Novels

BY MARY ALICE BURGAN

When Jane Austen talks about her novels, she often talks about the kinds of responses she means her characters to evoke. She speaks of her delight in Elizabeth Bennet, for example, and wonders "how I shall be able to tolerate those who do not like *her* at least."[1] She notes that her brother liked Henry Crawford "properly, as a clever, pleasant man."[2] She fears that Emma Woodhouse "may be a heroine whom no one but myself will much like,"[3] and she says of Anne Elliot in a letter to her niece, "You may *perhaps* like the Heroine, as she is almost too good for me."[4] After *Mansfield Park* had been published, Jane Austen went to the trouble of drawing up a catalog of the opinions of her family and friends about its characters; she did the same later for *Emma.*[5] The witty self-depreciation of some of these statements should not distract from their critical interest: they reveal a continuing and self-conscious encounter with the difficulty of placing moral sympathy where it belongs in a novel, without thereby forcing the reader to believe or admire. In one sense this concern for control is a mark of good manners in a kind of art that is secure about its mission to entertain.

[1] *Jane Austen's Letters to Her Sister Cassandra and Others,* ed. R. W. Chapman, 2nd ed. (London, 1952), p. 297.

[2] *Ibid.,* p. 378.

[3] Quoted by James Edward Austen-Leigh in *Memoir of Jane Austen,* ed. R. W. Chapman (Oxford, 1926), p. 157.

[4] *Letters,* p. 157.

[5] "Opinions of *Mansfield Park* and *Emma,*" in *Minor Works,* vol. VI of *The Works of Jane Austen,* ed. R. W. Chapman (London, 1954), pp. 431-39. Citations from the novels, incorporated in the text, are to Chapman's 3rd ed., 5 vols. (London, 1933).

Mary Lascelles has commented on this aspect of Jane Austen's fiction somewhat apologetically: ". . . whether or no it is capable of explanation or justification, it must be taken into account if her art is to be understood."[6] But apologies for Jane Austen's attention to the needs of her readers are unnecessary, for it is with the implications of such an attention that any investigation of her mature experiments with the novel must begin.

The development of Jane Austen's art has been studied carefully; it is now a general conviction that she was a conscious artist and an inventive creator of the novel form. Developmental studies have, however, tended to view her art in terms of its rejection of the sentimental and Gothic modes and have thus emphasized the movement from parody to a criticism of artificial values in human behavior as well as novel-writing.[7] It seems clear that after the publication and success of *Pride and Prejudice,* Jane Austen no longer worked simply out of the impulse to correct existing conventions. There was a growth intrinsic to her art — a more conscious knowledge of the experiential implications of her subject, an increasing tact in controlling the reader's response without dissipating the illusion of the narrative through literary burlesque, and a more sure and subtle psychological annotation of the mind in a state of crisis. In short, while no study of Jane Austen's development can afford to ignore the insights gained from the studies of what she owed to her predecessors — and by that I mean what she *deeply* owed, for I do not believe she simply lifted mere surface mannerisms and narrative tricks from the great eighteenth-century novelists — I am taking these insights for granted and thereby laying them aside. In doing so, I wish to push on to those "intrinsic" motives in her delineation of experience that pointed her novels toward the psychological density of James and Proust and away from the conventionality of Fanny Burney.

Jane Austen's concern for control of the reader's sympathies is involved in her consciousness of the difficulty and weight of the subject

[6] Mary Lascelles, *Jane Austen and Her Art* (London, 1939), p. 146.

[7] All the book-length studies of Jane Austen's novels have been developmental in some way or another, but those by Mary Lascelles; Q. D. Leavis, "A Critical Theory of Jane Austen's Writings," *Scrutiny,* X (1941), 61-87, and X (1941-42), 114-42, 272-94; and A. Walton Litz, *Jane Austen: A Study of Her Artistic Development* (New York, 1965), embody the important insights to be gained from the careful attention to what Jane Austen read and observed of the culture she moved in.

she had undertaken to explore in her fiction. The comments in her letters show that she is interested in depicting goodness. That interest places her capacity to control the reader under great pressure, for she wishes to depict goodness in such a way that, amid the various forms of folly which she can so sharply satirize, it will not be ridiculed or rejected.[8] The question of the dimensions and validity of Jane Austen's subject matter must always be raised by criticism; the answer lies not so much in the depth of her penetration into evil as in the subtlety and force of her penetration into good. As her mature novels commence their exploration of that most difficult kind of conventional character, the essentially virtuous young woman, they must also seek ways to establish the vitality and dramatic interest of good lives. They must begin to delineate the interior drama of commonplace experience; they must try to place wit and shrewdness at the service of the confused but well-meaning mind in action. Thus they will suggest that human morality depends not only on the creation of generally accepted norms but also upon that savoring of personal actuality which is a final justification for any kind of culture. "People themselves alter so much, that there is something new to be observed in them forever," Elizabeth Bennet observes in *Pride and Prejudice:* the kinds of alterations possible in the feelings of well-meaning people within the constraints of ordinary circumstances inform Jane Austen's later novels in ways that exhibit a subtle and moving vision of human life and that also strain and expand her art — challenging it to become more flexible, to attempt new ways of rendering experience so that finally it may be able to express a welter of fluctuating thought and confused emotions without losing the comic right to make some sense of it all.

Over all, Jane Austen's novelistic "alterations" may be briefly sketched, particularly in terms of their increasing use of time and place to express the emotional weight of experience. From the straightforward chronology of a year's growth and change in *Pride and Prejudice,* Jane Austen moves to the longer chronicle of a growth from childhood to maturity in *Mansfield Park,* losing some of the dramatic immediacy of the first novel in exchange for a broader spatial and temporal expanse in the second. *Emma* returns to the fully measured,

---

[8] Wayne Booth has analyzed the cross-currents of sympathy and their service to Jane Austen's interest in affirming the possibility of goodness — Emma's "relenting heart" — in his essay "Control of Distance in Jane Austen's *Emma,*" in *The Rhetoric of Fiction* (Chicago, 1961), pp. 243-66.

more compact dramatic form but intensifies it by creating a limited point of view that places the reader very close to the complications of Emma's quickly changing crises of self-awareness. Finally, *Persuasion* embodies a finely modulated psychological notation which is founded upon the echoes of a time that has passed but is held in consciousness by a memory forced to turn in upon itself by the demands of a social milieu that the novel renders with extraordinary attention to sensory detail. This last novel takes Jane Austen's art as far as it was to go in its effort to attain the interest of psychological subtlety without sacrificing the coherence of comedy.

It is impossible to annotate Jane Austen's fictional innovations fully within the scope of a single essay. Their major characteristics may be noted, however, by taking advantage of a sameness among the novels — by looking at a single kind of episode which recurs in significantly different treatments. The resolution of each of Jane Austen's novels depends upon the narration of a marriage proposal. In every novel but *Mansfield Park* this narrative presents a scene in which the mind of the heroine meets that of her lover, declaring itself openly, explaining the past, planning the future, in short, committing itself to the possibilities that the whole work has been setting up. The narrative always summarizes the moral character of the heroine in the reward it extends to her and in the way it handles her response to a last crisis of change. It provides a climax in the depiction of her goodness by dramatizing a final test of her capacity to choose rightly and to know the rightness of that choice, even in a flood of feeling. In the process it challenges the narrator's capacity to present rational choice in ways that will command the reader's assent both to the emotional sincerity of the heroine's response and to the validity of the psychological insight which accounts for it.[9]

It has been noted that the proposal scene is likely to present a point at which Jane Austen seems most uneasy with her control of the reader; this uneasiness forces her at times to retreat from or to intervene in the drama. When the emotions involved in a declaration of love are to be dramatized, she overdistances; she stops the dramatic rendition of

[9] In "The Comic Conclusions in Jane Austen's Novels," *PMLA*, LXXXIV (1969), 1582-87, Lloyd W. Brown has investigated Jane Austen's conclusion to *Mansfield Park* in terms of the requirements of comic justice. Clearly the endings of all the novels can be justified in terms of rational judgment, but when that is done, the question of whether or not they "work" still remains.

encounter; she steps in to summarize. Mary Lascelles describes what happens: "The dialogue gives place to direct narration and reported talk — we hear only the story-teller's voice — until those most private moments are past; and when the lovers become audible again they are still walking, and give the impression that if we were to press upon them they might draw away once more out of earshot."[10] One might assess this phenomenon as evidence of Jane Austen's limitations, and in some cases it does highlight important difficulties of whichever novel is at hand. For that reason it is, however, all the more interesting as the locus for a study of her experimentation with the fictional problems inherent in rendering psychological complexity within a comic framework.

The proposal scene in *Pride and Prejudice* constitutes the whole of Chapter Sixteen in volume III. In general outline, it forms the basic pattern for all of the proposal scenes to follow. There is the setting up of a situation in which the lovers can be alone, separated at last from the pervasive social milieu that has shaped their story. Once alone together, there is hesitation, then a quick announcement of feelings by the hero; following that, and at the center of interest, there is a delineation of the heroine's reply. Here the withdrawal noted above is most likely to be felt, for the heroine is rarely allowed a direct verbal response; she is too confused and emotional to speak well. The narrative must take over the task of dramatizing her consciousness. After the delineation of feeling has been accommodated, the characters resume their conversation, going over together all the misunderstandings and the understandings that have occurred. The scene usually ends with visions of future happiness, and the novel takes only one or two more chapters to completely resolve itself.

The single aspect of *Pride and Prejudice* that helps to enliven this rather dull formula is the wit of Elizabeth Bennet. Her irony helps to undercut any incipient sentimentality by asserting the limitations even in the best of human beings. Thus Elizabeth opens the conversation with a proclamation of her own egotism: "Mr. Darcy, I am a very selfish creature; and, for the sake of giving relief to my own feelings, care not how much I may be wounding your's" (p. 365). Throughout the exchange that follows, Elizabeth retains her capacity to cut through the pretensions of passion. When Darcy seeks to take on all the blame for the past, she replies, "We will not quarrel for the greater share of

---

[10] Lascelles, *Jane Austen and Her Art,* p. 126.

blame annexed to that evening. . . . The conduct of neither, if strictly examined, will be irreproachable . . ." (p. 367). And again, when Darcy accuses himself too sternly, she advises, "You must learn some of my philosophy. Think only of the past as its remembrance gives you pleasure" (pp. 368-69). Despite the charm of her frankness, it is important to note that Elizabeth Bennet is not all satire in this scene; she has learned the lessons of restraint. In the last paragraph of the chapter she checks her impulse to tease: "She remembered that he had yet to learn to be laught at, and it was rather too early to begin" (p. 371).

The ironic point with which Elizabeth adjusts Darcy's passion to the realities of human nature is, of course, illustrative of her whole character. Nevertheless, its lightness poses a threat to the feeling of the scene. The author seems alert to this threat; that may be why she follows the proposal episode with several scenes in which the analysis of Elizabeth's feeling is extended. In the following chapter there is an exchange with Jane in which Elizabeth, light-hearted and ironic as ever, directs her irony to the possibility of her own heartlessness. Jane asks her when she began to love Darcy, and Elizabeth replies, "It has been coming on so gradually, that I hardly know when it began. But I believe I must date it from my first seeing his beautiful grounds at Pemberley" (p. 373). The mercenary motive is a possibility that the reader dare not entertain if he is to judge Elizabeth's feelings sympathetically. In order to forestall his questioning of her heroine's motives, the author has her question them herself. In a second and more crucial exchange, between Mr. Bennet and Elizabeth, the possibility of unworthiness in her motives arises again. "He is rich, to be sure, and you may have more fine clothes and fine carriages than Jane. But will they make you happy?" Elizabeth's reply to this charge, and to further accusations about Darcy's pride, provides at last an occasion for uncontrolled feeling; her judgment is so completely suspended that she weeps openly before her father. It is interesting to point out that her verbal control is slightly impaired, made repetitive, by feeling. " 'I do, I do like him,' she replied, with tears in her eyes, 'I love him. Indeed he has no improper pride. He is perfectly amiable. You do not know what he really is; then pray do not pain me by speaking of him in such terms' " (p. 376). Mr. Bennet's irony, so irrepressible and so irresponsible, contrasts here with that of Elizabeth, who has learned that she must avoid giving pain. Her capacity to love truly is affirmed by her father's incapacity to take love seriously at all; he finishes their conversation by trivializing the affairs of all his daughters. As always,

Jane Austen shows what she means by dramatizing what she does not mean in pitting the claims of the head against those of the heart.

In *Pride and Prejudice* the masterly orchestration of episodes to point up the generosity of Elizabeth Bennet's wit confirms the reader's admiration and allegiance. Nevertheless, the narrative of the proposal scene proper seems to be seeking further ways to enlarge the reader's involvement by providing an immediate rendering of Elizabeth's consciousness as pure consciousness, isolated from its relations and ineloquent under the stress of feeling. It is important for Elizabeth to be at a loss for words if the emotional weight of her commitment to Darcy is to be completely felt. The narrator attempts to render this silence, with the following results:

> Elizabeth, feeling all the more than common awkwardness and anxiety of his situation, now forced herself to speak; and immediately, though not very fluently, gave him to understand, that her sentiments had undergone so material a change, since the period to which he alluded, as to make her receive with gratitude and pleasure, his present assurances. The happiness which this reply produced, was such as he had probably never felt before; and he expressed himself on the occasion as sensibly and as warmly as a man violently in love can be supposed to do. Had Elizabeth been able to encounter his eye, she might have seen how well the expression of heart-felt delight, diffused over his face, became him; but, though she could not look, she could listen, and he told her of feelings, which, in proving of what importance she was to him, made his affection every moment more valuable. [P. 366]

Jane Austen's prose is usually a source of wonder and delight, especially for the assurance with which it generalizes, asserting common truths forcefully without becoming encased in the stuffiness of common orthodoxy. Under the pressure of rendering Elizabeth's mental state, however, it falters. It is unsure, and in its unsureness, it shifts attention to Darcy, and then only to suggest how he "probably felt" or "what a man violently in love can be supposed to do." Embarrassment is the only psychic base provided to hold up such general words as "sentiment," "gratitude," "pleasure," "assurances," "importance," and "affection."[11] Moreover, formality of syntax belies the awkwardness of

---

[11] Many critics have analyzed Jane Austen's use of general words, none so helpfully as Howard S. Babb in the first chapter of *Jane Austen's Novels: The Fabric of Dialogue* (Columbus, Ohio, 1962). I do not wish to suggest that Jane Austen's vocabulary is inadequate because it is not "modern." Babb's analysis of the rhetorical effectiveness of the eighteenth-century vocabulary is

the situation to be rendered; there is no dislocation of phrasing to accommodate the confusions of feeling. In this passage one feels most strongly the limitation involved in the absence of metaphor in Jane Austen's prose style. Because of the richness of her dramatic invention and her masterful handling of dialogue, Jane Austen's prose rarely needs the aid of imagery, but in the proposal scenes, where gesture and speech have been severely restricted, the burdens of dramatic vividness must fall upon the style itself. At this point in her development Jane Austen cannot fully accommodate those burdens. Her vocabulary is too constricted, her syntax is too formal, and she is not yet ready to enrich her narrative with any of the images of the time and place in which the lovers make their vows.

Nevertheless, there are signs that Jane Austen perceives her problems. The very awkwardness of the passage just quoted, with its resort to hypothesis rather than authoritative assertion, denotes a consciousness of difficulty. The effort to lighten the summary with attention to the direction of Elizabeth's and Darcy's glances further indicates that a need to provide some image of them has been felt. Another point of interest lies in the device Jane Austen chooses for shifting out of the narrative of their immediate response into a summary of their talk as they continue, now sure of one another. "They walked on," the narrative continues, "without knowing in what direction. There was too much to be thought, and felt, and said, for attention to any other objects" (pp. 366-67). This sentence attempts to re-establish the proposal scene in time, and in the process it makes the setting of the scene — lightly sketched though it has been — symbolic of the relation between the outside world and the world of feeling.

The relation between objective, physical facts and the vagaries of feeling and desire is the subject of all Jane Austen's comedy. What we are dealing with in this instance, however, is not a thematic preoccupation but a technical effort to express the power of feeling uninhibited for a time by comic judgment. The effort to dramatize consciousness will never predominate over the comic allegiance to the adjudication between feeling and objective fact — the uses of setting in the proposal scenes will always imply the incipient and unavoidable demands of external forces — but more and more frequently Jane Austen will

---

convincing, but I believe that the effectiveness of general terms when used by masters like Samuel Johnson and Jane Austen depends upon a base supplied by a close annotation of the empirical facts of experience. Such a base is lacking in the passage at hand.

exploit physical environment for its power to convey the emotional interests of heroines who have less wit and self-assurance than Elizabeth Bennet. The contrast between time and place and the private world of feeling will become a characteristic resource of the proposal episodes to follow.

In *Pride and Prejudice* the temporal/spatial setting of the proposal is not fully exploited. In the end it merely helps, somewhat mechanically, to draw the scene to a close, for it is in "consulting" their watches, noting the unfelt passage of time, that Elizabeth and Darcy re-establish their contact with the outer world and head toward home.

In the light of the expressive price that wit must exact both from the character who possesses it in abundance and from the novel which embodies it almost as a self-sufficient value, the problems of *Mansfield Park* may be examined afresh. It is possible to see Fanny Price and the restraint with which she is presented as evidence of Jane Austen's effort to examine those aspects of moral choice and feeling unavailable to *Pride and Prejudice*.[12]

When one looks at *Mansfield Park* as a stage in Jane Austen's exploration of ways to make plain virtue artistically convincing, several significant departures in her art come to mind. First there is the conception of Fanny Price herself, a conception which, as Lionel Trilling has so brilliantly shown,[13] emphasizes weakness and passivity of both body and temperament, thereby testing the reader's capacity to agree to the moral interest of what Jane Austen calls "the consciousness of being born to struggle and endure." Another new departure is the conscious use of setting to provide a pervasive medium for feeling as well as theme. Although the contrast between Portsmouth and Mansfield is primarily emblematic of the novel's thematic concern for order, it also provides a framing device for Fanny's inner life. Her small sufferings are charged with pathos because they take place within extreme confines — those of her "little room" and of the cramped family house at Portsmouth — always brought into contrast with the free and harmonious expanse of the great country house.[14] Finally, *Mansfield Park* is the first of Jane

---

[12] A. Walton Litz has made a similar point about the relation of *Mansfield Park* to *Pride and Prejudice*. See "Counter-Truth: *Mansfield Park*," in *Jane Austen: A Study of Her Artistic Development*, especially pp. 122f.

[13] Lionel Trilling, "*Mansfield Park*," in *The Opposing Self* (New York, 1955), pp. 206-50.

[14] This aspect of setting in *Mansfield Park* has been suggested by Charles

Austen's novels to explore the narrative possibilities of time — time not only as the inevitable context of action but time as a force in action, in change, itself.

The action of *Mansfield Park* begins with Fanny Price's arrival at the Bertram household as a child of ten; it carries her through to her marriage with Edmund Bertram at nineteen. Such a span indicates interest in a kind of change which is different from that rendered in the other novels, which commence their action when the heroine is already ripe for whatever revelations may befall her — when her essential character is given. The changes in Fanny's life take place as a result of growth rather than sudden revelation. They are matters of gradual, almost imperceptible, process, and so the novel will never present her at a single pivotal moment, like Elizabeth Bennet's when she must say, "Till this moment, I never knew myself."

The exploration of the long, slow process of time creates several difficulties for the novel. It deprives it of the kind of pacing available when the narrative can move economically from one encounter to another with little need to annotate what has happened in the interim. *Mansfield Park* is admirably structured upon a number of major dramatic episodes, but the narrative between them carries a greater weight than in the other novels, and in some cases a single scene will not serve to render the gradual discoveries at issue. In point of fact, the proposal episode of this novel has no scene at all; it is really a summary of events that take many weeks to transpire. The necessity for summary places unusual demands on the author's stylistic resources; it calls for unusual tact in balancing prolonged analysis against the reader's tendency to reject static essays on human conduct. Jane Austen had refused the convention of first-person narration, which might have incorporated such analyses within the personality of a character (although she frequently does incorporate them in Fanny's judgment), and so she is forced to depend on the heavy convention of omniscience, though she tries to lighten it with satiric asides.

The problem of making time pass is not entirely new to Jane Austen. In *Northanger Abbey* she had written a comment on fictional chronology that is lightly critical of the sentimental novel's *longeurs* without completely dismissing the difficulty of bringing time and change together in the development of character: "Monday, Tuesday, Wednes-

Murrah, "The Background of *Mansfield Park*," in Robert C. Rathburn and Martin Steinmann, Jr., eds., *From Jane Austen to Joseph Conrad* (Minneapolis, 1958), pp. 23-34.

day, Thursday, Friday, and Saturday have now passed in review before the reader; the events of each day, its hopes and fears, mortifications and pleasures have been separately stated, and the pangs of Sunday only now remain to be described, and close the week" (p. 97). Jane Austen's early rhetorical strategy in coping with the passage of time is to admit its difficulties openly; thus she places both herself and her reader in the mechanics of the narrative. In doing this, to be sure, she runs the risk of distancing her heroine's experience; she must look upon it from the outside, as part of a purely narrative problem. In *Northanger Abbey* this distance enables her to make comic generalizations that undercut some outrageous claims of sentiment while allowing her to emphasize the simplicity of her heroine — reinforcing along the way the link connecting the heroine, the reader, and herself as ordinary, sensible people. In *Mansfield Park,* however, the heroine is not as simple as Catherine Moreland, and the moral issues are resistant to common, uninstructed sense. The narrative must therefore not only give a convincing illusion of time passing and change taking place, but it must also convince the reader of Fanny's capacity for growth and assure him of her genuine, though complicated, virtue and worth.

In the context of all that is involved in narrating the passage of time, the rhetoric in the concluding chapter of *Mansfield Park* becomes understandable if not entirely convincing. The chapter opens with a denial of the grave significance of what is to follow. Part of this denial seems concerned with a possible misplacement of sympathy, part seems preoccupied with the difficulty of tying up so many things in a short time, and part seems an effort to restore the comic mode to a novel that has extended itself far into the realm of pathos. The initial appeal to the reader and its self-conscious allusion to the difficulties of the author seek to create a distance in which pathos can be either ignored or laughed at. "Let other pens dwell on guilt and misery. I quit such odious subjects as soon as I can, impatient to restore every body, not greatly in fault themselves, to tolerable comfort, and to have done with all the rest" (p. 461). Despite this disclaimer, the chapter proceeds to paint pictures of failure that cannot be lightly dismissed — Sir Thomas surveying the ruins of his family pride, Maria Rushworth growing more and more bitter and finally banished in the company of Aunt Norris to an exile where "their tempers became their mutual punishment," Henry Crawford left to contemplate the destruction of his own character, Mary left divided between the consciousness of what she has lost in Edmund and the necessity to choose someone less worthy, and even poor Mr. Rushworth let loose again with his stupidity. There is so rigorous an allocation of mental pain that the author's depreciation of it seems an embarrassed apology.

At the end of the uneasy accounting of retributions, Jane Austen turns to the gradual awakening of Edmund Bertram's love for Fanny Price. There is no proposal scene proper in *Mansfield Park* because Fanny's character is so unassuming that her effects cannot be felt in a single episode. Once more the narrator is forced to summarize intensively, and once more she begins that summary with an open appeal to the reader to appreciate the difficulties of fixing time and change convincingly in a story.

> I purposely abstain from dates on this occasion, that everyone may be at liberty to fix their own, aware that the cure of unconquerable passions, and the transfer of unchanging attachments, must vary much as to time in different people. — I only intreat every body to believe that exactly at the time when it was quite natural that it should be so, and not a week earlier, Edmund did cease to care about Miss Crawford, and became as anxious to marry Fanny, as Fanny herself could desire. [P. 470]

In this passage from *Mansfield Park*, as in the whole of its conclusion, there is a strange intensity of authorial commitment that makes for the stiffness of dogma rather than the open delight in the haziness of human resolutions which the generalizations about time and change in the *Northanger Abbey* passage provide. There is an edge in the rhetorical demand made for cooperation from the reader; the danger of Mary Crawford's inspiring more sympathy than she should seems to lurk in the rhetoric of the narration. The crude irony in the antitheses between "unconquerable passion" and "unchanging attachments" and their "cure" or "transfer" makes the rejection of a definite date for such changes as Edmund's challenge the reader to deny that they have really occurred. Here the contrasts between generalizations about human behavior and the temporal facts of experience are not designed primarily as a comic invitation to engage with the author in a contemplation of human absurdity; they constitute a demand for agreement about a difficult case.

Lacking an even slightly drawn setting for this resolution in favor of the responsibilities of feeling, the narrative of Edmund's and Fanny's betrothal must depend entirely upon the stylistic resources of the narrator. That style is still unequal to the syntactical dislocations of emotion; it also lacks the specificity of imagery. Within its limitations, however, there is some attempt to form sentences that can mirror grammatically the complexities of feeling. There is certainly a rare occurrence of imagery in its effort to highlight the contrasts between Fanny Price and Mary Crawford, which make Edmund's change of heart so difficult to render.

> With such a regard for her, indeed, as his had long been, a regard founded on the most endearing claims of innocence and helplessness, and completed by every recommendation of growing worth, what could be more natural than the change? Loving, guiding, protecting her, as he had been doing ever since her being ten years old, her mind in so great a degree formed by his care, and her comfort depending on his kindness, an object to him of such close and peculiar interest, dearer by all his own importance with her than anyone else at Mansfield, what was there now to add, but that he should learn to prefer soft light eyes to sparkling dark ones. — And being always with her, and always talking confidentially, and his feelings exactly in that favorable state which a recent disappointment gives, those soft light eyes could not be very long in obtaining the pre-eminence. [P. 420]

The prose of this passage is so syntactically packed that it may not seem likely evidence for making a case about Jane Austen's attempts to loosen up her verbal formalism in favor of structures which would describe more fluently the varieties of feeling. However, it does seem to me that in attempting to encompass all that must take place in Edmund if he is to love Fanny, she avoids the epigrammatic precision of her usual antitheses and parallels and simply lists psychological details, and those in a series of participial phrases with unusual verbal force. "Loving, guiding, protecting" open an extremely complicated sentence that ends in an uncharacteristic imagery of "soft light eyes" and "sparkling dark ones." It is true that these images are so stereotyped that their specificity is submerged if not vulgarized by overfamiliarity. It is also true that this passage itself begins with another of those awkward rhetorical demands that carry on a continuing appeal for the reader to believe in what is happening as natural and inevitable. Nevertheless, the very insistences of such devices betoken the author's efforts to solve the special problems of dramatizing the feelings of her unusually virtuous lovers without the aid of a specific encounter.

Though the devices of rhetoric and style lend a recurrent note of formal and theoretical pleading to the narration of Edmund's discovery of his love for Fanny, it is important to notice the content of the theory. In these passages Jane Austen is making a survey of the states of a mind in action; she is talking about the mental acrobatics, hesitations, and reversals upon which any commitment must be made. Fanny's responses, as always, are more fixed than Edmund's, and so the passage that renders her reaction is somewhat less interesting and less effective.

> Her mind, disposition, opinions, and habits wanted no half concealment, no self deception on the present, no reliance on future improvement. . . . Timid, anxious, doubting as she was, it was still impossible that such tenderness as hers should not, at times, hold out the strongest hope of success, though it remained for a later period to tell him the whole delightful and astonishing truth. His happiness in knowing himself to have been so long the beloved of such a heart, must have been great enough to warrant any strength of language in which he could cloathe it to her or to himself; it must have been a delightful happiness! But there was happiness elsewhere which no description can reach. Let no one presume to give the feelings of a young woman on receiving the assurance of that affection of which she has scarcely allowed herself to entertain a hope. [P. 471]

The first element to notice in this passage is its dependence on superlatives to give a sense of unimaginable commitment on the part of the lovers. Besides the extraordinary exclamation point, which enforces the statement about the extent of Edmund's happiness, there is an extraordinary number of superlative phrases — "impossible," "strongest hope," "astonishing truth," and "any strength of language." This last phrase brings into play the sense that it is well nigh impossible to speak under the force of strong feeling. Jane Austen turns to the reader, asking him to join her in humility before Fanny's feelings, so great are they. This is a peculiarly extravagant request, and it causes the proposal summary to conclude with a strange tentativeness. The inability of the narrator to dramatize emotions concretely results in the aggressive assertion that they cannot be dramatized at all.

The last chapter of *Mansfield Park* is strangely flat and off-balance in tone. The author uses the problems of temporal summary to mask the greater problems of resolving the issues of the novel as a whole. She has spent the bulk of the novel on the tensions created by the presence of Mary Crawford and her brother, especially while Sir Thomas is away from the citadel of principle and propriety. Fanny has been left as the center of consciousness, the innocent center of consciousness, growing up under a painful awakening to the lure of trivial values created by an ultimately perverse collection of self-assured people. The creation of such an innocent eye presents the novelist with the task of convincing the reader that it is possible to maintain innocence under the pressure of knowledge. Modern novelists who have tried this feat have resolved the difficulty either by making their innocents relatively stupid or by killing them off before the end — one thinks of Milly Theale. If Jane Austen's imagination had been tragic, she might have concluded her novel with the death of Fanny and the complete disillusion of Edmund. But her mode requires a happy marriage; she does not believe in sudden death, and she does believe in the possibility of human happiness, even though it may be constrained by rational choice.

Despite elements of moral pathos in the whole, the ending of *Mansfield Park* returns to the format in which Jane Austen was easy philosophically and aesthetically. But her open proclamation of the difficulties of making the resolution acceptable advertises a sensitivity to the dislocations caused by imposing comedy on a novel of extreme sensibility. Perhaps the most jarring thing about the satire in *Mansfield Park*'s conclusion is the fact that its distrust of emotions works to the detriment of credibility on behalf of the lovers. Focuses for a sharp, ironic delineation of the differences between the aspirations of innocence and the sterility of unfeeling sophistication, they became victims of an irony that is only slightly blunted. The proposal narrative thus represents a mixture of modes that forces the author to plead for the lovers in the end as two quite ordinary young people who are somewhat ludicrous in the fuss they make about falling in love.[15]

Emma marks a recommitment to the comic mode and to the wittily vivacious heroine as well. Nevertheless, Emma Woodhouse is a heroine whom Jane Austen fears no one will much like, and it is clear from the very beginning that she knows the sources of that possible dislike. "The real evils indeed of Emma's situation were the power of having rather too much her own way, and a disposition to think a little too well of herself..." (p. 5). Lionel Trilling has characterized Emma as a snob,[16] and Jane Austen was conscious of the challenges of such a characterization.

[15] For a treatment of the resolution of the novel which does not admit the possibility that the novel fails, but wishes to say that it shows Fanny and Edmund as flawed creatures who work out a theme of limited happiness in a limited society and thus receive "rewards appropriate to their merits — each other," see Avrom Fleishman, *A Reading of "Mansfield Park": An Essay in Critical Synthesis* (Minneapolis, 1967), pp. 53-56.

[16] Lionel Trilling, *"Emma," Encounter,* VIII (1957), 49-59.

The scene which provides Emma with the saving grace of a "relenting heart" helps to resolve the problems of keeping sympathy for her alive. In the ebb and flow of consciousness that it succeeds in rendering, it also illustrates Jane Austen's victory over the difficulties involved in dramatizing climaxes of feeling without sacrificing comic pattern or clarity.

The scene has been carefully prepared. It comes at a point at which both Emma and Mr. Knightley are completely tangled up in their misinformation about each other and about themselves. Emma believes that Mr. Knightley is in love with Harriet Smith, or at least that his generous nature will require him to choose her. Knightley, on the other hand, thinks that Emma has been enamoured of Frank Churchill and that she must be laboring under extreme grief at the knowledge that he has always been engaged to Jane Fairfax. They meet one afternoon in the shrubberies, each determined to aid the other in his imagined troubles, and what results is a minuet of changing psychological postures that ends in a declaration and an acceptance.

One of the interesting developments in this episode is its use of setting. The chapter opens with a full notation of the state of the weather:

> The weather continued much the same all the following morning; and the same loneliness, and the same melancholy, seemed to reign at Hartfield — but in the afternoon it cleared; the wind changed into a softer quarter; the clouds were carried off; the sun appeared; it was summer again. With all the eagerness which such a transition gives, Emma resolved to be out of doors as soon as possible. Never had the exquisite sight, smell, sensation of nature, tranquil, warm, and brilliant after a storm, been more attractive to her. She longed for the serenity they might gradually introduce. . . . [P. 424]

It is clear that this passage is preparing for the familiar situation in which the lovers can be alone to walk and talk, and as in *Pride and Prejudice,* that walk will form a loose dramatic frame for their conversation. Mr. Knightley will appear in the shrubberies, and Emma will walk with him until she is so sure that he wishes to tell her of Harriet that she attempts to end the stroll by going inside. But her awareness of his distress will cause her to propose another turn so that he can continue, no matter how much his speech may pain her. As they continue on the second round, she will find out the happy truth. Despite its simplicity, Jane Austen has plotted the physical action of this episode carefully to accommodate a crisis and a resolution of feeling. The details of nature introducing it have been artfully arranged to express the change that has taken place in Emma, softening her feelings enough to enable her to think of another beyond her own pain or desires. There is a new mutuality between Emma and her surroundings.

The softening effects of feeling are not, however, to take precedence over the ironic play of judgment about Emma. The annotation of her feelings shows that, despite her natural generosity, she moves in a world of illusion until the very moment that she assents to Knightley's declaration. She has already been creating visions of Mr. Knightley's match with Harriet, which she is expecting to be verified as the walk continues; she has seen them married, and she has accepted a vision of herself nobly following the lonely paths of virtue, devoting her life to her father and to solemn thoughts. Her repentance is still misguided by the romantic imagination of herself as one who has learned to accept pain stoically. This last sentimentality must be dispelled and the triumph over it accepted if she is to be cured.

When Mr. Knightley begins to speak, we are aware of a new assurance in Jane Austen's handling of dialogue in the proposal situation. She is now willing to hazard a direct report of what he says; she has mastered the art of giving the illusion of emotional hesitance without permitting her dialogue to become sentimental or to lose its point.

"I cannot make speeches, Emma:" — he soon resumed; and in a tone of such sincere, decided, intelligible tenderness as was tolerably convincing. — "If I loved you less, I might be able to talk about it more. But you know what I am. You hear nothing but truth from me." [P. 430]

The narrator indicates Knightley's feeling through dashes and through his open protestations of inadequacy; as the lover continues, she also permits him rare words of endearment and an unusual "God knows." Nevertheless, his speech hangs together logically, and its short sentences are forceful. Only toward its conclusion do the hiatuses and repetitions begin to mirror Knightley's confusion.[17] And then the rhythm and asso-

---

[17] Several letters in the last chapters of *Mansfield Park* illustrate Jane Austen's experimentation with incoherence to render strong feeling. When Tom Bertram is not within her view, Lady Bertram writes too formally; his arrival at Mansfield inspires her to write in the "language of real feeling and alarm," and her letter to Fanny is a series of short, forceful clauses (pp. 425-27). A better example is offered by Mary Crawford's confused letter telling Fanny of Henry's elopement with Maria Rushworth. Here Jane Austen attempts as no-

nance of the last sentence, "only to hear, once to hear your voice," show
that sound as well as sense are being brought into play to express feeling.
We have noted the wit of Jane Austen's prose; here we must notice its
eloquence.

> " — I have blamed you, and lectured you, and you have borne it as no
> other woman in England would have borne it. — Bear with the truths
> I would tell you now, dearest Emma, as well as you have borne with
> them. The manner, perhaps, may have as little to recommend them.
> God knows, I have been a very indifferent lover. — But you understand
> me. — Yes, you see, you understand my feelings — and will return them
> if you can. At present, I ask only to hear, once to hear your voice."
> [P. 430]

Like Elizabeth Bennet, Emma is not to be given a directly reported
speech in reply. We find a familiar silence on the part of the heroine
that must be filled by the narrator's analysis of her consciousness.

> While he spoke, Emma's mind was most busy, and, with all the won-
> derful velocity of thought, has been able — and yet without losing a
> word — to catch and comprehend the exact truth of the whole; to see
> that Harriet's hopes had been entirely groundless, a mistake, delusion,
> as complete a delusion as any of her own — that Harriet was nothing;
> that she was every thing herself; that what she had been saying relative
> to Harriet had been all taken as the language of her own feelings; and
> that her agitation, her doubts, her reluctance, her discouragement had
> been all received as discouragement from herself. [Pp. 430-31]

Here an eighteenth-century vocabulary does not impede the author's
analysis of the way the mind works. Jane Austen searches that lexicon
for words like "velocity," which can convey the swiftness of thought and
the discrepancy between such speed and the temporal urgency of actual
events. The complex relation among feeling, fact, and sensation is noted
as an important aspect of the mind in motion. The narrative seeks
further to render this by packing all the fleeting thoughts into one sentence that builds, clause after clause, in almost random order. The
passage goes on, noting once again the temporal dimension of Emma's
reaction.

> — And not only was there time for these convictions, with all their glow

---

where else to give the effect of emotion through broken sentences and unex-
plained references (p. 437). These letters look back to Richardson's ideal of
"instantaneous descriptions" as well as forward to the flexibility of dialogue that
we see in Knightley's speech to Emma.

of attendant happiness; there was time also to rejoice that Harriet's secret had not escaped her, and to resolve that it need not and should not. — It was all the service she could now render her poor friend; for as to any of that heroism of sentiment which might have prompted her to entreat him to transfer his affection from herself to Harriet, as infinitely the most worthy of the two — or even the more simple sublimity of resolving to refuse him at once and for ever, without vouchsafing any motive, because he could not marry them both, Emma had it not. She felt for Harriet, with pain and with contrition; but no flight of generosity run mad, opposing all that could be probable or reasonable, entered her brain. She had led her friend astray, and it would be a reproach to her for ever; but her judgment was as strong as her feelings, and as strong as it had ever been before, in reprobating any such alliance for him, as most unequal and degrading. Her way was clear, though not quite smooth. [P. 431]

This passage sets up the possible mental debate between sentiment and true feeling. In managing this debate, it cleverly sketches an alternate, parodic ending consonant with the kind of novelistic plots Emma has indulged throughout the novel. Now, however, Emma is capable of rejecting romantic imaginings. The rejection is clothed in brisk phrases that mock the absurdity of the romanticizing imagination through formal hyperbole — "heroism of sentiment," "simple sublimity," "flight of generosity run mad" — these phrases, which point up the foolishness of sentimentality, take on added force because they are placed in an analysis of a mind truly moved. In her moment of truth Emma not only feels strongly, but she is able to judge well and choose rightly. The fact that this passage shows her in the process of using her judgment, while placing that process in the flight of consciousness with all its speed and confusion, enables Jane Austen to present the psychology of her character while maintaining stylistic control over its comic possibilities.

Jane Austen cannot let Emma speak if she is to let the comedy of her feelings have full play, if she is to exploit the contrast between Emma's last temptation to write a sentimental novel and the reality of the world she inhabits. When Emma does speak, Jane Austen once again avoids her exact words, not in a denial that they could be reported but in a deprecating statement about Emma's adequacy to the occasion: " — She spoke then, on being so entreated. — What did she say? — Just what she ought, of course. A lady always does. — She said enough to show there need not be despair — and to invite him to say more himself" (p. 431). The heroine's words have been avoided once again, but not defensively. The rhetorical question that introduces the shift away from Emma's speech, unlike those in *Mansfield Park*, gives no uneasy sense that the author is unsure of an answer. She moves on quickly through a summary of what Emma says to a short paragraph of interpretation that balances the ironies of psychological muddlement against the sincerity of generous motives. "Seldom, very seldom, does complete truth belong to any human disclosure; seldom can it happen that something is not a little disguised, or a little mistaken; but where, as in this case, though the conduct is mistaken, the feelings are not, it may not be very material. — Mr. Knightley could not impute to Emma a more relenting heart than she possessed, or a heart more disposed to accept of his" (pp. 431-32).

It would be hard to find a passage that would better illustrate the flexibility of Jane Austen's mature prose style. The ordering allegiance to the balanced sentence is still felt, especially in the precision of phrasing and the harmony of parallel constructions. But these grammatical elements are softened by repetition and enlarging modifying clauses. The repetition of "seldom" in the first sentence, and the enlargement of meaning in "a little disguised, or a little mistaken," denote an ease in letting sentences go back upon themselves to fill out the nuances of human behavior. The last sentence's openly sympathetic approval of the emotions of the lovers indicates that quality of feeling here is to preside over the stringencies of judgment.

The prose itself is relenting, and in being so, it is able to accommodate shades of feeling without indulging them in such a way that a particular case, like that of Emma and Mr. Knightley, can yield no general truth at all. The innovations in *Emma* are primarily matters of retrenchment, of the perfection of a style and form already well under control. But there is new facility in penetrating the flux of consciousness through attention to its temporal and physical frame. If I use phrases here that sound too psychological for Jane Austen's art, I do so by design. For it seems clear to me that as her creation of fiction progressed, she continually enlarged both her interest in the fluidity of experience and her capacity to express it.

In an important conversation with Frederick Wentworth in *Persuasion*, Anne Elliot makes an observation about time, place, and feeling that resonates throughout the novel. Wentworth is recalling the horror of an accident at Lyme, doubting that Anne would ever want to see the place again. She replies, "The last few hours were certainly very painful ... but when pain is over, the remembrance of it often becomes a pleasure. One does not love a place the less for having suffered in it, unless it has all been suffering, nothing but suffering . . ." (pp. 183-84). Rarely in Jane Austen's novels has a heroine spoken so openly of emotion, and rarely in such haunting tones. Anne Elliot is permitted to do so because of *Persuasion*'s peculiar emphasis on the passage of time and the poetry of place.

Time here is not merely a theoretical or technical aid to the rendering of moral awakening; it permeates the work's central insight into the effects of suffering. Anne Elliot is the kind of heroine that made Jane Austen "sick and wicked."[18] Her goodness is made interesting, and her choices are made vital, by the fact that she is the only one of Jane Austen's heroines who has a past. The memory of that past in the context of an unfeeling present provides the novel with a way to dramatize the pain of a choice that has been made patient and rich in moral significance through long years of secret retrospection. Place is related to time in its provision of specific images for memory to savor. The past can be recaptured and enjoyed if its incidents are attached to particular scenes.

In all the other novels time and place have their thematic and technical functions, but never are the two joined in such a purely expressive way as they are in *Persuasion*. One observation may serve to make this point quite clear. The result of the proposals heretofore has been the reward of a suitable abode for the heroine, and in each case that home has been previewed early in the novel. Elizabeth Bennet visits Pemberley, Fanny Price hears Edmund's plans for Thornton Lacey, Emma's visit to Donwell Abbey dramatizes the ideal of a reasoned control of nature. In *Persuasion* there is no dwelling that carries the stable assurances of such country estates; Kellynch Hall, to which Anne has attached the emotional allegiance of her childhood, must be rented out to strangers. The Musgrove residences are models of familial chaos: "I hope I shall remember, in future," Lady Russell observes, "not to call at Uppercross in the Christmas holidays" (p. 135). Anne's reward, then, is to be a new kind of place; she is the single heroine whose future must find its only stability in her relation with her husband. As if to symbolize this, Mrs. Croft speaks early in the novel of the homes she has shared with Admiral Croft. "When you come to a frigate, of course, you are more confined — though any reasonable woman may be perfectly happy

---

[18] This phrase is applied to heroines in general, but the letter in which it occurs goes on to speak of Anne Elliot as being "almost too good" for the author; see *Letters*, pp. 486-87.

in one of them; and I can safely say, that the happiest part of my life has been spent on board a ship. While we were together, you know, there was nothing to be feared" (p. 70). Anne Elliot's marriage to Captain Wentworth holds the promise of happiness attached to no single place itself, unless it be the ever-changing but entirely beautiful sea.

The sea itself is a presence in *Persuasion;* it evokes rare admiration on the part of the narrator for its timelessness.

> . . . and, above all, Pinny, with its green chasms between romantic rocks, where the scattered forest trees and orchards of luxuriant growth declare that many a generation must have passed away since the first partial fall-ing of the cliff prepared the ground for such a state, where a scene so wonderful and so lovely is exhibited, as may more than equal any of the resembling scenes of the far-famed Isle of Wight: these places must be visited, and visited again, to make the worth of Lyme understood. [Pp. 95-96]

There is no structural requirement for this passage; it exists as a free expression of feeling. The rare use of the word "romantic" in it strikes a new note in Jane Austen's art. But her attention to the sublimity of the sea and of nature is not the only peculiarity of setting in *Persuasion;* the novel also pays unusually specific attention to the details of town life.[19] "When Lady Russell, not long afterwards, was entering Bath on a wet afternoon, and driving through the long course of streets from the Old Bridge to Camden-place, amidst the dash of other carriages, the heavy rumble of carts and drays, the bawling of newsmen, muffin-men and milk-men, and the ceaseless clink of pattens, she made no com-plaint. No, these were the noises which belonged to the winter plea-sures . . ." (p. 135).

One does not expect to find lists of naturalistic details in Jane Austen; when one does in the Portsmouth scene of *Mansfield Park,* there is a slight disturbance of the harmony of the whole book. In *Persuasion* such lists are intrinsic; they serve to form not so much a contrast with the heroine's state of mind as its necessary context. Anne Elliot's retiring

---

[19] Critics like Virginia Woolf, "Jane Austen," in *The Common Reader; First Series* (New York, 1953), pp. 137-49; Frank O'Connor, "Jane Austen: The Flight from Fancy," in *The Mirror in the Roadway* (London, 1957); and A. Walton Litz have noted the unusual poetry of nature in *Persuasion,* with the suggestion that Jane Austen is at last beginning to feel the effects of the Ro-mantic movement. This is probably true, but it should be added that the presence of fully articulated town settings point to Jane Austen's affinities with the Romanticism of Lamb and Hazlitt as well as Wordsworth.

nature will be vivified by a portrayal rendered almost exclusively from the inside, but this inside will be enriched with poetic value through a pervasive attention to those random details of place that the remembrance of pain and the hope for surcease transmute. Several additional passages from the novel might be cited, but the one that portrays Anne's reception of Wentworth's changing sentiments just before she speaks to him of suffering must serve as a final illustration of the way *Persuasion* handles the buzz and hum of crowded places so as to evoke the private feelings of the heroine. The scene is a crowded concert room at Bath. ". . . and Anne, who, in spite of the agitated voice in which the latter part [of Wentworth's speech] had been uttered, and in spite of all the various noises of the room, the almost ceaseless slam of the door, and ceaseless buzz of persons walking through, had distinguished every word, was struck, gratified, confused, and beginning to breathe very quick, and feel an hundred things in a moment" (p. 183).

The proposal scene itself is a culmination of the tendencies we have already seen. There are several explanations for Jane Austen's revision of this episode, but we can see from the canceled chapters of *Persuasion* that she revised the proposal partly to provide it with the setting of the busy town.[20] In the earlier version she had maneuvered the lovers into a secluded corner of Admiral Croft's drawing room; in revision she places them first in the bustle of the Musgrove establishment, then in the public walks of Bath. The Musgrove setting points up the human environment that has forced Anne into the refuge of memory throughout the years. Even now, this environment will give the lovers no relief, no privacy. Overhearing Anne speak of a woman's claim to "loving longest, when existence or when hope is gone," Wentworth must compose his feelings in a hasty letter that Anne must read covertly. She cannot hide her reactions in the midst of all the Musgroves and pleads sickness as an excuse to return to the solitude of her room, perhaps to meet Captain Wentworth on the way. But still the insistencies of her environment bear in upon her, denying her even the private release of joy. Charles Musgrove cannot be prevented from taking her home.

---

[20] For a convenient summary of the various structural problems solved by the revised ending, see Litz, *Jane Austen: A Study of Her Artistic Development*, pp. 158-60. Robert Liddell prefers the setting of the first version in Admiral Croft's house for the view it gives of the admiral's happy life; see *The Novels of Jane Austen* (London, 1963), pp. 136-67. See also Louise D. Cohen, "Insight, the Essence of Jane Austen's Artistry," *Nineteenth-Century Fiction*, VIII (1953), 213-24.

As they proceed down the street, Anne hears the step of Captain
Wentworth. As so often before in the novel, she is aware of his presence
physically before she actually sees him; the notation of indirect physical
sensations gives her experience of him unusual physical density. It also
enables the narrative to plot the meetings in terms of temporal response. "They were in Union-street, when a quicker step behind, a
something of familiar sound, gave her two moments preparation for the
sight of Captain Wentworth. He joined them; but, as if irresolute
whether to join or to pass on, said nothing — only looked. Anne could
command herself enough to receive that look, and not repulsively. The
cheeks which had been pale now glowed, and the movements which
had hesitated were decided. He walked by her side" (pp. 239-40). The
crisis of the meeting is carefully rooted in details of gesture and sensation; these are all the more striking because Charles Musgrove is impervious to their import. He is anxious only for himself and an errand
he wishes to perform, so he asks Captain Wentworth to take Anne the
rest of the way home. In the process he gives an unusually precise street
guide to the city of Bath.

> "Captain Wentworth, which way are you going? Only to Gay-street, or
> farther up the town?" . . . "Are you going as high as Belmont? Are you
> going near Camdenplace? Because if you are, I shall have no scruple in
> asking you to take my place, and give Anne your arm to her father's door.
> She is rather done for this morning, and must not go so far without
> help. And I ought to be at that fellow's in the marketplace. He promised
> me the sight of a capital gun he is just going to send off; said he would
> keep it unpacked to the last possible moment, that I might see it; and if
> I do not turn back now, I have no chance. By his description, a good
> deal like the second-sized double-barrel of mine, which you shot with one
> day, round Winthrop." [P. 240]

The unimaginative rambling of Charles Musgrove's speech helps in
two ways to thicken the setting of the proposal to follow. First, its evo-
cation of the precise geography of Bath — the streets, the directions
they run, and the purposes they serve — emphasizes the publicity of the
lovers' encounter. The city and all its random concerns have formed
the context of the lovers' culminating experience of one another through
the last third of the novel. Charles's speech also provides a last illustration of that blank, meaningless self-absorption in the environment which
surrounds Anne and has forced her feelings inward. But in *Persuasion*
the contrast between external facts and the heroine's sensibility does not
inevitably lead to satirical judgments. Outside her own family the people

who undervalue Anne's right to her own consciousness are well-meaning, only slightly selfish people like Charles Musgrove, who at this point actually helps the situation by looking after his own interests. His presence is not a positive threat; it is part of a complicated physical setting that serves to illuminate the significance of Anne's silences with its unthinking chatter. Finally Charles leaves, and the reader is prepared for the familiar passage in which the narrative covers the first moments of the lovers' open commitment to one another. The whole thing takes a single paragraph.

There could not be an objection. There could be only a most proper alacrity, a most obliging compliance for public view; and smiles reined in and spirits dancing in private rapture. In half a minute, Charles was at the bottom of Union-street again, and the other two proceeding together; and soon words enough had passed between them to decide their direction towards the comparatively quiet and retired gravel-walk, where the power of conversation would make the present hour a blessing indeed; and prepare it for all the immortality which the happiest recollections of their own future lives could bestow. There they exchanged again those feelings and those promises which had once before seemed to secure every thing, but which had been followed by so many, many years of division and estrangement. There they returned again into the past, more exquisitely happy, perhaps, in their re-union, than when it had been first projected; more tender, more tried, more fixed in a knowledge of each other's character, truth, and attachment; more equal to act, more justified in acting. And there, as they slowly paced the gradual ascent, heedless of every group around them, seeing neither sauntering politicians, bustling house-keepers, flirting girls, nor nursery-maids and children, they could indulge in those retrospections and acknowledgements, and especially in those explanations of what had directly preceded the present moment, which were so poignant and so ceaseless in interest. All the little variations of the last week were gone through; and of yesterday and to-day there could scarcely be an end. [Pp. 240-41]

There are aspects of this passage that need no comment; we have seen them all before — the avoidance of direct quotation in favor of narrative summary of feeling; the notation of the passage of time unheeded by the lovers; the easy modulation of syntax from the formality of "all the immortality which the happiest recollections of their own future lives could bestow" to the more intuitive cadences of "more tender, more tried, more fixed in a knowledge of each other's character, truth and attachment; more equal to act, more justified in acting." And in it all is the presence of an ordering intelligence that can generalize about feelings without stultifying them. What is extraordinary, however, is the annotation of place. In this most public proposal of all the novels, Jane Austen uses the space provided by the lovers' private talk to list all the details that their emotion has for the moment shielded them from — "sauntering politicians, bustling house-keepers, flirting girls . . . nursery-maids and children." From this sharp elaboration of the quotidian world she returns to the inner place and time inhabited by the lovers; the painfulness of experience unrelieved by the soothing power of memory is dissipated as the lovers review the past. Their recollection, wrested from the distractions of trivial though lively surroundings, transmutes the present, making it timeless — "and of yesterday and to-day there could scarcely be an end." Temporal and physical notations here unite poignantly (the word belongs to the narrator) to create an eternal moment that is self-justifying in its beauty and its joy.

Persuasion is a comic novel; in spite of the unusual poetry of its proposal scene, it does end with judgments. In an exchange stolen from a crowded party later in the day, Anne Elliot tells Wentworth that after all she had been right in rejecting him the first time on the advice of Lady Russell: "I should have suffered more in continuing the engagement than I did even in giving it up, because I should have suffered in my conscience" (p. 246). And after Anne has expounded on the nature of duty and the relation between prudence and trust, Jane Austen turns to generalizations of her own about the irrationality of feeling. The first paragraph of the concluding chapter begins: "Who can be in doubt of what followed? When any two young people take it into their heads to marry, they are pretty sure by perseverance to carry their point, be they ever so poor, or ever so imprudent, or ever so little likely to be necessary to each other's ultimate comfort" (p. 248). In her last novel Jane Austen is aware of the dramatic power of time and place brought together to express the transcendence of the single, intensely felt moment, but she never gives up the sense that the moment must pass — it can sustain and soothe, but it cannot be the only guide to action.

There is a strong temptation in a study of her development to make guesses about where Jane Austen's art would have gone had she lived longer. Virginia Woolf surmises that "she would have devised a method, clear and composed as ever, but deeper and more suggestive, for conveying not only what people say, but what they leave unsaid; not only what they are, but what life is."[21] This study clearly shares the major thrust of such a hypothesis in its conception of the whole canon as illustrating a growth of competence in staging crisises of emotion and thought. Jane Austen becomes slightly more expert and free in her expressive use of time and place to set up human encounters. But the fact that the novels always come to a point in a scene which is designed to wrest moral significance from all that has gone before illustrates that clarity is always more important than suggestion for Jane Austen: her concern with quotidian reality is inevitably to be linked with her sense of the possibilities of order. We know that Jane Austen had a sense of the disorderly life that flowed beyond the confines of her novels; we know, for example, that Jane Fairfax would have died shortly after her marriage to Frank Churchill in *Emma*.[22] But the novels themselves always stop short of catastrophe, of death, of even natural diminution. Their endings affirm the ability of a generous intelligence to make sense of experience despite the uncertainties of human life. Wherever she would have gone, what Frank Kermode calls "the sense of an ending" would have remained constant in Jane Austen's art. The close of each new novel would have reiterated the possibility of creating living value in a time and space confused by distractions and beset by the temptation to bad choices.

[21] Woolf, "Jane Austen," p. 149.
[22] Marghanita Laski, *Jane Austen and Her World* (London, 1969), pp. 107-8.

FOUR

Jane Austen's Anatomy of Persuasion

BY DONALD RACKIN

Whether or not *Persuasion* is one of Jane Austen's best novels,[1] it surely calls for serious critical attention, for in it Jane Austen creates a new kind of protagonist and with her a new set of demands upon the reader. The only one of Jane Austen's heroines who does not mature significantly within the main story, Anne Elliot at twenty-seven has already matured almost to perfection when the novel begins. And the reader is faced at the outset not with the familiar questions: "How will this young girl learn to see more truly and behave more wisely, how will she grow up and realize her shortcomings?" but instead with a question like this: "Will this woman's now fully blossomed virtue be rewarded at such a late date not merely by virtue itself, but by that palpable prize one expects in Jane Austen's world — fulfillment embodied in the practical and emblematic reward of a satisfactory mar-

---

[1] Among recent Jane Austen critics, one finds considerable disagreement about the merits of *Persuasion*. For example, Rachel Trickett in "Jane Austen's Comedy and the Nineteenth Century," in Brian Southam, ed., *Critical Essays on Jane Austen* (London, 1968), p. 178, says: "There are, of course, many fine touches in *Persuasion* . . . . But by the standards we have used to judge her other works, it is a failure." For another, more thorough, recent argument that *Persuasion* is a failure, see Andor Gomme, "On Not Being Persuaded," *Essays in Criticism*, XVI (1966), 170-84. On the other hand, praise for *Persuasion* is pretty widespread, although rigorous critical corroboration of that praise is rare. See, for example, David Daiches's introduction to *Persuasion* (New York, 1958), p. v, where it is called "the most mature of Jane Austen's novels . . . the subtlest and most delicately wrought of all her novels, the novel which in the end the experienced reader of Jane Austen puts at the head of the list." Cf. Mark Schorer's introduction to *Persuasion and Lady Susan* (New York, 1959), p. 24, where Schorer calls it "Jane Austen's most intense and probably most moving novel." More recently, Malcolm Bradbury in "Persuasion Again," *Essays in Criticism*, XVIII (1968), 396, calls it "a classic of its author's maturity."

riage?" Moreover, although *Persuasion,* like all of Jane Austen's novels, sets its readers a problem in discrimination, unlike the others it does not dramatize the moral virtue under consideration by representing its failures, its growth, and its achievements through the dialectics of plot. Instead, because it confronts the reader immediately with a virtue already perfected, embodied in a heroine whose moral development has already taken place, the book might seem to some disappointingly static. To be sure, the reader will wonder whether Anne Elliot's goodness must continue to blush unseen to all but Lady Russell's narrow vision, but this kind of question is likely to appear relatively trivial in the context of the rigorous moral universe delineated by Jane Austen and inhabited by Anne Elliot.

In a way, however, the question is not trivial, for it relates closely to the questions the reader really wants to answer — not simply whether and how Anne's virtue will be discovered by the other characters, but what that virtue is and the means by which he, the reader, can fully understand that virtue himself. Jane Austen's own comment on Anne Elliot — "she is almost too good for me"[2] — suggests the difficulty in answering those questions: *Persuasion* is not so much a novel of moral development as it is an elaborate fictional anatomy of an achieved moral virtue in which that virtue is tested, refined, and rewarded, but above all in which that virtue is elegantly defined. The widespread critical dissatisfaction with the novel comes, I believe, from the critics' failure to recognize this structural principle. Although several critics note that what changes and grows as the novel progresses is not the protagonist but her world or her lover,[3] none seems to recognize that what must also grow is the reader's understanding, that the book is not so much the history of a character as it is the anatomy of her principal virtue.[4]

[2] Letter to Fanny Knight, Mar. 23, 1817, in *Jane Austen's Letters to Her Sister Cassandra and Others,* ed. R. W. Chapman (New York, 1932), p. 487.

[3] See, e.g., Bradbury, "Persuasion Again."

[4] Mark Schorer's well-known "Fiction and the Matrix of Analogy," *Kenyon Review,* XI (1949), 539-60, makes the serious mistake of approaching *Persuasion* in a way appropriate for many other Jane Austen novels but inappropriate for this special departure. Looking at what he calls the "texture" of Jane Austen's style in *Persuasion,* Schorer ferrets out a good sampling of hidden commercial metaphors, but surely not enough to justify his declaration that "this is a novel about marriage as a market" (p. 543). Schorer finds only "a patina of sentimental scruple and moral punctilio" (p. 540) in *Persuasion.* I hope my essay demonstrates that a closer look at the language will show that

That virtue, it seems to me, is persuasion. The word "persuasion" and closely related terms like "dissuade" and "persuade" occur over seventy times in this short book, and the entire structure depends on a wide-ranging but meticulous consideration of the moral issues involved in persuasion, persuadability, and persuasiveness. Most critics simply ignore this issue. When one finally does note that persuadability is of some importance in the novel, he immediately dismisses his own insight, declaring that "this particular theme-notion of persuadability was . . . too boring to repay Jane Austen's selection of it . . . she herself found that her story tended to break away from its rather flimsy ethical frame."[5]

A more careful examination of the persuasion theme reveals that it is much more interesting — and much more subtle, complicated, and pervasive — than such a declaration would suggest. For if Anne's former persuadability was a failing, her father's unpersuadability is no virtue. If Lady Russell was wrong to persuade Anne not to marry Wentworth, what are we to say when Anne persuades Wentworth to love Lady Russell as he would his own mother? In short, persuading and being persuaded involve a complicated network of moral values and resist the kind of simple equations with "firmness of character" or "lack of principle" we might be tempted to make if we read superficially. In fact, Jane Austen has the uninstructed Captain Wentworth make precisely this kind of simple equation when he overrates the headstrong Louisa Musgrove. Wentworth learns his mistake when Louisa falls from the Cobb at Lyme and Anne takes charge of the confused scene. Like Wentworth, the reader has to learn that mere unpersuadability is not sufficient equipment to cope with a universe in

morality, not money, is a truer stylistic base. Marvin Mudrick, in his generally excellent discussion of *Persuasion* in *Jane Austen: Irony as Defense and Discovery* (Princeton, N.J., 1952), pp. 207-40, makes another kind of mistake by treating *Persuasion* as if it is too great a departure from Jane Austen's other works. Thus, although he realizes *Persuasion* demonstrates that "Jane Austen has at last discarded the shield of irony" (p. 240), he ends by declaring the book something of a failure because she was apparently not ready artistically or temperamentally to destroy the distance between author and subject.

5 Gilbert Ryle, "Jane Austen and the Moralists," in Southam, ed., *Critical Essays*, pp. 109-10. Kenneth L. Moler, in the last chapter of *Jane Austen's Art of Allusion* (Lincoln, Nebr., 1968), pp. 187-223, does recognize the importance of persuasion as a motif, but he spends most of his time merely establishing the particular marital connotations of "persuasion" in eighteenth- and nineteenth-century fiction and society.

which surprises and misfortunes — moral as well as physical — are the only certainties, and an alert mind and a loving heart are required of all.

When we first come upon Anne Elliot in the late summer of 1814, at the beginning of her twenty-eighth year, her nearly flawless character is already complete and firm, if not completely tested by experience. However, "Anne, with an elegance of mind and sweetness of character, which must have placed her high with any people of real understanding, was nobody with either father or sister: her word had no weight; her convenience was always to give way; — she was only Anne."[6] The circular, static syntax of that last clause — "she was . . . Anne" — shows us how, at least in the narrow universe of Kellynch Hall, Anne must be defined by means of herself and measured by her own measure. Even the way Anne's one-syllable name stands out among the polysyllables of all the rest — Walter, Elizabeth, and Mary — helps to underscore her special relationship to her moral environment, as does the ironic "only" in "she was only Anne." Anne's very identity cannot be recognized by those who cannot recognize her moral virtue; for them she is "nobody." And the fact that she is "nobody" means she can persuade nobody. In spite of her manifest superiority to her father and sisters (the book's opening paragraph economically demolishes Sir Walter Elliot with one of Jane Austen's most savage and witty satiric descriptions), within that small family circle "her word had no weight," she had "always to give way."

Anne is thus trapped within that small and vicious family circle where she is constantly undervalued (Sir Walter, we read in the same paragraph, considers Anne, along with Mary, "of inferior value" to their older sister) because, for one thing, she allowed herself at the age of nineteen to be "persuaded" by Lady Russell "to believe the engagement [with Captain Wentworth] a wrong thing — indiscreet, improper, hardly capable of success, and not deserving it. But it was not a merely selfish caution, under which she acted, in putting an end to it. Had she not imagined herself consulting his good, even more than her own, she could hardly have given him up. — The belief of being prudent, and self-denying principally for *his* advantage, was her chief consolation, under the misery of parting — a final parting" (pp. 27-28).

---

[6] Jane Austen, *Persuasion,* ed. R. W. Chapman, 3rd ed. (London, 1933), p. 5. All subsequent text references to *Persuasion* are to this edition.

All this suggests that persuadability is a dangerous fault, for when
the nineteen-year-old Anne allowed herself to be persuaded to refuse
her lover, she condemned the twenty-seven-year-old woman to the
miserable condition in which we find her at the opening of the book,
in spite of the fact that the "elegance of mind and sweetness of character" she has now achieved would "have placed her high with any
people of real understanding." On the other hand, if Anne's persuadability has placed her in a trap, it is intimately related to the virtue
that will finally deliver her from it, even by etymology, for "sweetness" is related to "persuasion" by the Latin *suavis,* "sweet, pleasant,
agreeable," and it was sweetness that enabled Anne to be persuaded.[7]
She rejected Wentworth, not out of infirm, passive compliance with
those who thought him socially and financially unacceptable for the
daughter of a baronet, but out of active love — for Wentworth himself
and for Lady Russell. Without these reasons, we are told, "young and
gentle as she was, it might yet have been possible to withstand her
father's ill-will" toward the match (p. 27). For even at nineteen, Anne
had the strength to withstand the kind of "persuasion" her father
could bring to bear. Her solitary youth had been her best moral instructor, teaching her self-direction, self-denial, self-persuasion.[8]

At the end of the novel and after her total success with Captain
Wentworth, Anne herself is given the important role of passing judgment on her persuadability at nineteen. By this time she has surely
earned the readers' total respect — her voice is the voice of unambiguous authority — and she appropriately acts as our moral arbiter, telling
us and Wentworth:

> "I have been thinking over the past, and trying impartially to judge of
> the right and wrong, I mean with regard to myself; and I must believe
> that I was right, much as I suffered from it, that I was perfectly right in

[7] See Norman Page, "Standards of Excellence: Jane Austen's Language,"
Review of English Literature, VII (1966), 91-98. Page does an excellent job of
pointing out the need for a close reading of Jane Austen's use of such abstract
nouns as "elegance," "amiability," and "resolution." Unfortunately, he does
not do very much with "persuasion," but his discussion of "elegance" is very
helpful in understanding the precise meanings of Anne's "elegance of mind,"
while it suggests that we devote careful attention to Anne's "sweetness of
character."

[8] A. Walton Litz, *Jane Austen: A Study of Her Artistic Development* (New
York, 1965), considers difficulty of communication the major theme of *Persuasion.* This difficulty, he thinks, is expressed fictionally through Anne Elliot's
terrible loneliness. See, e.g., pp. 150-60.

being guided by the friend whom you will love better than you do now. To me, she was in the place of a parent. Do not mistake me, however. I am not saying that she did not err in her advice. It was, perhaps, one of those cases in which advice is good or bad only as the event decides; and for myself, I certainly never should, in any circumstance of tolerable similarity, give such advice. But I mean, that I was right in submitting to her, and that if I had done otherwise, I should have suffered more in continuing the engagement than I did even in giving it up, because I should have suffered in my conscience. I have now, as far as such a sentiment is allowable in human nature, nothing to reproach myself with; and if I mistake not, a strong sense of duty is no bad part of a woman's portion." [P. 246]

In speaking here of advice and submission, Anne speaks, of course, of persuasion and persuadability. In terms of plot, her analysis is fairly simple. As a moral evaluation of persuasion, however, such a statement is far from simple. In fact, what Anne says here about right and wrong, good and bad, submission and duty, directs us to the center of the rich and complex moral design woven through the novel from the various threads of persuasion. The ethical paradox here is mirrored in the miraculous paradox of the central love plot, where a blossoming springtime of romance follows and grows out of the autumnal harvest of experience. From nineteen to twenty-seven, Anne has grown from persuadability to conviction. "She had been forced," we read, "into prudence in her youth, she learned romance as she grew older — the natural sequel of an unnatural beginning" (p. 30). The progression from the passive voice of "had been forced" to the active voice of "learned" underscores her development to moral maturity. In *Persuasion,* becoming a moral agent is intimately related to self-direction and action; a true persuasion, like a true moral or religious belief or true prudence, results from the interaction of faculties in a single mind (frequently indicated by reflexive verb forms). Moreover, such a true persuasion will finally have concrete results in the material world.

Completing her outline of Anne's moral development before the events of the main story, Jane Austen informs us that by the age of twenty-two Anne had already displayed an unequivocal resistance to strong external persuasion and thereby an active sense of self-controlled morality. Once again, ethical action is triggered in that most important moral crucible of Jane Austen's world — marriage. Anne's suitor this time was her attractive and socially acceptable neighbor, Charles Musgrove. But neither he nor Lady Russell could now persuade Anne:

"She had been solicited. . . . Lady Russell had lamented her refusal. . . .
But in this case, Anne had left nothing for advice to do" (pp. 28-29).
So by the time Anne is twenty-seven and Captain Wentworth luckily
re-enters her life, she is thoroughly capable of resisting untoward persuasion. Few if any know this, of course. Louisa Musgrove, for example, tells the returned Wentworth that Anne refused her brother
Charles's suit because "Lady Russell . . . persuaded Anne to refuse him"
(p. 89). But the observant reader knows that Anne has already proven
herself perfectly capable, as an independent moral agent, of resisting
temptation or bad persuasion of any sort. And when, for instance,
Mary and Charles urge her to come to dine with the newly arrived
Captain Wentworth, Anne, alone aware of the moral dangers inherent
in that fearful if tempting meeting, finally prevails, because in this
clear-cut case of right, wrong, and practicality, "she was quite unpersuadable" (p. 58). Here Anne acts on principles that run counter
to her initial or primary desires; she has recognized those principles
independently and has schooled her own desires. Given the atmosphere
of selfish willfulness in the society that surrounds her (evident even in
her well-meaning mentor, Lady Russell), such principled acts even in
small matters take on a special moral significance.

Persuasion thus begins by presenting an Anne Elliot whose experiences with her difficult family and overbearing mother-surrogate have
taught her to become a self-sufficient moral agent. Very early we read:

> Anne, at seven and twenty, thought very differently from what she had
> been made to think at nineteen. — She did not blame Lady Russell, she
> did not blame herself for having been guided by her; but she felt that
> were any young person, in similar circumstances, to apply to her for
> counsel, they would never receive any of such certain immediate
> wretchedness, such uncertain future good. — She was persuaded that
> under every disadvantage of disapprobation at home, and every anxiety
> attending his profession, all their probable fears, delays and disappoint-
> ments, she should yet have been a happier woman in maintaining the
> engagement, than she had been in the sacrifice of it. [P. 29]

This passage measures the moral growth that occurred before the story
opened, measures it by the ethical distance between (1) "had been
made to think" or "been guided" and (2) "thought" or "felt." And
when we read that Anne now "was persuaded" that she had been
formerly mispersuaded, we know that the "was persuaded" is in this
instance an entirely internal act of conviction based on the evidence
presented to her elegant mind (cf. "thought") and her sweet character

(cf. "felt"). For here the passive voice of "was persuaded" has reflexive rather than passive connotations and indicates merely the passivity of part of her own mind and spirit to another part. It by no means suggests any weak passivity to external persuasion. At this point, then, we know that persuasion and persuadability are not necessarily opposites but, instead, two components of the same virtue, and we are ready to see Anne's persuasion further defined by its placement atop the book's scale of moral virtue.

As readers of Jane Austen would expect, *Persuasion* establishes its defining scale of virtue partly by satiric contrasts with vice and folly. But what is especially significant is that the measure of such vice or folly relates so closely to persuasion. Surely at the lowest rung of the book's moral ladder (along with William Elliot) stands the stupid and vain Sir Walter Elliot, object of the book's broadest satire. And his vices are perhaps best comprehended in the early episodes where he must be "persuaded" to relinquish Kellynch Hall, the family seat.

In his silly vanity Sir Walter has horribly bungled the stewardship of his inherited estate (a materialistic failure that has serious moral significance in Jane Austen's material-moral universe). The relationships between his weak stewardship, personal vanity, and moral blindness are summed up with exquisite precision: "The Kellynch property was good, but not equal to Sir Walter's apprehension of the state required in its possessor" (p. 9). His financial embarrassment, brought on by foolish ostentation, obviously demands a thorough retrenchment if the inheritance is to be saved from ruin. Hence the book's first plot complication: Chapter I ends with Sir Walter's muddled situation crying out for good advice, firm guidance, and, if possible, effective persuasion. Totally incapable of self-correction, Sir Walter and his equally vain eldest daughter, Elizabeth, look to others for help: "Their two confidential friends, Mr. Shepherd . . . and Lady Russell, were called on to advise them; and both father and daughter seemed to expect that something should be struck out by one or the other to remove their embarrassments and reduce their expenditure, without involving the loss of any indulgence of taste or pride" (p. 10).

But of all the characters in *Persuasion*, Sir Walter and Elizabeth seem the least advisable, the least persuadable. The shrewd lawyer, Mr. Shepherd, knows this, but the rather slow-witted, albeit well-meaning, Lady Russell does not. Falling back upon her overriding naive belief in simple persuasion, Lady Russell consults Anne, and together they mark out a scheme of retrenchment (the tables have already turned somewhat: in this case Anne is to a degree Lady Russell's persuader, and both are planning to persuade the willful Sir Walter and Elizabeth). Looking over that scheme, Lady Russell says to Anne, "If we can persuade your father to all this . . . much may be done . . . and I hope we may be able to convince him and Elizabeth, that Kellynch-hall has a respectability in itself, which cannot be affected by these reductions; and that the true dignity of Sir Walter Elliot will be very far from lessened ... by his acting like a man of principle" (p. 12). Although her general opinions are sound, she fails to understand that Sir Walter and Elizabeth are not like her beloved Anne; she fails to realize that, despite their social rank, these people are too vain and self-centered to be persuaded or convinced, that persuasion depends on the persuader's actuating within the persuaded some deep inner force of suprapersonal principle (what some might today call the superego).[9] Of course, Lady Russell's unimaginative attempts at persuasion prove unsuccessful: Sir Walter merely declares "he would sooner quit Kellynch-hall at once, than remain in it on such disgraceful terms" (p. 13).

In this declaration Mr. Shepherd immediately finds the opening he needs to suggest his solution — Sir Walter could lease Kellynch Hall, Mr. Shepherd being "perfectly persuaded that nothing would be done without a change of abode" (p. 13). Entirely convinced ("perfectly persuaded") of his client's incurable vanity, he knows Sir Walter can

---

[9] Sir Walter's self-centered vanity is best reflected in the emblematic mirrors of his dressing room. Admiral Croft — that bluff, open, and least vain of men — tells Anne of the few changes he has made since taking possession of Kellynch Hall: " 'I have done very little besides sending away some of the large looking-glasses from my dressing-room, which was your father's. A very good man, and very much the gentleman I am sure — but I should think, Miss Elliot' (looking with serious reflection) 'I should think he must be rather a dressy man for his time of life — Such a number of looking-glasses! oh Lord! there was no getting away from oneself' " (pp. 127-28). It is in "getting away from oneself" that the vain people in the book are so deficient. Such people, whose minds are filled with mirror images of their selves, rather than with "serious reflections," are of course incapable of true persuasions (moral convictions) or persuadability. Changing one's mind is an important element of moral virtue in many of Jane Austen's books. In *Persuasion* it is important too, and it is intimately related to persuadability. Sir Walter's constant reading of the Baronetage — especially the pages dealing with his own family — is the same sort of empty, circular activity that looking into mirrors is. Indeed, it is almost the same thing as looking into a mirror, and it neatly symbolizes the emptiness of looking-glass vanity.

only be tricked into giving up the property, as he must subsequently be tricked into avoiding London (with its innumerable expensive temptations for vanity) by settling on the more modest Bath. Like children incapable of acting on inner persuasion, Sir Walter and Elizabeth must be coaxed and flattered into what is good for them. Like mindless sheep, they require a shepherd.

Much of the third chapter's comedy rests upon Mr. Shepherd's devious strategies to move Sir Walter to the proper course. The vain child Sir Walter is cajoled and flattered — never "persuaded." His conceit cannot admit the thought of any tenant suitable to follow himself. Yet Mr. Shepherd is able to corral him, in one skillfully managed conversation, to the point not only of accepting a tenant but of accepting a mere sailor (Admiral Croft, who turns out to be Captain Wentworth's brother-in-law). And this just after Sir Walter — whose "book of books" is not the Bible but the Baronetage (p. 7) — has objected to the Navy "as being the means of bringing persons of obscure birth into undue distinction, and raising men to honours which their fathers and grandfathers never dreamt of" (p. 19). Sir Walter, we read, is "talked into allowing Mr. Shepherd to proceed in the treaty" (p. 24). In view of the high premium the book places on persuadability, we can appreciate the subtle but enormous moral difference between this passive act and the self-directed acts of a man amenable to true persuasion. Soon after, when Sir Walter meets Admiral Croft, he acts politely because he has "been flattered into his very best and most polished behaviour by Mr. Shepherd's assurances of his being known, to the Admiral, as a model of good breeding" (p. 32).

Like Sir Walter and Elizabeth, Mary, the youngest Elliot daughter, also serves as a satirical foil to delineate further the scale of persuasion and to define Anne's place on that scale. Anne's sweet and reasonable persuadability undergoes the severest tests in her many encounters with Mary, one of the silliest, most childish characters in *Persuasion*. Mary, we are told, "had not Anne's understanding or temper" (p. 37) (cf. Anne's "elegance of mind and sweetness of character" [p. 5] or her "nice tone of mind ... fastidiousness of ... taste" [p. 28]). For Mary has inherited "a considerable share of the Elliot self-importance" (p. 37) that precludes the objective thought and the selfless tractability of temperament that authentic persuadability requires. However, Mary does place a little higher on the moral scale than do Sir Walter and Elizabeth (even though through marriage she is lower on the social scale, as Anne will be by marrying a sailor), because, for one thing,

Mary is not "so inaccessible to all influence of [Anne's]" (p. 43). She has inherited a *share,* not all, of the Elliot self-importance.

In *Persuasion* forceful persuasiveness and compliant persuadability often play complementary roles in mature moral action. This complementary relationship is touched upon in many confrontations between Anne and Mary. Indeed, both Mary and her husband, Charles Musgrove, serve as foils to Elizabeth and Sir Walter in the matter of appreciating Anne's great persuasive powers as well as her persuadability. For both Charles and Mary have enough common sense and objectivity to realize Anne's superiority at persuasion. Early we read:

> Known to have some influence with her sister, [Anne] was continually requested, or at least receiving hints to exert it, beyond what was practicable. "I wish you could persuade Mary not to be always fancying herself ill," was Charles's language; and, in an unhappy mood, thus spoke Mary; — "I do believe if Charles were to see me dying, he would not think there was any thing the matter with me. I am sure, Anne, if you would, you might persuade him that I really am very ill — a great deal worse than I ever own." [P. 44]

Here we get a good view of the intricate web of persuasion upon which the book's fundamental structure and theme rest. Anne is bombarded, as she so often is, with the demands of would-be persuaders who by requests or "hints" attempt to persuade her to exert her admirable persuasiveness. If ever a reader encountered simple choices between right and wrong fleshed out in living complexity, it is in a delightful miniature like this, where the demands of two persuaders (one moderately selfless, the other immoderately selfish) press upon a sensitive, moral, and persuadable heroine to exert her powerful "influence" or persuasiveness. One tries to persuade her to be a false, lying persuader (for Mary's health is much *better* than she owns). The other tries to persuade her, partly for his own peace of mind, to be a "true" persuader. Furthermore, Anne herself, intelligent and sensitive, fully cognizant of the difficulties of moral action in a limited and imperfect world, must take into account the question of what is "practicable" as well as what is moral. Her ethical maturity becomes manifest in this incident. She realizes that her sister's mind is almost impervious to genuine persuasion and that the best practicable thing she can do is "listen patiently, soften every grievance, and excuse each to the other; give them all hints of the forbearance necessary ... and make those hints broadest which were meant for her sister's benefit" (p. 46).

Of course, petulant Mary is too shallow to be persuaded or to comprehend the workings of such an involved moral activity. Nevertheless, Mary can see the tangible results of Anne's persuasiveness. Speaking of her son, for example, Mary tells Anne, "You can make little Charles do any thing. . . . If I were to shut myself up for ever with the child, I should not be able to persuade him to do any thing he did not like" (p. 57). Unwittingly, Mary reveals here something about the nature of persuasion — it often involves taking action contrary to passion or desire. It resides thereby at the center of life's moral drama.

In numerous ways, then, Mary is used to further define her sister's overwhelming moral superiority as it relates to and is exemplified in persuasion. A final example should suffice. Mary's young sisters-in-law, Louisa and Henrietta Musgrove, pass by Mary's house one day as they set out on a walk. Out of politeness they ask Mary to join them. But "Anne felt persuaded, by the looks of the two girls, that it was precisely what they did not wish. . . . She tried to dissuade Mary from going, but in vain; and that being the case, thought it best to accept the Miss Musgroves' much more cordial invitation to herself to go likewise, as she might be useful in turning back with her sister, and lessening the interference in any plan of their own" (p. 83). Here Anne "felt persuaded" the girls wanted to be alone because to her clear intellect they were obviously out to meet and flirt with Wentworth (who is on a shooting expedition with their brother, Charles, in the vicinity). Anne's self-persuasion here depends on the objective, "elegant" reason that can perceive hidden motives (unseen by her slow-witted, subjective sister) and the "sweet" persuadability her selfish, headstrong sister also lacks. Anne's persuadability allows her to extinguish any selfish jealousy about these young and attractive, if silly, girls in pursuit of the one love of her lost youth — however unworthy they are of Wentworth's regard. Indeed, her persuadability allows her to plan how to make herself "useful" by somehow coaxing Mary away from the party when she realizes that attempts at persuasion will prove impracticable.

Mary is the youngest Elliot. Moreover, despite her marriage and motherhood, despite the fact that Charles Musgrove is evidently her superior in sense and sensibility and therefore might have some maturing influence upon her, she remains a very childish twenty-three. The book contains so many examples of her childishness that even to mention them would be superfluous, but in this theme of persuasion I am tracing, Mary's immaturity becomes noteworthy. For *Persuasion* carefully establishes a relationship between persuadability, persuasiveness, persuasion, and emotional maturity. Everyone recognizes the autumnal tone of the novel and the special maturity of its heroine. But critics fail to explore the relationship between the unpersuadability of characters like Sir Walter, Elizabeth, and Mary and their childishness. Like children, these people cannot practice self-correction, self-change; like children's egoism, their vanity incapacitates them for moral activity. If life blossoms for Anne in the autumn of her life, it does so, to a large extent, because her persuadability has aged into self-controlled persuasion. Time is an important topic in *Persuasion;* temporal metaphors abound. And it is significant that Sir Walter, who ranks lowest on the book's moral scale, sees time as the supreme enemy and growing old as the ultimate defeat, while Anne, who ranks highest, finds in time the ultimate ally and growing old a necessary, desirable step toward self-fulfillment. Sir Walter and Elizabeth rather miraculously (with some help probably from Gowland's skin lotion) retain their youthful beauty, and Mary remains an incorrigibly spoiled brat: all three are doomed to perennial infancy, and all three are almost entirely unpersuadable. Anne, on the other hand, loses her bloom but miraculously recaptures her "spring of felicity" (p. 252) because she has grown over the years and has nurtured her seeds of persuadability into the riches of moral harvest.

Louisa Musgrove serves as another foil for Anne, helping to make the scale of persuasion clearer and more usefully comprehensive. She also provides the central plot incident that allows Wentworth to see the true value of Anne's superior persuasiveness and persuadability so dramatically that he is persuaded to try once more for her hand.

When Wentworth first returns to Anne's neighborhood, he is almost the archetypal single man in possession of a good fortune and in want of a wife. As he good-humoredly tells his sister, Mrs. Croft, "Here I am, Sophia, quite ready to make a foolish match" (p. 62). Almost any suitable young lady will do: "He had a heart for either of the Miss Musgroves, if they could catch it; a heart, in short, for any pleasing young woman who came in his way, excepting Anne Elliot," who had "used him ill; deserted and disappointed him; and worse ... had shewn a feebleness of character in doing so, which his own decided, confident temper could not endure. She had given him up to oblige others. It had been the effect of over-persuasion. It had been weakness and timidity" (p. 61). Soon it appears that Wentworth has settled on Louisa; part of his reason is her charming, if rather immature, resistance to persuasion — what he likes to think of as her admirable "resolution." On an outing with Charles, Mary, Henrietta, Louisa, and

Wentworth, Anne from behind a hedgerow overhears an important conversation between Wentworth and Louisa concerning Louisa's younger sister, Henrietta, and Henrietta's suitor, Charles Hayter of Winthrop. Louisa speaks first, then Wentworth replies:

"And so, I made her [Henrietta] go. I could not bear that she should be frightened from the visit [to Winthrop] by such nonsense. What! — would I be turned back from doing a thing that I had determined to do, and that I knew to be right, by the airs and interference of such a person [Mary Elliot Musgrove]? — or, of any person I may say. No, — I have no idea of being so easily persuaded. When I have made up my mind, I have made it. And Henrietta seemed entirely to have made up hers to call at Winthrop to-day — and yet, she was as near giving it up, out of nonsensical complaisance!"

"She would have turned back then, but for you?"

"She would indeed. I am almost ashamed to say it."

"Happy for her, to have such a mind as yours at hand! — After the hints you gave just now, which did but confirm my own observations, the last time I was in company with him, I need not affect to have no comprehension of what is going on. I see that more than a mere dutiful morning-visit to your aunt was in question; — and woe betide him, and her too, when it comes to things of consequence, when they are placed in circumstances, requiring fortitude and strength of mind, if she have not resolution enough to resist idle interference in such a trifle as this. Your sister is an amiable creature; but *yours* is the character of decision and firmness, I see. If you value her conduct or happiness, infuse as much of your own spirit into her as you can. But this, no doubt, you have always been doing. It is the worst evil of too yielding and indecisive a character, that no influence over it can be depended on. — You are never sure of a good impression being durable. Every body may sway it; let those who would be happy be firm. — Here is a nut," said he, catching one down from an upper bough. "To exemplify, — a beautiful glossy nut, which, blessed with original strength, has outlived all the storms of autumn. Not a puncture, not a weak spot any where. — This nut," he continued, with a playful solemnity, — "while so many of its brethren have fallen and been trodden under foot, is still in possession of all the happiness that a hazel-nut can be supposed capable of." Then, returning to his former earnest tone: "My first wish for all, whom I am interested in, is that they should be firm. If Louisa Musgrove would be beautiful and happy in her November of life, she will cherish all her present powers of mind." [Pp. 87-88]

Of course, this whole incident bears an ironic resemblance to the Anne–Lady Russell–Wentworth persuasion affair of the past — here willful Mary, by her petulant orders, has tried unsuccessfully to persuade her young sister-in-law, Henrietta, away from her suitor, Charles Hayter. Her failure comes about partly because equally willful Louisa has "no idea of being so easily persuaded." But Captain Wentworth's opinions of the incident deserve our more careful attention: they are obviously related to his former experience with Anne. If Louisa is improperly impervious to all persuasion, good or bad, as her speech here implies, Wentworth's overconfident and simplistic convictions about the evils of persuadability and the virtues of decision, firmness, and resolution are rash, misinformed, and improper too. Louisa will soon learn the hard way that to be happy "in her November of life," her determined resistance to persuasion must be tempered by tractability. And Wentworth will learn from some of the same experiences that in "in *her* November of life," Anne is lovely and happy because she still retains the sweetness and light of a persuadable nature.

The proof comes, of course, in Louisa's disastrous fall from the Cobb at Lyme — the turning point of the plot and the occasion of Captain Wentworth's moral epiphany.[10] While the party enjoy their last walk in Lyme before setting off for Uppercross, they discover "a general wish to walk along [the Cobb] once more, all [are] so inclined, and Louisa soon [grows] so determined" that they take one more turn along the pier. "All were contented to pass quietly and carefully down the steep flight, excepting Louisa; she must be jumped down them by Captain Wentworth. . . . He advised her against it, thought the jar too great; but no, he reasoned and talked in vain; she smiled and said, 'I am determined I will' " (pp. 108-9). Through these words of what Wentworth admires as "resolution" — "determined," "must," "determined," and "will" — glares Louisa's infantile obstinacy against proper persuasion. The results are immediate: Louisa learns (along with Wentworth) her moral lesson through material consequences — "she fell on the pavement on the Lower Cobb, and was taken up lifeless!" (p. 109). And all because she refused to be persuaded.

Soon after, Wentworth cries out in anguish, "Oh God! that I had

10 "Epiphany" is not merely hyperbolic here. When the surgeon declares that Louisa is out of immediate danger, we read, "The tone, the look, with which 'Thank God!' was uttered by Captain Wentworth, Anne was sure could never be forgotten by her; nor the sight of him afterwards, as he sat near a table, leaning over it with folded arms, and face concealed, as if overpowered by the various feelings of his soul, and trying by prayer and reflection to calm them" (p. 112).

not given way to her at the fatal moment! Had I done as I ought! But so eager and so resolute! Dear, sweet Louisa!" (p. 116). While the exclamation marks here denote the pitch of his emotion, they also indicate the shock of his recognition: eager, youthful resolution remains no longer for him a pure, unalloyed virtue. And Anne, hearing his exclamations and thinking back to the conversation she overheard behind the hedgerow, speculates on his present conception of the morality of persuadability: "Anne wondered whether it ever occurred to him now, to question the justness of his own previous opinion as to the universal felicity and advantage of firmness of character; and whether it might not strike him, that, like all other qualities of the mind, it should have its proportions and limits. She thought it could scarcely escape him to feel, that a persuadable temper might sometimes be as much in favour of happiness, as a very resolute character" (p. 116).

This incident at the Cobb also provides us — and especially Captain Wentworth — with the means to perceive Anne's superiority in persuasiveness. Louisa's lifeless state obviously demands immediate attention, but of the entire group (which includes two naval officers with a good deal of combat experience), only Anne has the presence of mind to act, to command. Although the word "persuade" does not occur in the passage immediately following Louisa's fall (Anne "cried" her orders, "prompted" the others to attend to Louisa, "eagerly suggested" that Benwick run for a surgeon, etc.), it is nevertheless her persuasiveness that makes her position supreme. The immediate recognition by the others of her self-possession and sound, firm persuasions is manifested in their granting to her total command. Both Charles Musgrove and Captain Wentworth seem "to look to her for directions." Charles cries, "Anne, Anne.... What, in heaven's name, is to be done next?" Wentworth's "eyes [are] also turned towards her" as he awaits her every suggestion or order (pp. 110-11). And so in this emergency Anne's decisive, self-controlled, but morally correct resolution saves her rival Louisa's life at the same time that it recaptures her former lover's respect and admiration. The whole scene following Louisa's fall serves as a neat device to delineate further the scale of virtue I have been discussing: many important characters are present, including the hero and the heroine of the novel, and the reactions of each quickly but dramatically place him on the scale, with Anne coming out on top.

Louisa's fall, then, is symbolic as well as literal. As Louisa falls in Wentworth's regard, Anne regains her deserved supremacy in his estimation. At the end of the book, when Anne and Frederick have declared their love once again, he pinpoints his conversion to this incident at Lyme. He tells Anne that until that day on the Cobb, "he had not understood the perfect excellence of the mind with which Louisa's could so ill bear a comparison," thereby underscoring Louisa's function as another foil to establish Anne's place in the book's hierarchy of virtue. On the Cobb, he explains, "he had learnt to distinguish between the steadiness of principle and the obstinacy of self-will, between the darings of heedlessness and the resolution of a collected mind" (p. 242). In short, he had learned in that one incident the difference between selfish, childish determination and mature resolution based on persuadability and firm, living persuasions.

Almost every character finally gets placed on the book's refined scale of persuasion. Sometimes, however, Jane Austen merely hints at a character's placement or leaves his level rather ambiguous. Henrietta Musgrove, for example, is depicted as a good-natured, easily persuaded girl without any real convictions (for instance, she "was soon persuaded to think differently" about staying with Louisa at Lyme, although a minute before she had her heart set on it [p. 114]). In one brief conversation with Anne she reveals several simple-minded attitudes about persuasiveness (which she views as an almost magical talent) and thereby helps to enrich the persuasion theme. Wanting to see her fiancé, Charles Hayter, take over old Dr. Shirley's Uppercross curacy, she attempts to cloak her desire in charming, childlike disingenuousness and to persuade Anne that Dr. Shirley would somehow improve his health by moving permanently to Lyme. But, as she says, "My only doubt is, whether any thing could persuade him to leave his parish." "Do not you think," she asks Anne, "it is quite a mistaken point of conscience, when a clergyman sacrifices his health for the sake of duties, which may be just as well performed by another person?" And Anne "smiled more than once to herself during this speech," as well she might, considering her maturity and her own experiences with persuasion, points of conscience, sacrifice, and duties. Indeed, soon after, Henrietta unwittingly alludes directly to Anne's own experiences when she asserts, "I wish Lady Russell lived at Uppercross, and were intimate with Dr. Shirley. I have always heard of Lady Russell, as a woman of the greatest influence with every body! I always look upon her as able to persuade a person to any thing! I am afraid of her ... quite afraid of her, because she is so very clever" (pp. 102-3). Perhaps here Jane Austen ironically shakes up what the reader might, by this point in the novel, mistakenly feel is a simple or rather rigid hierarchy of persuasion: for out of the mouth of this moral infant comes a wisdom that the morally superior Anne could have profited by — Anne was never afraid of Lady Russell, and maybe she should have been. Or perhaps rather than undercut Anne's superiority (even nineteen-year-old Anne's superiority), these remarks by Henrietta merely enhance the moral complexity inherent in persuasion, showing that the scale of morality upon which all is strung is not simple or mechanistic but living and organic.

In general, the Musgroves are very persuadable people. Except for Louisa's obstinacy (which she significantly loses after her long recovery from the fall caused by that obstinacy), they display very little of the Elliot "self-importance." Indeed, although considerably lower on the social scale than the Elliots, the Musgroves are always the moral superiors to that proud family. Where the Elliots have but one persuadable member, the Musgroves have but one unpersuadable member (and that one capable of amelioration). And yet the Musgroves are too persuadable or, more accurately, too easily changed. It is as if their changes result not from intellectual persuasions but from morally insignificant changes in their emotional weather. Henrietta quickly gives up her infatuation for Wentworth, Louisa's "resolution" dissolves after physical injury, Mrs. Musgrove's sentimentality toward her dead son, Dick, runs counter to all rational evidence. Even Charles — the firmest, most mature of the Musgroves — is more lovable than admirable, to a large extent because he lacks solid convictions and the ability to resist persuasion or understand its nature.

Although Lady Russell's actions are central to the persuasion plot, and despite her reputation in the neighborhood among the naive like Henrietta and Louisa (or further afield with Frederick Wentworth), she is something of a failure as a persuader. Nevertheless, she does widen *Persuasion*'s anatomy of persuasion by representing one more type — the person who is quite unpersuadable, not, like Sir Walter, because of personal vanity but more because of slowness of mind and overfirmness of principle. Many of the adjectives Jane Austen employs in her descriptions of Lady Russell's character help to make this clearer: for example, she is described as "of steady age and character" (p. 5), "of strict integrity," "capable of strong attachments," "most correct in her conduct, strict in her notions of decorum" (p. 11). These steady, strict, strong, and correct attributes warrant a degree of approbation in a world populated by ill-mannered, selfish, fickle

people like Mary; or childishly coaxable, frivolous people like Sir
Walter and Elizabeth; or slippery flatterers like Mrs. Clay and her
father, Mr. Shepherd. But it is essential that we keep in mind what
Anne has said about firmness, persuadability, and the "proportions and
limits" of "all qualities of mind," just as we must remember the lessons
about resolution and flexibility Wentworth learned on the Cobb at
Lyme. Anne herself is not merely a strong persuader or a sweet per-
suadee — she is both combined, and she understands the fallacy of the
"too-common idea of spirit and gentleness being incompatible with
each other" (p. 172). In a sense, therefore, Lady Russell functions as
one more foil for Anne. Anne's principles, firm as they are, are
grounded in a flexibility and sense of proper limitations that stands
in sharp contrast to Lady Russell's rigid principles and rather mindless sense of strict decorum.

Contrasted with Anne's "elegant mind" is Lady Russell's "cultivated
mind," which could be "generally speaking, rational and consistent,"
but which succumbed to a number of firm "prejudices," particularly
"on the side of ancestry" (p. 11). For, unlike the clear-headed, objective Anne, Lady Russell lacks the intellectual tact to view moral
questions selflessly, universally. We are told at the end of the novel
what by that time we have already observed in action: "There is a
quickness of perception in some, a nicety in the discernment of character, a natural penetration, in short, which no experience can equal,
and Lady Russell had been less gifted in this part of understanding
than her young friend" (p. 249).

Here we see, as we do in many other places, that Lady Russell's
moral inferiority to Anne results to a great extent from her weaker
intellect. As Jane Austen told us in the beginning, Lady Russell is "a
woman rather of sound than of quick abilities" (p. 11). In many ways
Persuasion equates the morality of persuasion with intellectual power
— though there are exceptions, of course, like the intelligent but evil
Mr. William Elliot. That Anne is able to see beyond class ranking to
essential moral ranking is, for example, a function of her nimble reason as it is of her agreeable nature. She prefers the company of ordinary naval families like the Harvilles to that of aristocrats like Lady
Dalrymple because she is quick-witted enough to look beyond convention and see for herself the natural goodness of the one and the basic
emptiness of the other, regardless of social status. The same obtains
in her opinion of Admiral Croft — and again Lady Russell serves as
an intellectual-moral foil: "Admiral Croft's manners were not quite of

the tone to suit Lady Russell, but they delighted Anne. His goodness of heart and simplicity of character were irresistible" (p. 127). Finally, Anne suspects Mr. Elliot, and in the end the justice of her suspicions becomes evident. But Lady Russell can see in Mr. Elliot "nothing to excite distrust. She could not imagine a man more exactly what he ought to be than Mr. Elliot" (p. 161), for his manners are impeccable. "Imagine" seems the key word: Lady Russell's mind is incapable of the imagination to see beyond surface manners or pre-established social categories, the imagination that is required for such refined moral sensitivity as Anne embodies and exemplifies. That imagination, of course, results from both warm sentiments and quick reason, the sweetness and light Anne displays in vivid contrast to Lady Russell's merely "composed mind and polite manners" (p. 146). Imagination alone, however, can be dangerous. At one point Anne appears to allow Lady Russell almost to persuade her into a disastrous marriage with William Elliot — and imagination is partly responsible. Picturing her life as mistress of Kellynch Hall, Anne faces an imaginative "charm which she [can] not immediately resist" (p. 160). Later, after learning the full truth of Mr. Elliot's deceit, Anne shudders, because "it was just possible that she might have been persuaded by Lady Russell" to marry Mr. Elliot in order to make that imaginative charm into a reality (p. 211). But Anne has never been in real danger, for "her judgment, on a serious consideration of the possibilities of such a case, was against Mr. Elliot": only "her imagination and her heart were bewitched," and only "for a few moments." "Judgment," it seems, is a higher sort of "imagination," for what actually brings Anne to her senses in this scene is her mental "image of Mr. Elliot speaking for himself" (p. 160).

Thus, although Anne never becomes completely immune to Lady Russell's influence, she has a mind of her own when emergencies require it to resist persuasion in order to protect her serious moral and emotional requirements. Near the end of the story, at the concert in Bath where Anne has to decide what to do about Frederick Wentworth and has to endure the embarrassment of being with Lady Russell at such a crucial event, Anne, we are told, "was persuaded by Lady Russell's countenance" that she had seen Frederick in the concert room. But "she did not mean, whatever she might feel on Lady Russell's account, to shrink from conversation with Captain Wentworth, if he gave her the opportunity" (p. 189). Within Anne's delicate but trying moral dilemma, this "was persuaded" becomes something of an ironic locution — given the multiple meanings of "persuade" and "persuasion" already established in dozens of previous contexts. Anne makes her choice, and all that the former persuader Lady Russell accomplishes here is to act in a way that "persuades" (i.e., "makes clear to") Anne that Lady Russell sees the man she once had the power to persuade Anne to jilt. Lady Russell's loss of power is wittily symbolized by the shift from the clearly passive "she [Anne] was persuaded to believe the engagement a wrong thing" (p. 27) of the beginning to this reflexive "was persuaded" of the end. Now Lady Russell cannot — and of this we are by now completely sure — again persuade Anne of any action that goes against Anne's own judgments concerning her returned lover.

Although Lady Russell loses her persuasive influence over Anne, the question of Lady Russell's own persuadability still remains. Of course, Anne earns the just reward of her virtue — marriage and Captain Wentworth. But the book's web of persuasion and duty is imperiled because Anne's impending marriage runs counter to the wishes of the woman to whom she owes filial obedience. Duty and persuasion seem now to oppose rather than complement one another. Here at the end, then, this final plot complication maintains the book's moral suspense because Anne's almost perfect virtue hovers in jeopardy.

In the final chapter, when Anne and Frederick's marriage is assured, we read that

> Anne knew that Lady Russell must be suffering some pain in understanding and relinquishing Mr. Elliot, and be making some struggles to become truly acquainted with, and do justice to Captain Wentworth. This however was what Lady Russell had now to do. She must learn to feel that she had been mistaken with regard to both; that she had been unfairly influenced by appearances in each; that because Captain Wentworth's manners had not suited her own ideas, she had been too quick in suspecting them to indicate a character of dangerous impetuosity; and that because Mr. Elliot's manners had precisely pleased her in their propriety and correctness, their general politeness and suavity, she had been too quick in receiving them as the certain result of the most correct opinions and well regulated mind. There was nothing less for Lady Russell to do, than to admit that she had been pretty completely wrong, and to take up a new set of opinions and of hopes. [P. 249]

Several of the verbs here ("Lady Russell *had* now *to do*," "She *must learn*") and the general imperative force of many of the other verb constructions in the passage indicate a burden of duty — one that has shifted ironically from Anne's shoulders to her advisor's. Now the tables have been completely turned: Lady Russell "must" relinquish her favorite the way Anne at nineteen had to relinquish hers. But Lady Russell is, as we have seen, too deficient in mental acuity to be persuaded solely on the basis of principle or on the mere perception of Captain Wentworth's fine character as opposed to Mr. Elliot's deceptive politeness and "suavity" (a kind of slick, calculating, and limitless persuadability). How, one wonders, will the book accomplish this reversal: how will this rigid, close-minded woman come to "admit that she had been completely wrong"?

It might be argued that Jane Austen settles this problem rather flimsily in her haste to bring her composition to its proper and properly swift resolution. In any case Lady Russell's motherly love for Anne leaps all obstacles. Her first object, we are told, is "to see Anne happy. She loved Anne better than she loved her own abilities"; in the end, this "very good woman" finds "little hardship in attaching herself as a mother to the man who [is] securing the happiness of her other child" (p. 249). Parental love (which Anne's literal parent completely lacks) here performs the requisite persuasive miracle (in somewhat the same fashion that filial love moved Anne to perform her duty eight years before). If this miracle is not as convincing as, say, the "spring of felicity" that springs in Anne's warm autumnal heart, probably that is because Lady Russell finally plays a subordinate role in the story and the swift ending is more important than is an explanation of her conversion. It suffices that love is her persuader, and that the imperative force of Anne's manifest happiness works where full, genuine moral and intellectual persuasion would fail. Lady Russell does turn out to be in some ways a "very good woman." Thus at the end Anne's regard for her is justified, and Anne's paramount virtue remains secure.

Finally, Captain Wentworth completes the scale of moral measurement, marking the rank just below Anne's apex; again the hierarchy depends on maturation, moral growth, and persuasion. Of all the characters besides Anne, Frederick demonstrates most capability for moral development — for being persuaded to new and better persuasions. His ethical understanding deepens because he comes to perceive the intricate relationships between self-denial and self-willed action, persuasion and resolution. And he comes to this sophisticated perception through his experiences with Anne. Thus we have a hero (in place of the typical Jane Austen heroine) whose perceptions and moral position change radically within the novel. It would be foolish to argue that Anne undergoes no moral changes — what I have already outlined makes it clear that she does not remain static, but her changes within the main story are very subtle and ones of degree rather than kind. Indeed, many are actually changes in our perception of Anne rather than changes in Anne herself. Frederick's changes, on the other hand, are drastic and depend on a rather basic moral conversion.[11] What he considers Anne's former "feebleness of character," her "weakness and timidity" in succumbing to "over-persuasion" (p. 61), he shortly learns to respect as an integral part of a character that is "perfection itself, maintaining the loveliest medium of fortitude and gentleness" (p. 241). What he is persuaded to respect, cherish, and even emulate in Anne is her rare blend of ordinarily separate virtues, her temperate fusion of persuasions and persuadability whose spiritual loveliness is perhaps best symbolized by the miraculous fusion of the two temperate seasons of man's life and nature's year — spring and fall. During the walk to Winthrop through the autumn countryside, Anne's mind is struck by the thought of "declining happiness . . . images of youth and hope, and spring, all gone together." But along with that she observes "the ploughs at work, and the fresh-made path [which] spoke the farmer, counteracting the sweets of poetical despondence, and meaning to have spring again" (p. 85). This paradoxical, bittersweet mixture, in life as well as in the life of moral perception and ethical action, finally comes clear for Frederick as he learns to understand and value all that Anne Elliot is and has been.

He learns, too, the nature of his pride. He sees that he has been his own enemy more than Lady Russell has, for Anne surely would have renewed the engagement two years after their separation had he but asked again. He has reached the point of moral maturity when he can say, " 'I was proud, too proud to ask again. I did not understand you. I shut my eyes, and would not understand you, or do you justice. This is a recollection which ought to make me forgive every one sooner than myself. . . . Like other great men under reverses,' he added with a smile, 'I must endeavour to subdue my mind to my for-

---

[11] It is almost as if Frederick plays the role of an Emma and Anne the role of a Mr. Knightley. Cf. W. A. Craik, *Jane Austen: The Six Novels* (New York, 1965), p. 184. See also Moler, *Jane Austen's Art of Allusion*, pp. 187-223. Moler argues cogently that Anne is the moral norm or center of the novel and that Wentworth is the chief character to undergo significant moral growth, learning from Anne's example.

tune. I must learn to brook being happier than I deserve'" (p. 247). Though he ends this little confession facetiously, it is full of the serious morality his relationship with Anne has always embodied and has finally taught him. Pride, justice, and the "oughts" and "musts" of this passage are important in understanding a heroine who is "almost too good" and yet quite human enough to serve as the reader's and Frederick's living moral norm.

At the end Frederick tells Anne of his agony at seeing her in the concert hall with Lady Russell: the sight of the two together reminded him of the harm "persuasion had once done" and made him fear that Anne would once again submit to Lady Russell's persuasions and marry his rival, Mr. Elliot. Anne, now his moral instructor, replies, teaching him of the delicate relationships inherent in persuasion and duty: "You should have distinguished. . . . You should not have suspected me now; the case so different, and my age so different. If I was wrong in yielding to persuasion once, remember that it was to persuasion exerted on the side of safety, not of risk. When I yielded, I thought it was to duty; but no duty could be called in aid here. In marrying a man indifferent to me, all risk would have been incurred, and all duty violated" (p. 244). Anne thus instructs Frederick that yielding to persuasion is not the simple matter he has always assumed it to be, that "duty" is intimately bound up with "persuasion" (repetition of the two terms stresses this relationship). Her complex perception of these complicated issues — symbolized by the association of yielding, a passive behavior, with doing one's duty, an active one — goes far beyond Frederick's rather simplistic understanding of her actions. True, months before, back in Lyme, he "had learnt to distinguish between" the deceptively similar motives of "principle and . . . self-will" (p. 242). But he still has to learn in his reunion with Anne to perceive how seemingly dissimilar moral virtues combine in paradoxically organic relationships.

Captain Wentworth thus places below Anne on the moral scale, not because he lacks the requisite wit, will, or spirit for potential moral excellence but because his moral and mental capacities require refinement, instruction toward genuine elegance and nicety of understanding. Anne provides him with both precept and example. Moreover, from Anne he learns to mediate his positions, not to be (like Lady Russell or Louisa Musgrove) merely firm or rash but to be firm and yet changeable, truly open-minded and yet principled, in short, a man of real persuasion.

For Anne and Frederick, the rewards of such moral growth are

manifest (and appropriately swift after their long separation): their
renewed love has gained immensely; it has deepened into a kind of
spiritual persuasion. The enlightened Frederick has learned from
Anne how to act properly on self-direction, how to make fully principled choices, and how to allow his judgments to be persuaded into
steady, measured growth. Now no false external "persuasion," no force
whatsoever, can stand in the way of their union. Jane Austen begins
the last chapter with this observation:

> Who can be in doubt of what followed? When any two young people take
> it into their heads to marry, they are pretty sure by perseverance to carry
> their point, be they ever so poor, or ever so imprudent, or ever so little
> likely to be necessary to each other's ultimate comfort. This may be bad
> morality to conclude with, but I believe it to be truth; and if such parties
> succeed, how should a Captain Wentworth and an Anne Elliot, with the
> advantage of maturity of mind, consciousness of right, and one inde-
> pendent fortune between them, fail of bearing down every opposition?
> [P. 248]

With such "independent fortune," "maturity of mind," and "consciousness of right," these seasoned lovers are ready to begin a predictably
successful marriage. If marriage is the ultimate testing ground for
morality in everyday material circumstances, of all Jane Austen's cou-
ples, Frederick and Anne are best qualified for that test. Certainly
they are romantic lovers, but their love enjoys strong moral (as well
as necessary financial) underpinnings, underpinnings achieved by the
passage of time, the acquisition of fortune, and the growth of moral
understanding. In some ways, then, Anne's initial rejection of Wentworth has paid off handsomely, and her paradoxical view of the rightness and wrongness of that rejection is corroborated. By waiting and
suffering, both lovers have prepared their characters for their union
and have established for their future the firmest material-moral base.
Their reunion, we read, finds them "more tender, more tried, more
fixed in a knowledge of each other's character, truth, and attachment;
more equal to act, more justified in acting" (pp. 240-41). All the
"more"'s indicate growth and harvest; the "justified," "act," and
"acting" indicate its ethical significance; the whole passage indicates
the deeply moral nature of their love and of the book within which it
has been chronicled.

Only one important character seems to fall outside the pattern I
have been discussing. William Walter Elliot, Anne's hypocritical cousin,

contributes directly little if anything to the persuasion theme. True, he does demonstrate further how easily the foolish characters can be fooled by appearances that appeal to their vanity rather than to any powers of authentic persuadability. True, he indirectly helps to document the human shortcomings in Anne's "almost" perfect nature, and he helps to show Lady Russell's inferior imagination and superficial standards of behavior. But as for the villainous William Elliot himself and his own actions, little can be said about his position on *Persuasion*'s scale of persuasion. Indeed, his perfidy might be a bit too gratuitous, revealing a rather serious flaw in the novel. However, we must keep in mind that, regardless of the strong patterns I have been tracing, *Persuasion* is not a regimented discursive essay attempting merely to rank in ordered exposition various moral positions vis-à-vis persuasion. It is, rather, a dramatic representation of those positions that quite successfully molds the rich welter of human experience into a satisfying, neat aesthetic pattern, without violating the vitality of that welter. As such, perhaps *Persuasion* deserves a Mr. Elliot — representative of self-willed, intelligent, attractive evil — as the obverse of Anne Elliot — representative of self-persuaded, intelligent, lovely goodness.

Another way of accounting for Mr. Elliot is to remind ourselves that *Persuasion* is doubtless an unfinished work. If Jane Austen had lived to complete her revisions, he probably would have played a more significant role in the persuasion theme than he now does. For her revisions of *Persuasion* graphically demonstrate her desire to strengthen the persuasion motif. Indeed, some of the book's most important treatments of persuasion appear in the penultimate chapter, added after completion of the original manuscript.[12]

Of course, Mr. Elliot is the main reason for the existence of the clumsy interviews with Mrs. Smith — at least the main reason in terms of plot. Despite their admitted weaknesses in plotting and characterization, those episodes aid substantially in exposing just how the mature Anne is persuaded by evidence and comes to firmly grounded persuasions. Because critics fail to recognize the great importance of persuasion in *Persuasion*, they fail to see Anne's interviews with Mrs.

[12] For a discussion of the revisions of *Persuasion,* see Brian Southam, "The Two Chapters of *Persuasion,*" in *Jane Austen's Literary Manuscripts* (London, 1964), pp. 86ff. For a full text of the two canceled chapters, see *Two Chapters of "Persuasion" Printed from Jane Austen's Autograph,* ed. R. W. Chapman (Oxford, 1926).

Smith as more than a weak device to reveal Mr. Elliot's deception and true villainy — a feeble performance instead of the careful plotting Jane Austen's readers have come to expect. But if we look again at the scene where Anne is finally persuaded by Mrs. Smith of Mr. Elliot's treachery, we see that it gives us an excellent view of Anne's elegant mind at work in the actual process of self-persuasion.

Mrs. Smith begins by pleading Mr. Elliot's suit for Anne's hand in marriage. "Let me plead ... for my former friend," she says. "Let me recommend Mr. Elliot" (p. 196). Thus she starts out as one more good old respected friend attempting to persuade Anne to make the wrong marital decision. But as soon as Mrs. Smith (who incidentally seems, because of her flexibility, to rank above Lady Russell) is persuaded by Anne's forthright protestations that Mr. Elliott is unacceptable, she begins to tell Anne of "Mr. Elliot's real character." She asserts, "Hear the truth. . . . He is totally beyond the reach of any sentiment of justice or compassion. Oh! he is black at heart, hollow and black!" Anne's strength of character and unambiguous, honest assertions of her solid persuasions have therefore elicited change and valuable evidence (actual truth) from Mrs. Smith. Mrs. Smith tells Anne that "facts shall speak" (p. 199), knowing that Anne's intelligence requires genuine evidence and strict proof before she will change her opinions or think ill of anyone. Over and over in the long conversation, Anne demands facts and unassailable proof. Finally Mrs. Smith produces her most material piece of evidence, a letter from Mr. Elliot to her dead husband, proving beyond a doubt that Mr. Elliot despised Sir Walter, Kellynch Hall, even the Elliot name. This clear corroboration of William Elliot's hypocrisy and deceit seems to clinch the persuasion of Anne's demanding intellect, and her immediate emotional response is evident: she is put "in a glow," and Mrs. Smith observes "the high colour in her face." Both mind and temper have now been persuaded; yet because of her almost infinite moral delicacy, she endures some ethical misgivings: "She was obliged to recollect that her seeing the letter was a violation of the laws of honour, that no one ought to be judged or to be known by such testimonies, that no private correspondence could bear the eye of others, before she could recover calmness enough to return the letter which she had been meditating over, and say, 'Thank you. This is full proof undoubtedly, proof of every thing you were saying. But why be acquainted with us [her family] now?'" (p. 204).

After her initial shock and moral indignation, then, Anne regains her characteristic coolness and fairness. She is still demanding here the proof that her sound judgment needs to be fully persuaded to change. Mrs. Smith's response underscores that need for immaculate proof: she says, "I have shewn you Mr. Elliot, as he was a dozen years ago, and I will shew him as he is now. I cannot produce written proof again, but I can give as authentic oral testimony as you can desire, of what he is now wanting, and what he is now doing" (p. 204). Mrs. Smith recognizes Anne's paramount moral integrity in her ability to suspend judgment, even in such personal matters, even despite her roused passions. But Mrs. Smith is by no means the equal of Anne, and her next bit of proof, her "oral evidence," coming as it does third- or fourth-hand, is rejected: "Indeed, Mrs. Smith, we must not expect to get real information in such a line," says Anne. "Facts or opinions which are to pass through the hands of so many, to be misconceived by folly in one, and ignorance in another, can hardly have much truth left" (p. 205).

And so it goes in this episode — full of dialogue and terminology that could fit comfortably into a courtroom scene, building a clearer and clearer portrait of Anne's mind and the scrupulous means by which she persuades herself to revise her persuasions. Anne's "shudder" at the end of the interview, when she realizes that "she might have been persuaded by Lady Russell" to marry this man whom she now finally perceives as a consummate villain, indicates how her reason, imagination, and emotions work in concert.

Several scholars have pointed out that the title *Persuasion* was probably not chosen by Jane Austen.[13] Whether or not Jane Austen's brother Henry actually did select the title, it seems to me a good choice. I have tried to show in this essay the centrality of persuasion in the book and the value to the reader of appreciating that centrality. Numerous episodes I have not discussed also take on new meanings when we observe their relations to the moral issues inherent in persuasion. Indeed, such an understanding of the novel's great dependence on the meanings of persuasion can enrich our comprehension of other Jane Austen works (*Emma*, for example, has much to say about persuasion — the word itself occurring in many dozens of significant contexts). Most impor-

[13] See R. Brimley Johnson, *Jane Austen: Her Life, Her Work, Her Family, and Her Critics* (London, 1930), pp. 165-66. Cf. R. W. Chapman, "Jane Austen's Titles," *Nineteenth-Century Fiction,* IX (1954), 238.

tant, I believe, is our need to recognize the complexity of moral vision in *Persuasion,* a complexity discoverable in the numerous, different, and yet often closely related meanings attached to all the nouns, verbs, and verbals based on "persuade." Such a recognition should afford the reader instructive pleasures otherwise hidden. Then, like Mrs. Smith's homely nurse Rooke, or like any really good storyteller or story, Jane Austen's final creation will be "sure to have something to relate that is entertaining and profitable, something that makes one know one's species better" (p. 155).[14]

[14] I am indebted to Professor Phyllis Rackin for helping me revise this essay.

FIVE

Empathy and the Daemonic in *Wuthering Heights*

BY CHARLES I. PATTERSON, JR.

In his monumental *History of the English Novel,* E. A. Baker makes two germinal pronouncements concerning Emily Brontë's stark and powerful novel *Wuthering Heights.* He proclaims that it is the first novel in English with a cosmic background,[1] a penetrating insight obviously foreshadowed by Lord David Cecil's brilliant discussion of the ways in which the characters in their responses and actions are very largely motivated and governed by inexorable laws that are in fact the laws governing the universe.[2] Also, concerning the delayed entry of the full force of Romanticism into the English novel, Baker maintains that "the deeper romanticism, the romanticism of Wordsworth and his fellows, did not enter fully into English fiction until the time of the Brontë sisters, with their deep-rooted sense of a material world transfused with spirit." But with the advent of the Brontës "imagination and instinct claimed their share" in the genre at last. Then, contends Baker, "fiction regains a place beside or only a little below poetry, dares to speak for the soul, to sound the deeps of personality, to face the enigmas of evil and death."[3] These statements, just as do those of Lord David Cecil concerning the cosmic element in the story, point toward profound depths in this novel that can fruitfully be examined further.

The more obvious Romantic elements of *Wuthering Heights* are easy to recognize: the Gothic traits in the character of the hero, the Gothic aura of the house and the lonely isolated location exposed to storm winds from the moors; the suspense that stems from mystery, terror,

---

[1] E. A. Baker, *History of the English Novel,* 10 vols. (New York, 1950, first published in 1937), VIII, 70-72.

[2] Lord David Cecil, *Early Victorian Novelists* (New York, 1935), pp. 157-206.

[3] Baker, *History of the English Novel,* VI, 15; VIII, 19.

and the supernatural; the representation of nature as an ever-present source of both the aesthetic and the spiritual; and the idea that external nature is both an influence upon the inner mind of man and an outward image of it. More deeply interfused throughout the novel as a shaping force upon the characters, upon the action, and upon the tone and atmosphere of the whole is the relentless Romantic drive for experience more richly fulfilling than ordinary life affords. This drive manifests itself in Heathcliff and Cathy Earnshaw in two modes that continually appeared at the deepest levels of the poetry of the preceding age, especially the poetry of Coleridge, Byron, Keats, and Shelley. The first mode is the daemonic urge to pierce beyond all human limitations in the search for the heart's desire, an urge that unfortunately has been confused with the Satanic; the second is a great capacity for empathy, for what John Keats termed "Negative Capability," the capacity to become so fully united with another being or object as to feel that the self and the beloved object are one and the same. This latter capability is augmented by the emotional force of the former, and both interact upon each other throughout the story. Both have been discussed in previous criticism, but both have been considerably garbled and blurred. It is the purpose of this essay to attempt to clarify the nature and function of these two great principles of empathy and the daemonic in *Wuthering Heights* and to suggest that these are the elements that contribute most to its tremendous power and appeal.

Dorothy Van Ghent discusses both of these elements at some length, mentions the "daemonic character" of Heathcliff, and labels him a "demon-lover."[4] However, she then maintains that it is difficult to define precisely the quality of the daemonic in the conception of Heathcliff. She does so in terms that at times point unmistakably toward the particular concept of the daemonic involved and reveal how it has become confused with the Satanic, which is significantly different:

> There is still the difficulty of defining, with any precision, the quality of the daemonic that is realized most vividly in the conception of Heathcliff, a difficulty that is mainly due to our tendency always to give the "daemonic" some ethical status — that is, to relate it to an ethical hierarchy. Heathcliff's is an archetypal figure, untraceably ancient in mythological thought — an imaged recognition of that part of nature that is "other" than the human soul (the world of the elements and the ani-

4 Dorothy Van Ghent, *The English Novel: Form and Function* (New York, 1953), pp. 154, 156, 161, 163, 164-65, 168.

mals) and of that part of the soul itself which is "other" than the conscious part. But since Martin Luther's revival of this archetype for modern mythology, it has tended to forget its relationship with the elemental "otherness" of the outer world and to identify itself solely with the dark functions of the soul. As an image of soul work, it is ethically relevant, since everything that the soul does — even unconsciously, even ignorantly (as in the case of Oedipus) — offers itself for ethical judgment, whereas the elements and animals do not. Puritanism perpetuated the figure for the imagination; Milton gave it its greatest splendor, in the fallen angel through whom the divine beauty still shone.[5]

Although more is involved in this archetype than the world of the elements and animals, and although it is not as untraceable in mythology as she claims, Van Ghent clearly perceives that Heathcliff is strikingly different from those individuations of the archetype that are customarily related to ethical thought:

> The exception is Heathcliff. Heathcliff is no more ethically relevant than is flood or earthquake or whirlwind. It is as impossible to speak of him in terms of "sin" and "guilt" as it is to speak in this way of the natural elements or the creatures of the animal world. In him, the archetype reverts to a more ancient mythology and to an earlier symbolism. *Wuthering Heights* so baffles and confounds the ethical sense because it is not informed with that sense at all. . . . But Heathcliff does have human shape and human relationships; he is, so to speak, caught in the human; two kinds of reality intersect in him — as they do, . . . indeed, in the other characters. Each entertains, in some degree, the powers of darkness. . . . Even in the weakest of these souls there is an intimation of the dark Otherness, by which the soul is related psychologically to the inhuman world of pure energy, for it carries within itself an "otherness" of its own, that inhabits below consciousness.[6]

Penetrating and fruitful as these insights are, they do not offer sufficient definition and clarification of the concept of the daemonic involved, and the resort to "animism" is too vague to be helpful in particularizing it. Consequently, Van Ghent envisions the central conflicts in the novel too much as "a tension between . . . the raw, inhuman reality of anonymous natural energies, and the restrictive reality of civilized habits, manners, and codes." She is quite accurate in the latter but not so in the former. She sees the lovers as entirely too brutish and suggests that they are like animals who rend each other when they kiss.

[5] *Ibid.*, p. 163.
[6] *Ibid.*, pp. 164-65.

On the basis of this erroneous attribution, she then draws a conclusion quite far afield, I think: "But since no conceivable *human* male and female, not brutish, not anthropologically rudimentary, could be together in this way as adults, all that we can really imagine for the grown-up Cathy and Heathcliff, as 'characters' on the human plane, is what the book gives them — their mutual destruction by tooth and nail in an effort, through death, to get back to the lost state of gypsy freedom in childhood."[7]

This view completely overlooks the grandeur of their mutual love and the remarkable empathy between them, which makes them nobly selfless for the most part in spite of their possessive moments and utterances. Van Ghent shows that she does not fully understand the nature of empathy when she declares their love inevitably sexless because a person cannot mate with himself and because in empathy he feels that the other person *is* himself. She thus concludes that their relationship is not an adult one. But empathy does not involve complete delusion. During empathic union one does not simply confuse his identity with another person's but feels a pronounced lessening of awareness of his separate identity and a simultaneous filling up of his selfhood by the other person's selfhood *in idea,* all the while remaining to some degree conscious of his own being. Empathy therefore enhances sexual consummation and spiritualizes it. Heathcliff and Cathy are not sexless; they are adult human lovers with high sexuality. They yearn for something far more compelling than the lost state of gypsy freedom in childhood, and they yearn forward, not backward.

Similarly, Professor John Hagan perceives that Heathcliff and Cathy have daemonic characteristics, but he does not differentiate between the Christian and pre-Christian conceptions of the daemonic.[8] Hence he makes what I believe to be serious misjudgments concerning the novel and is led to assert that critics are attempting "to discover in the novel more metaphysical concreteness than it can yield."[9] In actuality it will reveal considerable metaphysical concreteness if the particular metaphysics involved is defined and clarified. Not having this very necessary equipment in hand, Professor Hagan slips into the mistake of applying conventional moralistic standards to Heathcliff's and Cathy's actions, with critical results that are not acceptable. For example, he

[7] *Ibid.,* pp. 157, 159.

[8] John Hagan, "Control of Sympathy in *Wuthering Heights,*" *Nineteenth-Century Fiction,* XXI (1967), 305-23.

[9] *Ibid.,* p. 314.

states, "If Edgar is not Heathcliff's equal for passion, neither is he so merely contemptible. Heathcliff's speech is a piece of special pleading and deplorable vainglory," especially outrageous because Heathcliff has just performed his horrible act of revenge, marrying Isabella. And yet Professor Hagan concludes as follows: "The dominant image of Heathcliff that emerges, then, is neither that of a 'moral force' nor a 'demon,' but that of a tragic sufferer. And this is finally our image of Catherine, too. We do not condone their outrages, but neither do we merely condemn them. We do something larger and more important: we recognize in them the tragedy of passionate natures whom intolerable frustration and loss have stripped of their humanity."[10]

Hagan thus pares down the stature of Heathcliff and Cathy at the same time that he designates them tragic sufferers. He has ignored all the author's efforts to endow their *emotional life* with suprahuman intensity while steadily asserting that *they* are certainly within the human family. It is true that they are not motivated by "moral force" nor by the love of evil as is the case in the Christian "demonic." But surely they are markedly enhanced as tragic protagonists by the force and power of the pre-Christian daemonic, which flows through them and motivates their enormously passionate natures and fierce attachment, human beings though they are. The impetus of their daemonic search for fulfillment, centering intently upon each other alone, drives them into an empathic union as relentless as the union of two planets in orbit around each other. And this empathy then functions like the cosmic principle of inertia, the opposite of motion, resisting change of direction or separation and bringing cataclysmic eruptions when the two are forced apart.

Lord David Cecil points unerringly in this direction when he maintains with uncanny insight that their "deeds and passions do not spring from essentially destructive impulses, but impulses only destructive because they are diverted from pursuing their natural course," that Emily Brontë's outlook is neither moral nor immoral but *pre-moral*.[11] This is indeed what it is, as Dorothy Van Ghent in effect perceives, and this points the way to clarification of the daemonic element in the book. In essence, the universal principles of empathy and the daemonic can be subsumed under Lord Cecil's majestic conception of a single cosmic principle of dual modes that underpins and pervades the entire novel

[10] *Ibid.,* pp. 320, 323.
[11] Cecil, *Early Victorian Novelists,* pp. 164-65.

and all its parts. The daemonic is a particular aspect of one of these dual modes and empathy an aspect of the other — the world of storm and motion as opposed to the world of inertia and stasis. Both, working together, vividly reveal how the universal principles of the cosmos operate just as unerringly within the human psyche as within a solar system.

Among the various notions of daemons in Greek mythology there is a conception, ancient but not entirely untraceable, of daemonic creatures living outside the pale of all human limitations and therefore neither good nor evil but neutral to both.[12] Hence they were thought to dwell in joy and ecstasy without stint. And since they were not subject to human restrictions of any kind, all their emotions — even their griefs — could be considered to be stronger and more engulfing than those within the human breast. They could experience attachments and aversions with fierce intensity and total preoccupation; they could not experience what is given in human morality — obligation, duty, restraint, moderation. However, they were thought to have an important connection with human beings, for they supposedly had assisted Saturn in the creation, later ruled over men for a time and brought them great happiness, and subsequently served as messengers between gods and men. Sometimes they carried a human being away into eternal bliss and joy, as did their counterparts in fairy lore and in the medieval romances, for example, in William Butler Yeats's *The Stolen Child* and Thomas Cestre's fifteenth-century romance *Sir Launfal*. Emily Brontë probably gained much of her knowledge of such a daemonic world from fairy lore.

These daemonic creatures and their relationships with human beings are frequently mentioned in the Platonic dialogues, although Plato evidently did not believe in them literally. Knowledge of them was handed down to modern times by many of the neo-Platonists. In the dialogues "Statesman" and "Laws" the following is spoken by two of the lesser disputants:

> Blessed and spontaneous life does not belong to the present cycle of the world, but to the previous one, in which God superintended the whole

[12] Discussions of various conceptions of daemons appear in Robert H. West, *The Invisible World* (Athens, Ga., 1939), and James Hastings, ed., *Encyclopedia of Religion and Ethics* (New York, 1925). I have discussed various aspects of the daemonic in *The Daemonic in the Poetry of John Keats* (Urbana, Ill., 1970), Chapter I. The spelling "daemon" is more frequent for the pre-Christian conception, "demon" for Christian; but the distinction is not always kept.

revolution of the universe; and the several parts of the universe were distributed under the rule of certain inferior deities . . . and each one was in all respects sufficient for those of whom he was the shepherd . . . and I might tell of ten thousand other blessings, which belong to that dispensation.

There is a tradition of the happy life of mankind in days when all things were spontaneous and abundant. And of this the reason is said to have been as follows: . . . God, in his love of mankind, placed over us the demons, who are a superior race, and they with great ease and pleasure to themselves, and no less to us, taking care of us . . . made the tribes of men happy and united.[13]

In sum, such a conception is useful today only as an objective correlative to an inner proclivity within man — the relentless proclivity to seek joy, beauty, and knowledge beyond what is afforded by the ordinary human lot even at its best. This insistent drive is readily apparent in some men, though not in all, but it may be latent in all human beings. Goethe elevates the conception into a universal principle in passages of his autobiography, *Dichtung und Wahrheit,* Part IV (first published in 1833), which sound at times as if he is speaking directly of the central characters in *Wuthering Heights* fourteen years before the novel was created. Emily Brontë could have seen the passages or heard them discussed. Goethe does more than anyone else to clarify the concept of the daemonic reflected in the novel, to distinguish it from the evil and the Satanic and to suggest the evidences of it in human conduct and human minds (Goethe is using the third person to speak of himself as a youth) :

He believed he could detect in nature — both animate and inanimate, spiritual and non-spiritual — something which reveals itself only in contradictions, and which, therefore, could not be encompassed under any concept, still less under a word. It was not divine, for it seemed without reason; not human, for it had no understanding; not diabolical, for it was beneficent; not angelic, for it took pleasure in mischief. It resembled chance, in that it manifested no consequence; it was like Providence, for it pointed toward connection. All that restricts us seemed for it penetrable; it seemed to deal arbitrarily with the necessary elements of our

[13] *The Dialogues of Plato,* tr. B. Jowett (New York, 1937), II, 299, 385. Keats expresses ideas akin to these frequently, for example, in "I Stood Tiptoe," ll. 185-87, and "Sleep and Poetry," ll. 29-34. It is possible that Emily Brontë had seen the translations of Plato and commentaries by Thomas Taylor; in some of the latter, daemonic lore is summarized, for example, in Taylor's note 2 on "The First Alcibiades."

existence; it contracted time and expanded space. It seemed to find pleasure only in the impossible and to reject the possible with contempt. To this entity, which seemed to intervene between all others, to separate them and yet to link them together, I gave the name daemonic, after the example of the ancients and of those who had perceived something similar. I tried to shield myself from this fearful entity by seeking refuge, in accordance with my usual habit behind an imaginary representation. . . .

Although this daemonic element can manifest itself in all corporeal and incorporeal things, can even manifest itself most markedly in animals, yet with man especially has it a most wonderful connection that creates a power which while not opposed to the moral order of the world still does so often cross through it that one may be considered the warp and the other the woof. . . .

However, the daemonic appears most fearful when it becomes predominant in a human being. During my life I have observed several. . . . They are not always the most eminent men either in their intellect or their talents . . . but a tremendous power seems to flow from them; and they exercise a wonderful power over all creatures, and even over the elements; and who can say how far such influence may extend? All the combined forces of convention are helpless against them.[14]

[14] Johann Wolfgang von Goethe, *Dichtung und Wahrheit*, Part IV, Book 20, ed. Georg Witkowski, from *Goethes Werke*, X (Leipzig, [193]), 317-19. The translation is essentially mine, with help from that of J. Oxenford (Boston, 1882), II, 321-23, and with helpful suggestions from my colleague Professor Calvin Brown. The German text is as follows:

"Er glaubte in der Natur, der belebten und unbelebten, der beseelten und unbeseelten, etwas zu entdecken, das sich nur in Widersprüchen manifestierte und deshalb unter keinen Begriff, noch viel weniger unter ein Wort gefasst werden könnte. Es war nicht göttlich, denn es schien unvernünftig; nicht menschlich, denn es hatte keinen Verstand; nicht teuflisch, denn es war wohltätig; nicht englisch, denn es liess oft Schadenfreude merken. Es glich dem Zufall, denn es bewiess kein Folge; es ähnelte der Forsehung, denn es deutete auf Zusammenhang. Alles, was uns begrenzt, schien für dasselbe durchdringbar; es schien mit den notwendigen Elementen unsres Daseins willkürlich zu schalten; es zog die Zeit zusammen und dehnte den Raum aus. Nur im Unmöglichen schien es sich zu gefallen und das Mögliche mit Verachtung von sich zu stossen.

"Dieses Wesen, das zwischen alle übrigen hineinzutreten, sie zu sondern, sie zu verbinden schien, nannte ich dämonisch, nach dem Beispiel der Alten und derer, die etwas Ähnliches gewahrt hatten. Ich suchte mich vor diesem furchtbaren Wesen zu retten, indem ich mich nach meiner Gewohnheit hinter ein Bild flüchtete. . . .

"Obgleich jenes Dämonische sich in allem Körperlichen und Unkörperlichen

It is discernible at once that this passage particularizes the nature of the underlying daemonic force that imperiously motivates Heathcliff and Cathy and also that the passage suggests many of the specific manifestations of the daemonic that are apparent in their thoughts and actions. Their love for each other revealed itself continually in contradictions — extremes of tenderness and of cruelty, great selflessness and marked possessiveness, godlike thoughtfulness for each other as well as the fierce desire to hurt and torture, condemnation of each other's actions along with soul-stirring expressions of unextinguishable devotion, tremendous joy in each other and also the most searing pain. As Van Ghent says, two realities did intersect in them, one the warp and the other the woof, according to Goethe. Moreover, they continually flouted reason, pierced through what restricts ordinary people, found pleasure in the impossible while rejecting the possible with contempt, exhibited a tremendous power over others, and indeed managed to render the combined forces of convention quite helpless against them.

For example, Heathcliff admitted neither Cathy's marriage to another nor her death nor the lapse of twenty years as a deterrent to his love, and he flung off the trammels of dire poverty and lack of status as easily as he broke through the restraints of conventional life in a rigidly hierarchical social structure. Cathy, for example, assumed that her husband, Edgar, would welcome Heathcliff into the household when he suddenly returned from his three-year absence, and she was indignant that he was not thus received. A subtle evidence of the daemonic nature of her underlying mental life and basic assumptions is that in her dreams and conceptions of the hereafter she shows no affinity whatever with the Christian Heaven nor with the world of conventional humanity but only with a metaphorical daemonic realm of freedom

manifestieren kann, ja bei den Tieren sich aufs merkwürdigste auspricht, so steht es vorzüglich mit dem Menschen im wunderbarsten Zusammenhang und bildet eine der moralischen Weltordnung wo nicht entgegengesetzte, doch sie durchkreuzende Macht, so dass man die eine für den Zettel, die andere für den Einschlag könnte gelten lassen. . . .

"Am furchtbarsten aber erscheint dieses Dämonische, wenn es in irgend einem Menschen überwiegend hervortritt. Während meines Lebensganges habe ich mehrere teils in der Nähe, teils in der Ferne beobachten können. Es sind nicht immer die vorzüglichsten Menschen, weder an Geist noch an Talenten . . . aber eine ungeheure Kraft geht von ihnen aus, und sie üben eine unglaubliche Gewalt über alle Geschöpfe, ja sogar über die Elemente, und wer kann sagen, wie weit sich eine solche Wirkung erstrecken wird? Alle vereinten sittlichen Kräfte vermögen nichts gegen sie. . . ."

from restraint that has the characteristics of neither Heaven nor Hell nor earth. This realm is represented physically for her by the wild countryside surrounding Wuthering Heights and is constituted spiritually for her by her engulfing empathic union with Heathcliff, a union so complete that it very nearly blots out every other consideration. When telling Nelly Dean that she had dreamed of being in Heaven, Cathy states:

> Heaven did not seem to be my home; and I broke my heart with weeping to come back to earth; and the angels were so angry that they flung me out into the middle of the heath on top of Wuthering Heights; where I woke sobbing for joy. That will do to explain my secret as well as the other. I've no more business to marry Edgar Linton than I have to be in heaven; and if the wicked man in there had not brought Heathcliff so low, I shouldn't have thought of it. It would degrade me to marry Heathcliff now; so he shall never know how I love him; and that not because he's handsome, Nelly, but because he's more myself than I am. Whatever our souls are made of, his and mine are the same, and Linton's is as different as a moonbeam from lightning or frost from fire.[15]

Even the imagery at the end suggests the daemonic aspects of their love and of their souls — she likens hers and Heathcliff's to lightning and fire and Linton's to pallid moonbeams and frost. Her joyous, unrestrained life on the vast heath in company with this kindred soul made of the same elemental fire as herself indicates for her the characteristics of the only heaven that she can conceive to be desirable — a neutral region, metaphorically speaking, that is neither heaven nor earth but a place where she can be entirely free of the restrictions and limitations of conventional life. This conception of life after death appears again and again in her thoughts. She shows that she envisions something beyond this life, something to which she is related but which has no characteristics whatever of the Christian Heaven in her expression of it. She says to Nelly, "Surely you and everybody have a notion that there is, or should be, an existence of yours beyond you. What were the use of my creation if I were entirely contained here" (pp. 73-74). Similarly, when her death is near, she longs for release from earthly limitations and entrance into what she calls a "glorious world," but it seems in her conception to be a world of pure energy and uninhibited life, from which her daemonic lover Heathcliff will not be absent:

[15] Emily Brontë, *Wuthering Heights,* ed. W. M. Sale, Jr., Norton Critical Editions (New York, 1963), p. 72; cf. p. 107. All subsequent citations, incorporated in the text, are to this edition, evidently now the most reliable.

The thing that irks me most is this shattered prison, after all. I'm tired, tired of being enclosed here. I'm wearying to escape into that glorious world, and to be always there; not seeing it dimly through tears, and yearning for it through the walls of an aching heart; but really with it, and in it. Nelly, you think you are better and more fortunate than I; in full health and strength. You are sorry for me — very soon that will be altered. I shall be sorry for you. I shall be incomparably beyond and above you all. I *wonder* he won't be near me. [P. 134; italics in original]

good

In sum, the metaphysical reality that Cathy expects to join after death more nearly resembles what Goethe had brilliantly described as the universal principle of the daemonic than it does the Christian Heaven, with its tranquillity, peace, and hymns of praise to the Almighty. The consistency and homogeneity of this girl's basic character, on both the conscious and subconscious levels, is remarkably well sustained throughout the book. In the light of the mighty force that motivates her being, her perversity and recalcitrance are understandable and are removed from the sphere of what we are expected to accept, condone, or blame.

Whereas Emily Brontë easily depicted Cathy as still belonging to the human family in spite of her daemonic qualities, the control of reader response to Heathcliff presented a more difficult problem. In order for his gross breaches of convention and for his sustained love beyond death to be sufficiently motivated to seem credible to readers, she repeatedly suggested that he is beyond mortality in the fierceness of his daemonic passions. Yet, in order for him still to retain enough of the reader's sympathy to appear a tragic figure, she found a way to remind readers repeatedly of his human identity at the same time. She accomplished this difficult feat through having Nelly Dean, the principal narrator, indicate in a continual dual pattern that he *seems* supramortal and yet *is* fully human, as evidenced through her own knowledge of him. By this clever manipulation of the technical narrative point of view, Emily Brontë has things both ways at once, throwing over Heathcliff the glamour of the suprahuman and at the same time maintaining reader sympathy for a very human sufferer in tragic circumstances. She keeps us ever mindful of the two kinds of reality that intersect in him. Emphasis on his pre-moral daemonic nature is carried about as far as possible without placing him beyond the pale of humanity. Even the author's sister Charlotte did so in her "Editor's Preface" to her "New Edition" of the book (1850), in which she makes the common mistake of conceiving him as basically a supramortal evil demon with little evidence of humanity. But Emily Brontë, when she created him, had masterfully projected his true lineaments through Nelly Dean.

At the very beginning of her narrative, she relates that Mr. Earnshaw found him as a deserted child on the streets of Liverpool and brought him home to be cared for in his household. Mr. Earnshaw said to the family as he unwrapped the child and set him upon his feet before them, "You must e'n take it as a gift of God, though it's as dark as if it came from the devil." His speech indicates at once that the child is to be considered within the whole human family under God and also that this child bears an aura of the extrahuman from the mystery of his origin, a mystery that is never cleared up and that continues throughout the book to suggest his difference from ordinary humanity (p. 38). Earnshaw's words, "dark as if it came from the devil," are simply convenient terms for him to use for the purpose and cannot be taken to indicate serious belief in an evil origin of the boy, as the first part of Earnshaw's sentence clearly shows. Shortly afterward the other children, as well as their mother, draw away from this child and refuse to have him in their bedroom, as if he were a stranger to the human race. Nelly, who admitted hating him unjustly at first, put him on the landing of the stair, hoping he might be gone on the morrow (p. 39). But the little fellow immediately asserted his humanity by creeping to Mr. Earnshaw's door during the night, They later gave him the name Heathcliff, which had been the name of a son who had died in infancy, suggesting his full acceptance in this human family. But since "Heathcliff" served him throughout life as both given name and surname, it was simultaneously a constant reminder of his difference from them (p. 39). Further, he clung to Nelly in human need when seriously ill in childhood, wanting her always near. And Nelly reported, "Cathy and her brother harassed me terribly; he [Heathcliff] was as uncomplaining as a lamb" (p. 40). Yet he early revealed a fierce, daemonic intentness upon his own purposes regardless of powerful opposition, as shown in his getting possession of Hindley's pony to replace his own lame one (pp. 40-41). But the very human Mr. Earnshaw took to the fatherless boy inordinately, favoring him above his own children and believing all he said; Nelly reported that the boy "said precious little, and generally the truth" (p. 40), an ideal human trait.

The same dual pattern of human and daemonic qualities is continued throughout Nelly's account of his adult life after his and Cathy's love has locked them into an orbit together from which there could never be egress. When as a grown man, returned and well-to-do, Heathcliff appears for the first time at Thrushcross Grange, he is seen by all as an admirable blend of fine human traits with the traces of his old fire now subdued. Nelly describes him thus:

> He had grown a tall, athletic, well-formed man, beside whom my master seemed quite slender and youth-like. His upright carriage suggested the idea of his having been in the army. His countenance was much older in expression and decision of feature than Mr. Linton's; it looked intelligent, and retained no marks of former degradation. A half-civilized ferocity lurked yet in the depressed brows and eyes full of black fire, but it was subdued; and his manner was even dignified, quite divested of roughness, though too stern for grace.
>
> My master's surprise equalled or exceeded mine. [P. 84]

Shortly thereafter Cathy tells Edgar and Nelly that Heathcliff is now "worthy of any one's regard, and it would honour the first gentleman of the country to be his friend" (p. 86). On the other hand, after the ensuing days of terrible conflict between the two men and growing danger to Hindley, Nelly designates Heathcliff "an evil beast . . . waiting his time to spring and destroy" (p. 94). Later, when she sees the enormity of his anguish at Cathy's impending death, Nelly says, "I did not feel as if I were in the company of a creature of my own species" (p. 134). And in his terrible grief after Cathy's death, Nelly reports that he dashed his head against a knotty tree trunk and "howled, not like a man, but like a savage beast getting goaded to death with knives and spears. . . . It appalled me" (p. 139). By the beast imagery she does not mean actually to suggest the bestial but rather the extramortal — that is, emotion beyond the extremes of the human. Yet her human sympathies embraced him, for she says, "I was weeping as much for him as for her" (p. 138). To Isabella's terming him a "monster," Nelly cries out, "Hush! Hush! He's a human being. . . . Be more charitable; there are worse men" (p. 143). Finally at the very end just before his death she puts both strains together; two kinds of reality meet in him to the very end:

> "Is he a ghoul, or a vampire," I mused. I had read of such hideous, incarnate demons. And then I set myself to reflect how I had tended him in infancy; and watched him grow to youth; and followed him almost through his whole course; and what absurd nonsense it was to yield to that sense of horror.
>
> "But where did he come from, the little dark thing, harboured by a

good man to his bane?" muttered superstition, as I dozed into uncon-
sciousness. And I began, half dreaming, to weary myself with imaging
some fit parentage for him. [P. 260]

Without thus establishing and sustaining both the human and the
daemonic qualities of her lovers, Emily Brontë could never have successfully handled in the novel the elements that chiefly provide dramatic depth and power — the strong empathic union of their souls and
the cataclysmic consequences of their being wrenched apart — and she
could never have made credible and acceptable the stark and bare
emotions in their speeches, which render forth the heights and depths
of their joy and suffering. Their speeches would have seemed over-
laden with emotional excess, and the extent to which their consciousnesses had actually merged would not have been made palpable. But
their daemonic intensity and the circumstances of their childhood, when
each was everything meaningful to the other, make probable the fullness of their empathy. Therefore, we can accept unquestioningly Cathy's
simple and beautiful statement of the central truth of her being, that
she felt no self-identity apart from the companion of her soul, a matter
which clinical psychologists could validate:

> My great miseries in this world have been Heathcliff's miseries, and I
> watched and felt each from the beginning: My great thought in living is
> himself. If all else perished, and *he* remained, I should continue to be;
> and, if all else remained, and he were annihilated, the Universe would
> turn to a mighty stranger. I should not seem a part of it. My love for
> Linton is like the foliage in the woods. Time will change it, I'm well
> aware, as winter changes the trees. My love for Heathcliff resembles the
> eternal rocks beneath — a source of little delight, but necessary. Nelly,
> I *am* Heathcliff — he's always, always in my mind — not as a pleasure,
> any more than I am always a pleasure to myself — but as my own being
> — so, don't talk of our separation again — it is impracticable. [P. 74]

And Heathcliff, perceiving from her wasted condition that her death is
inevitable, voices with piercing directness the central fact of his existence, followed soon after her death by his anguished plea for con-
tinuance of their union beyond the grave:

> Oh, Cathy! Oh, my life! how can I bear it? [P. 132]

> Be with me always — take any form — drive me mad! only do not leave
> me in this abyss, where I cannot find you! Oh, God! it is unutterable!
> I *cannot* live without my life! I *cannot* live without my soul! [P. 139]

What is expressed here occurs repeatedly in real life: the consciousnesses of two persons deeply attached to each other over a long period finally intermesh, so that each constitutes a large part of what fills up the other. When one of them is taken away, the mind of the other actually loses a significant part of its content, and the loss is felt profoundly below the levels of thought in the depths of the psyche. I remember vividly a strong and gracious lady, seventy-one years of age, who, after a lifetime of devotion to her husband, bore his death bravely and said that she would not wish to have him back suffering from disease as he was. But after a few weeks the emptiness and vacuity of her mind, divested of her thoughts of him, impelled her into a state of apathy and dejection that lasted for years. In her novel Emily Brontë has managed to present this psychological truth in the lives of two people who lived only a short span of years, not an easy task for a novelist to attempt.

In the art medium the elements of life must be heightened and emphasized for the rendering to have force and point. One great aspect of Emily Brontë's achievement is that she found a way to motivate the unleashing and expressing of the most powerful human emotions resulting from the loosening of the strongest human ties, somewhat as Shakespeare had done in *King Lear*. And in this novel, as in *King Lear*, the results of the loosening of these ties are likened and related to the workings of tremendous forces in the cosmos. Heathcliff and Cathy came to be remarkably similar to two celestial bodies in orbit round each other, like Sirius and its companion, held in orbit by interaction of the velocity of their motion and the attraction of their mass responding to the law of gravity. Their being wrenched apart, first by her marriage to another and then by her death, released into the human cosmos that energy which had been held in check as it held them together (if we may extend Lord David Cecil's conception). It had to spend its force in collisions and chaotic attractions and repulsions (such as that of Isabella to Heathcliff) before equilibruim and stasis could be restored, as it is indeed finally restored both in Heathcliff's last days before death and in the calm lives of the second generation. The deeper Romanticism had truly entered the English novel: the ways in which the instinctive, the irrational, the transcendental union of the self with the "other," the depths of the subconscious, and the human relationship to the cosmos influence our decisions and actions — all are powerfully set forth in Emily Brontë's picture of life. Her skilled use of empathy and the daemonic, which are like cosmic motion and stasis within the human sphere, are among the chief means that enabled her to emerge with admirable success in this difficult undertaking and to produce in her one novel a presentation, unparalleled in the century, of the elemental power and grandeur of human longing.

SIX

The Control
of Emotional Response in
David Copperfield

BY GEORGE J. WORTH

Beginning with the deeply involved author himself, who called it his "favourite child," most perceptive readers of Dickens's fiction have assigned *David Copperfield* a special place of honor in the canon of his novels. Not only does it hold great interest for its superb craftsmanship and obvious autobiographical elements, but it astonishes and captivates because of the wide range of powerful emotions — from profound sadness to uproarious laughter — that it arouses in persons of normal sensibility.

There have been those, of course, who have disparaged *David Copperfield* for its emotional excesses — its "sentimentality," its "melodrama" — and there are undeniably aspects of the novel that might seem puzzling or even offensive to a tough-minded, hard-hearted twentieth-century audience. Nonetheless, it can be shown that in *David Copperfield* Dickens carefully husbanded his affective resources so as to deploy them with the greatest possible impact where they were most needed. He refrained from calling forth strong responses unnecessarily, and indeed he sometimes took great pains to avoid arousing them at all. The result is a masterfully controlled and on the whole subtly orchestrated emotional texture.

Dickens's decision to tell the story from David's point of view, probably inevitable given the genesis and the nature of *David Copperfield,* not only lends the novel much of its fresh immediacy but — perhaps paradoxically — also makes large portions of it less pathetic and less indignant than an omniscient narrator would have rendered them. I am thinking chiefly of the first quarter of the book, in which young David's formidable sufferings before his arrival at Aunt Betsey's little cottage at Dover are recounted. A fatherless boy with an ineffectual mother, neglected and tyrannized after the Murdstones move in and take over, banished first to Salem House and then — after the death of his beloved mother — to the unspeakable wine and spirits warehouse, forced to flee on foot and without money from London to the Kentish coast, bullied and gulled by confidence tricksters, petty crooks, and other scoundrels, David leads a truly pitiful existence until Betsey Trotwood takes him under her wing.

The *quality* of the pity David's plight arouses is interesting. Dickens's fiction is full of suffering children, but nowhere else is this subject treated as it is in David's case. Some examples from *Dombey and Son,* which immediately precedes *David Copperfield* in the chronological list of Dickens's novels, and from *Bleak House,* which immediately follows it, will perhaps help to make my point clear.

Paul and Florence Dombey in *Dombey and Son* and Jo the crossing sweeper in *Bleak House* are pitiable, suffering children too. But whether their ordeals are rendered in omniscient narrative or in dramatic episodes only somewhat less obviously manipulated by the omniscient narrator than his narrative is, one cannot easily escape the suspicion, which Dickens's technique encourages, that such ordeals are in these novels largely to prove a point, about Dombey and Dombeyism in the first case, about an utterly irresponsible society in the second. Paul and Florence and Jo exist chiefly not as feeling young human beings in their own right but as ready means to arouse the reader's emotions in the service of ends that Dickens is trying to further.

Among many passages from these two novels that might be cited in this connection, there is the death scene of Paul, a little boy who is less lonely in these ultimate moments than he has ever been in the chilling company of his father:

> "Remember Walter, dear papa," he whispered, looking in his face. "Remember Walter. I was fond of Walter!" The feeble hand waved in the air, as if it cried "good-bye!" to Walter once again.
>
> "Now lay me down," he said, "and, Floy, come close to me, and let me see you!"
>
> Sister and brother wound their arms around each other, and the golden light came streaming in, and fell upon them, locked together.
>
> "How fast the river runs, between its green banks and the rushes, Floy! But it's very near the sea. I hear the waves! They always said so!"
>
> Presently he told her that the motion of the boat upon the stream was lulling him to rest. How green the banks were now, how bright the

flowers growing on them, and how tall the rushes! Now the boat was out at sea, but gliding smoothly on. And now there was a shore before him. Who stood on the bank! —

He put his hands together, as he had been used to do at his prayers. He did not remove his arms to do it; but they saw him fold them so, behind her neck.

"Mama is like you, Floy. I know her by the face! But tell them that the print upon the stairs at school is not divine enough. The light about the head is shining on me as I go!" [Chapter 16]

Or, in *Bleak House,* the narrator's denunciation of the worthies who have allowed Jo to die: "Dead, your Majesty. Dead, my lords and gentlemen. Dead, Right Reverends and Wrong Reverends of every order. Dead, men and women, born with Heavenly compassion in your hearts. And dying thus around us every day" (Chapter 47).

Even if first-person narrative were not impossible in Paul's case and inconceivable in Jo's, it is pointless to speculate how their experiences might have emerged if they had been rendered from the suffering children's point of view. What we do know is that in *David Copperfield* Dickens's narrative method produces a remarkable blend of feelings in which pity for the unhappy child and indignation against his tormentors, though certainly present, are not the predominant ingredients.

Young David's clear-eyed but necessarily imperfect perception of what is happening alternates with the mature David's retrospective musings on the significance of these childhood events. In that majority of instances when we see things pretty much as young David saw them, a variety of effects is achieved, of which comedy is not the least frequent. We know so much more about life than this stripling that we are able to catch meanings and nuances that elude him, and in the resultant amused superiority that we feel toward David, much of the humor of the novel resides. When, for example, Murdstone and his Lowestoft friends make merry over Murdstone's allusion to "Brooks of Sheffield" (Chapter 2), we get the joke (which, regarded objectively, is more cruel than funny) and David does not, and so we smile. Or when, a little later on (Chapter 5), the greedy waiter in the inn at Yarmouth makes fun of David when he is en route to Salem House, takes advantage of the lad, and frightens him, we understand exactly what is happening and view the situation as comical rather than threatening.

At other times David's detailed and occasionally fanciful accounts of his boyhood experiences and impressions, sad though these may be in themselves, actually modify the pathos of his circumstances and qualify with other emotions the pity that we feel for him. When David bites Mr. Murdstone's hand and his stepfather retaliates by beating him brutally, we are told of David's rage and sense of guilt but hear little about the pain and nothing about any self-pity. What might the omniscient narrator of *Dombey and Son* or *Bleak House* have made of scenes like this? As a consequence of his act of rebellion, David is confined to his room for five days — not the "old dear bedroom" he had had before his mother's remarriage, but a different one — and he stores up his vivid perceptions of that unhappy time like the future novelist he is:

> The length of those five days I can convey no idea of to any one. They occupy the place of years in my remembrance. The way in which I listened to all the incidents of the house that made themselves audible to me; the ringing of bells, the opening and shutting of doors, the murmuring of voices, the footsteps on the stairs; to any laughing, whistling, or singing, outside, which seemed more dismal than anything else to me in my solitude and disgrace — the uncertain pace of the hours, especially at night, when I would wake thinking it was morning, and find that the family were not yet gone to bed, and that all the length of night had yet to come — the depressed dreams and nightmares I had — the return of day, noon, afternoon, evening, when the boys played in the churchyard, and I watched them from a distance within the room, being ashamed to show myself at the window lest they should know I was a prisoner — the strange sensation of never hearing myself speak — the fleeting intervals of something like cheerfulness, which came with eating and drinking, and went away with it — the setting in of rain one evening, with a fresh smell, and its coming down faster and faster between me and the church, until it and gathering night seemed to quench me in gloom, and fear, and remorse — all this appears to have gone round and round for years instead of days, it is so vividly and strongly stamped on my remembrance. [Chapter 4]

Because it is anything but maudlin, that paragraph evokes not only pity for David but admiration as well. The pity it engenders arises from the situation as David rather matter-of-factly describes it rather than from an indignant narrator's clever attempt to call forth stock responses.

On leaving home for Salem House, David weeps copiously, soaking his handkerchief with his tears. But, as he tells it, this poignant incident is as funny as it is sad.

> Having by this time cried as much as I possibly could, I began to

think it was of no use crying any more, especially as neither Roderick Random, nor that captain in the Royal British Navy had ever cried, that I could remember, in trying situations. The carrier seeing me in this resolution, proposed that my pocket-handkerchief should be spread upon the horse's back to dry. I thanked him, and assented; and particularly small it looked, under those circumstances.

I had now leisure to examine the purse. It was a stiff leather purse, with a snap, and had three bright shillings in it, which Peggotty had evidently polished up with whitening, for my greater delight. But its most precious contents were two half-crowns folded together in a bit of paper, on which was written, in my mother's hand, "For Davy. With my love." I was so overcome by this, that I asked the carrier to be so good as to reach me my pocket-handkerchief again; but he said he thought I had better do without it, and I thought I really had, so I wiped my eyes on my sleeve and stopped myself. [Chapter 5]

Upset as he is, David is still able to take in details (the "stiff leather purse, with a snap," the "three bright shillings"). We also see his brave efforts to behave like the heroes he has read about in books, as well as Barkis's gruff attempts to be kind, in a different light from that in which he perceives them.

Dickens's treatment of David's awful period "in the service of Murdstone and Grinby" is handled somewhat differently. We know it was awful because the mature David *tells* us so (and because we know about its real-life analog), but beyond a rather tame paragraph or two in Chapter 11 he actually *shows* us nothing of its horrors. He renders this stage of his early life with a kind of detachment, almost as if he were writing about another boy. His use of the word "compassion" in Chapter 10 strikes the keynote: compassion, after all, is an emotion we feel toward other people, not ourselves. It is the *memory* of the period, burned into the sensitive psyche of this writer, rather than the sufferings of the child, that we are asked to respond to: "The deep remembrance of the sense I had, of being utterly without hope now; of the shame I felt in my position; of the misery it was to my young heart to believe that day by day what I had learned, and thought, and delighted in, and raised my fancy and emulation up by, would pass from me, little by little, never to be brought back any more; cannot be written." Or:

I see myself emerging one evening from some of these arches, on a little public-house close to the river, with an open space before it, where some coal-heavers were dancing; to look at whom I sat down upon a bench. I wonder what they thought of me!

I was such a child, and so little, that frequently when I went into the bar of a strange public-house for a glass of ale or porter, to moisten what I had had for dinner, they were afraid to give it to me. I remember one hot evening I went into the bar of a public-house, and said to the landlord:

"What is your best — your *very best* — ale a glass?" For it was a special occasion. I don't know what. It may have been my birthday. [Chapter 11]

For whatever reason, Dickens is retreating in passages like these from the directness of the accounts quoted earlier. Might it be that he could not bring himself to have David recount these searing experiences, with all their parallels to Dickens's own term in Warren's blacking warehouse, in comparably vivid detail? Had he done so, the emotional effect might well have been in excess of what he wanted to achieve.

Surely there is nothing intrinsically humorous in David's desperate journey from London to Dover. His account of that ordeal combines realism with a ready eye for the grotesque (as in the encounter with the "dreadful old man" in the second-hand clothing shop), but once again self-pity plays virtually no part. The closest he comes to feeling sorry for himself is during the night he spends outside Salem House, but even here what we have is the ability of a sensitive young observer to see his particular plight in a wider human, spatial, and temporal context. His capacity to perceive and record concrete details is unimpaired.

Sleep came upon me, as it came upon many other outcasts, against whom house-doors were locked, and house-dogs barked, that night — and I dreamed of lying on my old schoolbed, talking to the boys in my room; and found myself sitting upright, with Steerforth's name upon my lips, looking wildly at the stars that were glistening and glimmering above me. When I remembered where I was at that untimely hour, a feeling stole upon me that made me get up, afraid of I don't know what, and walk about. But the fainter glimmering of the stars, and the pale light in the sky where the day was coming, reassured me: and my eyes being very heavy, I lay down again, and slept — though with a knowledge in my sleep that it was cold — until the warm beams of the sun, and the ringing of the getting-up bell at Salem House, awoke me. . . . So I crept away from the wall as Mr. Creakle's boys were getting up, and struck into the long dusty track which I had first known to be the Dover Road when I was one of them, and when I little expected that any eyes would ever see me the wayfarer I was now, upon it. [Chapter 13]

One reason the novel changes in character after David leaves Dr. Strong's school is that such narrative and descriptive devices as those to which I have been referring are no longer available to him in quite the same way. He is still the same clear-eyed observer, and he goes on periodically modifying his immediate perceptions in the light of later consideration and judgment. But it makes some difference that it is no longer a fallible and vulnerable child who has these experiences and recounts them. Not only are such grim stories and events as the Em'ly affair and the deaths of Dora, Ham, and Steerforth less susceptible of wryly comic treatment than aspects of his boyhood life, but the point of view from which we see them has altered as David has been growing up.

Nevertheless, the mature narrator David is still given to converting pathos into comedy, for example, by calling attention to the self-delusion of such victims of circumstance as the Micawber family and Tommy Traddles, and to the absurdity of the predicaments in which they find themselves. The comic irony here resides in the discrepancy between the true plight and the fancied situations of these other characters, and not — as was the case earlier — in the inconsistency between what the boy David imagined to be the truth and what we, experienced and worldly readers, knew about the real state of affairs.

Even poor Dora, whom Dickens saw fit to kill off, is as much a figure of fun as she is a fated victim. Of course, I do not mean simply that we are invited to laugh at her ineptness and her pouting selfishness — nothing in *David Copperfield* is that simple. We also laugh *with* David (do I dare to say through our tears?) as his "child-wife" tries to cope with her domestic responsibilities, learn about things that matter to her husband, and be of some help to him in his work. It is a curious and marvelous mixture of effects that Dickens gives us: we are amused by Dora's silliness; we feel sorry for her as we see the shadow of death growing larger upon her; we admire her attempts to be what David would have her be; we deplore David's stuffiness about her, his inability to fight down his growing sense that he has married someone who is unworthy of him — all this even as we share his later feelings of remorse at the unfortunate direction which his relationship with her has taken and, ultimately, his rather guilty grief.

In connection with Dora's demise it is worthwhile to note that there is no actually represented deathbed scene. Though the chapter in which she expires is carefully contrived to arouse the right sort of emotional

response, Dickens attempts to avoid the obvious and to deflect our
attention from the dying young woman to the remorseful David and,
to a lesser degree, to the saintly Agnes. This is one of the retrospective
chapters in the novel, in which everything is seen in the strange light
of time suspended that Dickens's use of the present tense casts over his
material. Dora talks of Agnes, wants Agnes, and has Agnes — and not
David — by her bedside when she dies. But we are with David and
Dora's decrepit dog as they wait downstairs in the parlor.

> How the time wears, I know not; until I am recalled by my child-wife's
> old companion. More restless than he was, he crawls out of his house,
> and looks at me, and whines to go up-stairs.
>
> "Not to-night, Jip! Not to-night!"
>
> He comes very slowly back to me, licks my hand, and lifts his dim
> eyes to my face.
>
> "Oh, Jip! It may be, never again!"
>
> He lies down at my feet, stretches himself out as if to sleep, and with
> a plaintive cry, is dead.
>
> "Oh, Agnes! Look, look, here!"
>
> — That face, so full of pity, and of grief, that rain of tears, that awful
> mute appeal to me, that solemn hand upraised towards Heaven!
>
> "Agnes?"
>
> It is over. Darkness comes before my eyes; and, for a time, all things
> are blotted out of my remembrance. [Chapter 53]

Much earlier in the novel, when David's mother dies, there is not,
properly speaking, a deathbed scene either. Here, too, Dickens eschews
the obvious potential for pathos, in which his material is so rich, and
gets his effects in a different way. We first learn of Mrs. Copperfield's
death, with David, at Salem House. Mrs. Creakle has received a letter
containing the news, and she breaks it to the boy as kindly as she can.
Within the space of a very few lines, as the dreadful truth dawns upon
David, his reaction escalates from trembling, to a mist in his eyes, to
"burning tears" running down his face, to a "desolate cry" — all rendered with his customary fidelity to precise detail. As he broods over
his bereavement a little later on, his grief imperceptibly becomes mixed
with other — less worthy, perhaps, but intensely human and even
amusing — emotions.

> I thought of our house shut up and hushed. I thought of the little baby,
> who, Mrs. Creakle said, had been pining away for some time, and who,
> they believed, would die, too. I thought of my father's grave in the
> church-yard by our house, and of my mother lying there beneath the tree

I knew so well. I stood upon a chair when I was left alone, and looked into the glass to see how red my eyes were, and how sorrowful my face. I considered, after some hours were gone, if my tears were really hard to flow now, as they seemed to be, what, in connexion with my loss, it would affect me most to think of when I drew near home — for I was going home to the funeral. I am sensible of having felt that a dignity attached to me among the rest of the boys, and that I was important in my affliction. [Chapter 9]

To be sure, Peggotty does give David an account of his mother's dying moments at the end of the same chapter, but this takes on a special twist of its own as the result of being imbedded in a longer narrative in Peggotty's own words and of having been anticipated by Mrs. Creakle's disclosure.

Regarding the supposed "melodramatic" nature of *David Copperfield*, it should be pointed out that, like most of Dickens's novels after *Nicholas Nickleby*, it does not in fact depend on big *scènes à faire* to arouse feelings of admiration for virtue asserting itself, or concern for innocence threatened, or indignation at the fulminations of villainy, or triumph at the defeat of vice.

When virtue does assert itself in *David Copperfield*, and this happens rarely, it does so in a quiet, self-deprecating voice. One has only to contrast David, for example, with Nicholas Nickleby, or Agnes with Nicholas's sister Kate, to appreciate that we are in a different moral world in the later novel. Nicholas is a self-righteous prig next to David, and though we are quite prepared to believe in David's essential goodness, we can see for ourselves that it is shot through with a very strong sense of his own blindness and inadequacy. When he lets us know how virtuous he was at certain stages of his life, like the marriage with Dora, we are meant to take these professions ironically.

As for Agnes, she is never threatened sexually by Uriah Heep in the way Kate Nickleby is threatened by Sir Mulberry Hawk or, also in *Nicholas Nickleby*, Madeline Bray is threatened by Arthur Gride. Though Heep is in a strong position to exert pressure on Agnes, as Sir Mulberry and Gride are vis-à-vis their intended victims, there is never any real question of Agnes's accepting him in marriage, much less in an irregular relationship. She simply tells David, quietly, to stop worrying about her giving herself to the monstrous Uriah, and that is that.

"There has been no change at home," said Agnes, after a few moments.

"No fresh reference," said I, "to — I wouldn't distress you, Agnes, but I cannot help asking — to what we spoke of, when we parted last?"

"No, none," she answered.

"I have thought so much about it."

"You must think less about it. Remember that I confide in simple love and truth at last. Have no apprehensions for me, Trotwood," she added, after a moment; "the step you dread my taking, I shall never take."

Although I think I had never really feared it, in any season of cool reflection, it was an unspeakable relief to me to have this assurance from her own truthful lips. [Chapter 42]

Victorian melodrama has become a contemporary laughingstock, especially among persons who have little or no first-hand knowledge of the genre, partly because our modern sensibility does not permit us to respond to villainy as audiences did in the nineteenth century. We refuse to cringe before supposedly odious characters, and we tend to dismiss contemptuously, as empty bombast, speeches in which evil men (or women) unashamedly display their rotten souls before us. In this regard, too, melodramatic effects are virtually absent from *David Copperfield*. Who, after all, are the villains of the piece? Steerforth? He does most of his dirty work off stage or through his agent Littimer, and when we do see him, our vision is clouded by David's unreasoning affection for him. Jack Maldon? A very sketchy and inconsistent figure indeed. Rosa Dartle? She certainly employs the language of melodrama, for example, in the scene with Steerforth's mother after David's friend has drowned (Chapter 56), but surely she is as much victim as villainess and, by this point in the novel, more than a little demented. Uriah Heep, perhaps? Perhaps, but in his case, too, there are features that significantly qualify our sense of his villainy. For he is, first and foremost, a repellent caricature, and it is seriously to be asked if the threat to Agnes he represents is really objectively there or if it exists largely in David's jealous imagination.

Certainly Heep refuses to behave like a self-righteously indignant villain when he engages in confrontation with David. When, for example, Heep has attempted to make trouble for Agnes's friend Annie Strong by speaking to her husband of her alleged indiscretion with Jack Maldon, David abuses him verbally and actually strikes him. But Heep declines to retort in kind, and his words are hurt-conciliatory rather than eloquent-justifying.

"Copperfield," he said at length, in a breathless voice, "have you taken leave of your senses?"

"I have taken leave of you," said I, wrestling my hand away. "You dog, I'll know no more of you."

"Won't you?" said he, constrained by the pain of his cheek to put his hand there. "Perhaps you won't be able to help it. Isn't this ungrateful of you, now?"

"I have shown you often enough," said I, "that I despise you. I have shown you now, more plainly, that I do. Why should I dread your doing your worst to all about you? What else do you ever do?" . . .

"Copperfield," he said, "there must be two parties to a quarrel. I won't be one."

"You may go to the devil!" said I.

"Don't say that!" he replied. "I know you'll be sorry afterwards. How can you make yourself so inferior to me, as to show such a bad spirit? But I forgive you."

"You forgive me!" I repeated disdainfully.

"I do, and you can't help yourself," replied Uriah. "To think of your going and attacking *me,* that have always been a friend to you! But there can't be a quarrel without two parties, and I won't be one. I will be a friend to you, in spite of you. So now you know what you've got to expect." [Chapter 42]

And of course the marvelous scene in which Heep's evil deeds are exposed by Micawber is funny rather than melodramatic: in fact, in Micawber's lip-smacking use of absurdly inflated stage diction it becomes a sort of comic mock melodrama.

"Then it was that — HEEP — began to favour me with just so much of his confidence as was necessary to the discharge of his infernal business. Then it was that I began, if I may so Shakespearingly express myself, to dwindle, peak, and pine. I found that my services were constantly called into requisition for the falsification of business, and the mystification of an individual whom I will designate as Mr. W. That Mr. W. was imposed upon, kept in ignorance, and deluded, in every possible way; yet, that all this while, the ruffian — HEEP — was professing unbounded gratitude to, and unbounded friendship for, that much-abused gentleman. This was bad enough; but, as the philosophic Dane observes, with that universal applicability which distinguishes the illustrious ornament of the Elizabethan Era, worse remains behind!" [Chapter 52]

And so on.

That *David Copperfield* was meant to arouse emotional responses in its audience is undeniable. In fact, the reader who finds himself unmoved by it would do well to scrutinize the mind and the imagination he brings to his reading. But to condemn the novel unthinkingly for its sentimental and melodramatic excesses is to be insufficiently aware of the numerous strategies Dickens employs to keep his readers' emotions under control, by qualifying obvious and expected reactions with unlooked-for modifications and additions. May we not say that it is largely in such devices that *David Copperfield*'s unending capacity to surprise and delight resides?

SEVEN

Time in *Little Dorrit*

BY MIKE HOLLINGTON

The purpose of this essay is to suggest the importance of temporal process in *Little Dorrit,* both as a theme and as an aspect of Dickens's narrative technique. The topic is neither new nor recondite, but it is, I believe, vitally important, especially so because *Little Dorrit* easily gives rise to the impression that it is not very much concerned with time at all. When we read John Wain's round assertion that "it is his most static novel; its impact is even less dependent on plot than is customary throughout Dickens's work; its development is by means of outward radiation, rather than linear progression," we recognize the overt "spatial" emphases of the New Critics — the tendency to look for an "expanded metaphor" as the principle of organization. Certainly *Little Dorrit,* with its ubiquitous prison, yields considerable rewards to such an approach. But if some aspects of the novel can be described as static, the novel as a whole is certainly also pessimistic about stasis; it has none of the "spatial rapture" that metaphoric critics normally uncover in the works, recent and ancient, that they admire. Its authorial perspective, I want to argue, upholds the importance of change and growth, even if these are felt to be almost entirely absent in the society that the novel describes and analyzes.

To ask ourselves at the outset whether the stasis belongs to this society or to Dickens's imagination, we enter the critical debate about the nature of Dickens's creative power in *Little Dorrit.* If we follow the trend that started with Forster but received its most important recent charge from Trilling, and perceive in the novel an augmented power of abstraction, a diminished vitality of imaginative detail, we are more likely to be satisfied by "spatial" accounts of the novel. We can, on the other hand, respond to the arguments put forward in the chapter on *Little Dorrit* in *Dickens the Novelist* by F. R. and Q. D. Leavis, indebted though the chapter is, more substantially than it acknowledges, to the insights gained by that tradition. It invites us to see, *within* the novel itself, the abundant evidence of an imagination concerned with the particularities of reality, by its presence defining what the society portrayed inhibits and destroys. Thus we are also likely to seek positive signs of an alternative attitude toward time.

It seems important, then, to note straight away that the "redeemed" characters of *Little Dorrit*, those in whom imaginative vitality is not suppressed or is only superficially distorted, differ from other characters in their perception of time. There are two kinds of difference — one between precision and imprecision about time, the other between a sense of history and an absence of that sense. The first contrast is established very distinctly between John Baptist Cavalletto and Rigaud in the very first chapter, when Rigaud asks to be told what time it is: " 'Say what the hour is,' grumbled the first man. 'The mid-day bell will ring — in forty minutes.' When he made the little pause, he looked round the prison-room, as if for certain information. 'You are a clock. How is it you always know?' 'How can I say? I always know what the hour is, and where I am' " (I, i, 4). Cavalletto has an instinctive sense of time that he can't explain. He displays a keen and resourceful attentiveness to the scanty means of telling the time at his disposal, patiently checking the state of the faint prison light as a means of verification. What is apparent is a sensitive attunement to natural process; the contrast with Rigaud is brought out when Rigaud curses the hostile autumnal wind and darkness on his road to Chalons (I, xi, 124), betraying an egoistic sense of being slighted by natural elements. At another level the contrast is between the relations of perceiving subject and surrounding reality; Rigaud, for whom anything outside himself is mere matter, can regard Cavalletto only as an object, and calls him a clock.

Cavalletto is not a clock; his capacity to tell the time accurately signifies his hold upon reality. We are made aware of it on another occasion much later in the novel, when he confers with Arthur Clennam about the chronology of Rigaud's disappearance into the mysteries of London: "In his passionate raptures, he at first forgot the fact that he had lately seen the assassin in London. On his remembering it, it suggested hope to Clennam that the recognition might be of later date than the night of his visit at his mother's; *but Cavalletto was too exact about time and place,* to leave any opening for doubt that it has preceded that occasion" (II, xxii, 677-78; my italics). Mysteries and doubts are clarified by Cavalletto's accuracy; his capacity to remember events in clear and ordered sequence establishes the reality of things.

This precision about time is reminiscent of Doyce's professional pains-taking in another sphere, and it is through him that we may introduce the second aspect of the creative response to temporal process in *Little Dorrit*: a historical imagination, a capacity to imagine and envisage other times, past and future, besides one's own. Doyce understands that his frustrations at the Circumlocution Office belong in historical per-spective; others have suffered before, and more will suffer after him: "You see, my experience of these things does not begin with myself" (I, i, 121). Doyce is able to make projections into the future, basing them on the probabilities of individual and historical outcomes. He expresses, in contrast to Clennam's hesitations, his own gloomy cer-tainties about the marriage of Pet Meagles and Henry Gowan:

> "I see him bringing present anxiety, and, I fear, future sorrow, into my old friend's house. I see him wearing deeper lines into my old friend's face, the nearer he draws to, and the oftener he looks at, the face of his daughter. In short, I see him with a net about the pretty and affectionate creature whom he will never make happy."
>
> "We don't know," said Clennam, almost in the tone of a man in pain, "that he will not make her happy."
>
> "We don't know," returned his partner, "that the earth will last an-other hundred years, but we think it highly probable." [I, xxvi, 307-8]

As his last remark implies, time for Doyce is an objectively real and shared phenomenon; his projections are not inspired divinations but appeals to a logic of sequential probability. When we first meet him outside the Circumlocution Office, he is presented "looking into the distance before him, as if his grey eye were measuring it" (I, xi, 121).

Likewise Little Dorrit herself, during her visit to Italy, is imagina-tively stirred by a realization that the places she visits have had an existence previous to her own: "One of my frequent thoughts is this: — Old as these cities are, their age itself is hardly so curious, to my reflections, as that they should have been in their places all through those days when I did not even know of the existence of more than two or three of them, and when I scarcely knew of anything outside our walls" (II, xi, 553). Little Dorrit is here countering the idealist per-ceptual notions of Rigaud and many other characters by recognizing the separate existence of other phenomena, independent in time and space of herself as a necessary perceiving object. She feels life going on before and after and outside herself.

The contrasting state, the absence of any sense of history and change, is perhaps most emphatically stated in Mrs. Clennam. In one passage we find Dickens analyzing her "subjective time" — from a perspective entirely different from that of Proust or Mann:

> The wheeled chair had its associated remembrances and reveries, one may suppose, as every place that is made the station of a human being has. Pictures of demolished streets and altered houses, as they formerly were when the occupant of the chair was familiar with them; images of people as they too used to be, with little or no allowance made for the lapse of time since they were seen; of these, there must have been many in the long routine of gloomy days. To stop the clock of busy existence, at the hour when we personally were sequestered from it; to suppose mankind stricken motionless, when we were brought to a standstill; to be unable to measure the changes beyond our view, by any larger standard than the shrunken one of our own uniform and contracted existence; is the infirmity of many invalids, and the mental unhealthiness of almost all recluses. [I, xxix, 339]

The perspective is first sensed in the hint of irony in the withheld omniscience; Dickens as narrator has to "suppose" even the limited amount of contact with past reality that is outlined here. But the imagery of size is the most telling and characteristic feature; the vast extent of time and space outside here and now is reduced to the compass of the self and its preoccupations. Habitually, self-centeredness in *Little Dorrit* is manifested in a denial of history, a contraction of its scope to make it an instrument of selfish desire. So the Bohemians of Hampton Court await a private apocalypse for the irritating Sunday visitors, expecting "the earth to open and swallow the public up . . . which desirable event had not yet occurred, in consequence of some reprehensible laxity in the arrangements of the Universe" (I, xxvi, 312).

Ultimately, the alternative to this private fantasy is provided by the attempt, in the linear structure of *Little Dorrit,* to make the novel a real "history." For the moment, however, we must substantiate the varieties of subjective experience of time; the extreme dissociation from reality of Mr. F's aunt, for instance, is accompanied by an equally "original" sense of time. When Clennam follows Miss Wade to the Casby house, appearing there for the first time in three months, she exclaims, "Drat him if he an't come back again!" Dickens, pointing the theme even at this grotesque — but illuminating — distance from Mrs. Clennam, offers the supposition that she is "measuring time by the acuteness of her own sensations and not by the clock" (II, ix, 534). More poignantly, perhaps, there is William Dorrit's bitter complaint to

Clennam as he waits impatiently to be released from prison, " 'A few hours, sir!' he returned in a sudden passion. 'You talk very easily of hours, sir! How long do you suppose, sir, that an hour is to a man who is choking for want of air?' " (I, xxxiii, 421). The affront is that Clennam appears incapable of projecting himself into Dorrit's personal time; clock time, as something objective and shared, is vigorously and ominously repudiated.

Increasingly in the novel we feel that "subjective time" is the equivalent of the experience of time in dreams, and perhaps the fundamental contrast is that between living in a dream and living in reality. No doubt Dickens's own sense of time in dreams provided the basis of this theme. Not many years before writing *Little Dorrit*, he had noted in a letter to his doctor how his dreams followed their own peculiar temporal laws: "My own dreams are usually of twenty years ago. I often blend my present condition with them, but very confusedly. . . ." Likewise, the dreamers of *Little Dorrit* both habitually revert to the past and mingle different phases of development in their reveries. Clennam, "dozing and dreaming" in his Marshalsea imprisonment, just before he is awakened by Little Dorrit's nosegay of flowers, is "without the power of reckoning time, so that a minute might have been an hour and an hour a minute" (II, xxix, 755). The condition is elaborated upon by Mrs. Tickit, in the marvelous eccentric monologue explaining how Tattycoram appeared at the Meagles house when she was "what a person would strictly call watching with my eyes closed": "As I was saying, I was thinking of one thing, and thinking of another, and thinking very much of the family. Not of the family in the present times only, but in the past times too. For when a person does begin thinking of one thing and thinking of another, in that manner as it's getting dark, what I say is, that *all times seem to be present,* and a person must get out of that state and consider before they can say which is which" (II, ix, 529; my italics). Mrs. Tickit's dream associations are not about herself but about "the family"; her evident unselfish devotion to them cancels any temptation to consider this disquisition as merely ludicrous. She is talking, significantly, to Arthur Clennam, the central dreamer of *Little Dorrit*, afflicted by a traumatized fixation on the past and impeded in his dream from action and progression: "It was like the oppression of a dream, to believe that shame and exposure were impending over her and his father's memory, and to be shut out, as by a brazen wall, from the possibility of coming to her aid" (II, xxvii, 720). Thus Mrs. Tickit, a minor character in the novel, points to a

major theme — the development of Clennam. Her wisdom is trustworthy; in order to wake up, Clennam has eventually to "get out of that
state and consider." He does so in the Marshalsea at the end of the
novel. Experiencing a "marked stop from the whirling wheel of life,"
he at last finds a vantage point from which he can separate present and
past: "he could think of some passages in his life, almost as if he were
removed from them into another state of existence" (II, xxvii, 720).

Another dreamer in the novel, Affery, illuminates a very similar progress. In her dream state she is a "Heap of confusion," uncertain of her
own identity, and very vague about time; "she looked at the candle
she had left burning, and, measuring the time like King Alfred the
Great, was confirmed by its wasted state in her belief that she had been
asleep for some considerable period" (I, iv, 41). Once she eventually
wakes up in the novel, she is capable of progressive action and development: "I have broken out now, and I can't go back. I am determined
to do it" (II, xxx, 766).

Thus dreaming in the novel implies inertia, a blurred sense of time,
an inability to find any sequence in events; Dickens's critical analysis
of the society of *Little Dorrit* establishes this as the state induced by
the practitioners of fraud and injustice. The labyrinthine images in the
novel, noted by J. Hillis Miller, have as their temporal equivalent
the absence of intelligible temporal relationships. Plornish, turning "the
tangled skein of his estate about and about, like a blind man who was
trying to find some beginning or end to it" (I, xii, 143), reflects in a
direct way the confusions fostered by Casby's thumb-twirling, "so typical to Clennam of the way in which he would make the subject revolve
if it were pursued, never showing any new part of it nor allowing it to
make the slightest advance" (II, ix, 539). The circular imagery is pervasive; for the natural linearity of events in time, the confidence tricksters of the novel have substituted a confusing cyclical *perpetuum mobile.*

Timelessness, then, is analyzed and placed in the novel; again a clear
alternative attitude is discernible. History for Dickens followed a linear
pattern, its natural tendency being toward progression; he never tired
of repeating that the "good old days" were really the "bad old days."
The approved image of history is conveyed, revealingly, in a comparison
where its rightful onward flow is related to the cheer from the Bleeding-
Heart Yarders that accompanies Doyce's departure to the country that
"knows how to do it": "In truth, no men on earth can cheer like Eng-
lishmen, who do so rally one another's blood and spirit when they cheer
in earnest, that the stir is like the rush of their whole history, with all

its standards waving at once, from Saxon Alfred's time downwards"
(II, xxii, 675). There is undoubtedly something disagreeable in the
naive "heartiness" of this image, and yet the stress on a collective historical momentum does effectively function as a contrast to "subjective
time."

The private and fictional versions of history that hold sway in *Little
Dorrit* perpetuate superseded stages of its progression, mingle them in
confusing juxtaposition with their advanced sharp practices, and impede forward movement. Thus it is that "the ugly South Sea Gods in
the British Museum might have supposed themselves at home again"
in the enlightened taboos of the Victorian Sunday (I, iii, 28). The
expatriate society in Rome may still be described as "Island Savages"
(II, xv, 609), as at the time of the Roman occupation of Britain.
Indeed, the fiercely sarcastic treatment of Mrs. Merdle's lament that
she and her fellow members of society cannot, alas, behave as primitive
savages stresses that they in fact do. Footmen lounge around like "an
extinct race of monstrous birds" (I, xxvii, 327), and the "Spartan boy
with the fox biting him" still presides as a model, in this society, for
the repressive upbringing of children (I, xxiv, 284). In imitation, the
feudal society within the Marshalsea is out of phase with the times, its
father patronizing it "like a baron of the olden time" (I, xxvi, 425)
and dispensing platitudes on Christian fortitude "like Sir Roger de
Coverley going to Church" (I, xxvvi, 428). The pitiable passivity of
the Plornishes is expressed in their adherence to a vision of the past,
of a renewed innocence, "the Golden Age revived" (II, xiii, 574).

Such anomalous hangovers are bolstered by entrenched rationaliza-
tions. Historical reality is blurred over with mystifying abstractions;
evading any recognition of cause and effect, and blocking progress, the
Circumlocutory powers erect false historical inevitabilities. By inventing
abstract "nobodies" who are hypocritically presented as determinisms —
Society, Precedent, Fate — responsibilities are evaded and initiative effort stifled. "If we could only come to a Millennium, or something of
that sort," sighs Mrs. Merdle (I, xx, 242); but Society prevents it,
and she, like Mrs. Gowan, resigns herself "to inevitable fate" (I, xxxiii,
388). "Treasury" is similarly wistful in contemplating future possibilities — more mundane though their object is (the entry of Merdle into
Parliament) — and trusting to "accident": "If we should ever be
happily enabled, by accidentally possessing the control over circumstances, to propose to one so eminent to — to come amongst us . . ." (I,
xxi, 250). Against these supernatural agencies determining the course

of history, "mere actions are nothing" — the phrase and the theology
are Mrs. Clennam's (I, xxx, 357), but rationalization of stasis is the
habit of the whole society.

Throughout *Little Dorrit* the conception of historical movement
forms an impressive unity with the conception of individual growth,
and this applies equally to their perversion. Fictions about historical
determinism have their counterparts in fictions about the necessity of
one's nature; in Fanny Dorrit, for instance, they are to be found side
by side. Little Dorrit urges her to consider love as a relinquishing of
self; "if you loved anyone, you would no longer be yourself, but you
would quite lose and forget yourself in him." But for Fanny these are
"degenerate impossibilities" (II, xiv, 591) — she echoes the lament of
the Hampton Court Bohemians over the "degeneracy of the times" (I,
xxvi, 313) — that the conditions of history will not permit. To lose herself would be to fly in the face of her "fated" personality: "Other girls,
differently reared and differently circumstanced altogether, might wonder at what I say or may do. Let them. They are driven by their lives
and characters; I am driven by mine." These justifications are in some
sense compensatory; they register the habitual Dorrit insecurity about
the Marshalsea disgrace, which also governs her father's pathetic boasts
about his adaptation to "Necessity": "Consider my case, Frederick.
I am a kind of example. Necessity and time have taught me what to
do" (I, xix, 223). And so they do engage our sympathy. But a cruder
instance, the running commentary of Rigaud on the "fatalities" of his
character, makes the point obvious; these fictions insulate their perpe-
trators from any form of self-scrutiny that might lead to a change in
their behavior. Personal development, like historical development, is
negated; these characters remain statically imprisoned within themselves.

At this point it is necessary to shift focus somewhat and develop
some other aspects of the contrast between characters bound within
themselves and characters receptive to experience outside themselves.
As I noted earlier in discussing Mrs. Clennam's imprisonment, the
imagery of size is characteristic. For the ego-bound characters of *Little
Dorrit,* other experience is felt to be an unfortunate encumbrance, to
be crushed or reduced in size. The most extraordinary instance of this
is Fanny's outburst at Sparkler, in their London house: "You look so
aggravatingly large by this light. Do sit down. . . . Oh, you *do* look so
big!" (II, xxiv, 694). But it is apparent not only in the way of treating
other people but in a careless insensitivity toward things, especially
little things. Gowan kicks stones in a way "that Clennam thought had

an air of cruelty in it. Most of us have more or less frequently derived a similar impression, from a man's way of doing some very little thing; plucking a flower, clearing away an obstacle, or even destroying an insentient object" (I, xvii, 201). Likewise Rigaud, staying at the coffee-house near Mrs. Clennam, displays his nature in the way he violates the furniture: "His utter disregard of people, as shown in his way of tossing the little womanly toys of furniture about, flinging favourite cushions under his boots for a softer rest, and crushing delicate coverings with his big body and his great black head, had the same brute selfishness at bottom" (I, xxx, 352).

The importance of size in this novel is announced by the stress of its title, *Little Dorrit*. All its redeemed characters are small in stature: Cavalletto is a "sunburnt, quick, lithe, little man" (I, i, 4); Doyce is short, "not much to look at, either in point of size or in point of view" (I, x, 118); Pancks is a "short dark man" with "a scrubby little black chin" (I, xiii, 148). Their size has metaphoric significance; they are in consequence more responsive to the vastness of everything outside themselves. By contrast, many of the fraudulent impostors and hypocrites in the novel are very large: Merdle has "large unfeeling handsome eyes" and a "broad unfeeling handsome bosom" (I, xx, 238); Casby has "a shining bald head which looked so large because it shone so much" (I, xiii, 145) and moves around like a "heavy selfish drifting booby" with a history of "unwieldy jostlings against other men" (I, xiii, 149). The imagery of clumsiness in Casby suggests a trampling disregard of anything not related to his selfish concerns.

Likewise, moral perceptiveness in *Little Dorrit* is a matter of a capacity to discriminate carefully between minutely different signals. The coarse mind, like Gowan's, sees humanity only as an indiscriminate lump and reduces distinctive features to the same scale. Rigaud serves him equally well as an artist's model for a large number of entirely different human types. Rigaud himself boasts of making "few weak distinctions" (I, xi, 132); this is so, for instance, when he fails to perceive any difference between the way the jailor's daughter reacts to him and to Cavalletto (I, i, 5). Finer and more practiced observers of behavior, like Pet Meagles and Little Dorrit herself, notice something slightly special in Rigaud's manner of behaving toward them: "The difference was too minute in its expression to be perceived by others, but they knew it to be there. A mere trick of his evil eyes, a mere turn of his smooth white hand, a mere hair's-breadth of addition to the fall of his nose and the rise of his mouth in the most frequent movement of

his face, conveyed to them equally a swagger personal to themselves"
(II, vii, 509). The narrative voice, too, is always attentive to subtle
nuances of change in behavior, even in such an apparently impenetrable person as Mrs. Clennam: "As there are degrees of hardness in
the hardest metal, and shades of colour in black itself, so, even in the
asperity of Mrs. Clennam's demeanour towards all the rest of humanity
and towards Little Dorrit, there was a fine gradation" (I, v, 52).

With these images in mind, I think we can now press home the importance of the precise calculation of time in *Little Dorrit*. To do things
"inch by inch," to take painstaking care over detail in the specification
of time and change, is the corollary of finely tuned moral sensitivity,
and of meticulous concern with real, other life. When Pancks an-
nounces his discovery of the inheritance that is owed to the Dorrits,
he dwells upon the gradual stages of his investigations: "How he had
felt his way inch by inch, and 'Moled it out, sir' (that was Mr. Pancks'
expression), grain by grain" (I, xxxv, 410). When Tattycoram has
emancipated herself from the perverse gratifications that Miss Wade
can offer, she signals her release by resolving on patient effort in small
stages of time: "I shall get better by very slow degrees" (II, xxxiii, 811).
When Fred Dorrit makes a real (and not illusory, as in the case of his
brother) transformation from his old self, the change expresses itself
in "a certain patient animal enjoyment" of the world about him (II,
iii, 457); he passes "hours and hours" in front of historic Venetians
and venerates them "with great exactness" (II, v, 481).

Patient exactness is the key virtue in *Little Dorrit*, the essential condition of lasting change and real development. When Cavalletto goes
searching for Rigaud in London, he follows the "moling-out" tactics
of Pancks and expresses the moral attitudes that lie behind them:

> "But! — After a long time when I have not been able to find that he is
> here in Londra, some one tells me of a soldier with white hair — hey? —
> not hair like this that he carries — white — who lives retired secret-
> tementally, in a certain place. But! — " with another rest upon the word,
> "who sometimes in the after-dinner, walks, and smokes. It is necessary,
> as they say in Italy (and as they know, poor people), to have patience.
> I have patience. I ask where is this certain place. One believes it is here,
> one believes it is there. Eh well! It is not here, it is not there. I wait
> patientissamentally. At last I find it. Then I watch; then I hide, until he
> walks and smokes. He is a soldier with grey hair — But! — " a very de-
> cided rest indeed, and a very vigorous play from side to side of the back-
> handed forefinger — "he is also that man you see." [II, xxviii, 743]

Cavalletto's method of narration harmonizes with the patient watchfulness and minute attention to slender detail (Rigaud is betrayed only by "walking and smoking") that the discovery displays. It is a careful unfolding of the stages of the process of discovery, with significant pauses at the points of change. His suffixes ("patientissamentally") convey finer shades of meaning than a more standard English provides; his gestures add enriched nuances of suggestion.

I want to say more about patience as a theme in *Little Dorrit* a bit further on, but the time has come to examine Dickens's own method (which is very much like Cavalletto's) of conducting the temporal flow of his narrative. Not only is *Little Dorrit about* patience; it also, by means of its narrative technique, attempts to make its readers aware of the necessity of patience, and of its moral significance, by very gradual unfoldings and very frequent withholdings. Future outcomes are very often anticipated in oblique or ironic ways, but they are held back in a regard for proper sequence, and the reader is returning to a still-developing plot. Like Cavalletto's investigations, the plot will eventually clear up the "mysteries" proliferated by Circumlocution, and gives continual promise of its intention to do so. But the mysteries are of so convoluted and deep-seated a nature that no sudden revelation will suffice to show their full extent or effect.

The way in which this technique operates locally can best be suggested by exploring some of Dickens's narrative anticipations. The introduction of Merdle's mysterious complaint occasions one of them: "Had he that deep-seated recondite complaint, and did any doctor find it out? Patience. In the meantime, the shadow of the Marshalsea wall was a real darkening influence, and could be seen on the Dorrit family at any stage of the sun's course" (I, xxi, 254). Narrative expectation is aroused, but satisfaction is deliberately withheld. The appeal for patience is an urging of essential priorities; the circumlocutory plot mystification ("deep-seated recondite complaint" is a cunning euphemism) is ironic, and the word "real" consequently receives a powerful stress. The real offense, the existence of the Marshalsea, is available for inspection "at any stage of the sun's course." The phrase makes overt reference to the novel's own trajectory and justifies its gradual patient unfoldings by linking them to natural process.

The deliberateness of Dickens's narrative art is once more apparent when he makes a second ironic reference to the still unrevealed outcome of Merdle's career: "At dinner that day, although the occasion was not foreseen and provided for, a brilliant company of such as are not made of the dust of the earth, but of some superior article *for the present unknown,* shed their lustrous benediction upon Mr. Dorrit's daughter's marriage" (II, xvi, 618-19). Merdle's end is by no means "unforeseen and unprovided for" by the art of the novel; the "superior article" of which Merdle is made will be revealed when the Star of Bethlehem following him stops "over certain carrion at the bottom of a bath" (II, xxv, 710) — dust to dust, with savage new overtones, despite the pretentious detour. The care of Dickens's art is in conscious contrast to the hypocritical laissez-faire kowtowing to the "unforeseen." The gradual and "natural" revelation of the actuality beneath the pretense protests against the illusory shimmer of Merdle's revelation, "sprung from nothing, by no natural growth or process" (II, xxv, 709-10).

The experience of reading the novel is therefore in part the experience of a succession of present moments, linked with others before and after, but not transcending time, and clearly of importance in themselves as distinct stages of a process. Despite what John Wain says, plot is indeed important in *Little Dorrit,* and another of Dickens's narrative foreshadowings — of the death of William Dorritt — provides what is perhaps the fundamental reason for this: "Only the wisdom that holds the clue to all hearts and all mysteries can surely know to what extent a man, especially a man brought down as this man had been, can impose upon himself. Enough, for the present place, that he lay down with wet eyelashes, serene, in a manner majestic, after bestowing his life of degradation as a sort of portion on the devoted child upon whom its miseries had fallen so heavily, and whose love alone had saved him to be even what he was" (I, xix, 231).

The metaphoric connections between this lying-down and his final lying-down are clear enough — the self-pitying legacy he offers here, "a life of degradation," anticipates what he will actually bestow on her after his death, at a point in the plot where expectation is entirely different. But the temporal connection isn't; only God, the narrative voice asserts, can know when this mystery will be revealed, and the reader is returned to "the present place." The plot of *Little Dorrit,* in its gradual unraveling of mysteries, imitates the way in which Divine Providence is revealed; individual outcome and historical destiny are withheld until the scheme is completed.

To amplify this point, a passage in one of Dickens's letters, dating from 1863, is helpful: "What these bishops and suchlike say about revelation, in assuming it to be finished and done with, I can't in the least understand. Nothing is discovered without God's intention and assistance, and I suppose each new knowledge of his works that is conceded to man to be distinctly a revelation by which men are to guide themselves" (Letters, III, 351; to Cerjat, 21/5/63). In Dickens's conception of the divine plot, then, "revelation" is not limited to the Book of Revelation; it is the gradual, piecemeal process of discovery, continuous and progressive, and not a sudden enlightening. The plot of *Little Dorrit* imitates the providential scheme, deliberately and purposefully leading the reader in a process of gradual enlightenment.

Once again there is essential contrast in the novel; this passage about revelation helps us to understand the critical eschewal of false and premature millennia in *Little Dorrit*. They are distinguished by a transcendent flight from the medium of time and history in which the plan of creation is to be fulfilled. The messianic Merdle, "the rich man who had in a manner already entered the Kingdom of Heaven" (II, xvi, 616), represents an obvious perverse short-circuiting of temporal process. So does Mrs. Clennam, who mounts "on wings of words to Heaven" (I, xxvii, 319), disdaining action and involvement in the temporal world. Dorrit's millennial "castles in the air" attempt a more pitiable flight; his attempt to effect a discontinuity — "sweep that accursed experience off the face of the earth" (II, v, 479) — displays a shakier Old Testament rhetoric than Mrs. Clennam's. With tragic irony he achieves separation from himself: up above, the fastnesses of imaginary satisfactions; down below, the threatening contingencies of a real past and a real world; in between, a paranoid schizophrenic.

In opposition to these chimera, Dickens's novel concerns itself with minute details of real growth and change. "To combine what was original and daring in conception with what was patient and minute in execution" (I, xvi, 188) — the phrase describes Daniel Doyce's habit of working, but it also intentionally suggests what Dickens himself was trying to achieve in *Little Dorrit*: to reflect, in the careful and precise notation of a specific stage history, the continuing presence of a divine scheme. The novel frequently refers to itself as a history, implying thereby a particular narrative stance and a particular relation to its readership. The narrator stands firmly in the present of the mid-1850s, recording the changes and legacies of thirty years ago: the Marshalsea "is now gone, and the world is none the worse without it" (I, vi, 57); the Adelphi Terrace is a place where "there is always, to this day, a sudden pause . . . to the roar of the great thoroughfare" (II, xi, 531). He shares the present with his readers and, as Leavis perceives — my indebtedness to his essay will be particularly apparent here — seeks to engage "colloborative" contemplation of that present. He appeals to shared experience of historical realities — experience of frustration at the Circumlocution Office, accounts of which "we all know by heart" (I, x, 120), experience of mournful dinners at houses like the Merdles': "Everybody knows how much like the street, the two dinner-rows of people who take their stand by the street will be" (I, xxi, 246).

Of course, "everybody" doesn't know. The assumption of a readership whose members all attend Merdle dinners is ironic, but if the *carte d'entrée* is limited, imaginative understanding need not be. The appeal to everybody establishes a corrective to the more common appeal in the novel to "nobody." The version of artistic vocation that Dickens portrays in Daniel Doyce involves a special respect for intelligent self-projection: "No man of sense, who has been generally improved, and has improved himself, can be called quite uneducated as to anything. I don't particularly favour mysteries" (I, viii, 515). Doyce thus sets himself up against the sacred abstract professionals like Treasury and Bar, for whom the rest of the world is a collection of jurymen: "In my calling . . . the greater usually includes the less" (I, xvi, 194).

The "greater" is perhaps in the first place, then, the vast audience of whom Dickens was always aware. But it is also the complexity and variety of reality, of individual lives and their changes — hence the sarcastic dismissal of a "host of past and present abstract philosophers, natural philosophers, and subduers of Nature and Art in their myriad forms" (II, xv, 605). And, finally, it is certainly God and the vast providential scheme of history — hence the hatred of such notions of relative scale as Mrs. Clennam's "process of reversing the making of man in the image of his Creator to the making of his Creator in the image of erring man" (I, xiii, 165).

If God is greater, then everything else, novelist and novel included, is less — hence the egalitarian relation of novelist and reader. The novelist can see to the end of his novel, but he can't see to the end of the creation which it attempts to render and upon which is depends. As the reader is to the novel, as the plot unfolds, so the novelist is to God; both can only see that segment of time and space that is immediately about them, and only God can perceive the whole scheme. But not to be able to see the rest, does not mean that it doesn't exist; it is the function of the imagination to make present what is in reality absent. To fall into the temptation of Mrs. Clennam, "the whimpering weakness and cruel selfishness of holding that because such a happiness or such a virtue had not come into his little path, or worked well for him, therefore it was not in the great scheme, but was reducible, when found in appearance, to the basest elements" (I, xiii, 165), is to be wanting in historical and moral imagination.

And so, to return to this theme in the novel, the redeemed characters of *Little Dorrit* are often to be found stationed at windows, looking out at the "overwhelming rush of reality" (II, xxxi, 787). Affery goes at the House of Clennam "to the ripped-up window, in the little room by the street door, to connect her palpitating heart, through the glass, with living things beyond and outside the haunted house" (I, xv, 180). And Little Dorrit in Rome, as earlier at Venice, sits at an irregular bay window "commanding all the picturesque life and variety of the Corso, both up and down" (II, xiv, 594). As a child she perceived "that it was not the habit of all the world to live locked up in narrow yards surrounded by high walls with spikes on the top" (I, vii, 69). She exhibited already the capacity of projection and the capacity to make distinctions, of which many characters in the novel seem incapable.

These windows in the novel are treasured for being a source of light: Little Dorrit as a child sits in the lodge of the Marshalsea "looking up at the sky through the barred window, until bars of light would arise" (I, vii, 69), and Pet Meagles in Rome is discovered by Little Dorrit "looking up at the sky shining through the tops of the windows" (II, xi, 550). Though not simple and single in its meaning, the light imagery of *Little Dorrit* is certainly connected with revelation, and the yearning may be felt as a looking for redemptive deliverance from the present blight that the novel analyzes. But what the windows illuminate is real life; the fake messiah Merdle is a mere "shining wonder." The true millennium is a much more distant phenomenon, to be reached only through patient effort in time: "We must be patient, and wait for day" (I, xiv, 173) is Little Dorrit's symbolic appeal to Maggie when they are out on the streets for a night.

Thus it is, at this symbolic level, that in the Alps only "unaccustomed eyes" mistake the distance between themselves and the luminous mountaintops, "cancelling the intervening country ... slighting their rugged height for something fabulous ... [measuring] them as within a few hours' easy reach" (II, i, 431). Their eyes are akin to those of speculators, who represent a kind of secularized false prophecy, "conditionally speculating, upon this that and the other, at uncertain intervals and distances" (II, xxxiii, 813), and they contrast with Doyce's, "looking into the distance before him as if his grey eyes were measuring it" (I, x, 121). Progression in time toward real and not illusory fulfillment can only be achieved in the novel through Doyce's method of "making everything good and everything sound, at each important stage, before taking his hearer on a line's breadth further" (II, viii, 515-16). Thus it is that the liberating morning sun in the Alps is illusory: "The bright morning sun dazzled the eyes, the snow had ceased, the mists had vanished, the mountain air was so clear and light, that the new sensation of breathing it was like the having entered on a new existence. To help the delusion, the solid ground itself seemed gone, and the mountain, a shining waste of immense white heaps and masses, to be a region of cloud floating between the blue sky above and the earth far below" (II, iii, 452). The betraying touch is the disappearance of solid ground. The progress of *Little Dorrit* is along the ground — "restitution on earth, action on earth: these first, as the first steep steps upward" (I, xxvii, 319) — and not through the air. If the static present of *Little Dorrit* appears hopelessly unalterable, it is nonetheless only through the medium of time that it will be cast away.

"But you know we always make an allowance for friction, and so I have reserved space to close in" (II, xxxiv, 824). These are Doyce's words once more, following an orderly three-point exposition of his rehabilitation of Arthur Clennam at the end of the novel. They reflect the flexibility that goes with Dickens's concern for precision and careful deliberation, and they permit me to attempt a slight correction of my approach in this essay. In this case the space must be filled with a few more words about Dickens's imaginative vitality in *Little Dorrit*, in order to avoid a subtler kind of utilitarian view of the imagination than that which Dickens satirizes in Gradgrind or Podsnap. In perceiving the theme of growth and change in *Little Dorrit*, we are liable to misleading abstraction and to neglect of an inventiveness of mind beyond explanation and appreciation in terms of its moral purpose. In the scene where John Chivery protests at what he takes to be Arthur's feigned ignorance of Little Dorrit's love, the theme stands out obviously enough: ". . . that can't make it gentlemanly, that doesn't make it honourable, that can't justify throwing a person back upon himself after he has struggled and strived out of himself like a butterfly" (II, xxvii, 727). But if we pin the thematic specimen without regard for the sheer playful exuberance with which Dickens creates the absurd rhetorical redundancies of his indignation, we miss the poise of the passage altogether.

Indeed, time is not really felt primarily as an abstract theme in the novel at all. We are conscious of time, first and foremost in the *texture* of the novel: in the extraordinary improvisatory *swiftness* of Dickens's imagination, in its quick and deft linking of incongruities. It is the capacity to move with lightning speed between spheres of experience and registers of language that makes the rendering of the "myriad forms" of nature in *Little Dorrit* something other than solemn cliché. In a sentence like this one describing Mrs. Merdle we have a characteristic example: "And if ever there were an unfeeling handsome chin that looked as, for certain, it had never been, in unfamiliar parlance, 'chucked' by the hand of man, it was the chin curbed up so tight and close by that laced bridle" (I, xx, 238). The sentence moves from circumlocutory style, with a hint or two of anachronism — appropriately enough, in the phrase "unfamiliar parlance" — through the familiar and vulgar present of "chucked" with its feel of genuine affection, and back out again by way of the disembodied "hand of man" to the language of horseriding in "curbed up" and "bridle." The sentence closes with an oxymoron reminding us that restraint chokes the society of the novel not only by means of prison bars but also by means of lace. Nothing appropriate about the powerful moral charge of the sentence can be said without a realization of its fluidity of movement.

A similar swiftness is to be felt in metaphor as it establishes connection between disparate worlds. On one page, where John Chivery makes his nervous attempt to woo Little Dorrit, the items of clothing include "pantaloons so highly decorated with side-stripes, that each leg was a three-stringed lute," and a great hat turning in John Chivery's hand "like a slowly twirling mouse-cage" (I, xviii, 215). It is not surprising, then, that there is such admiration in the novel for the rapid movements of mind and body in characters of small stature, or for "a woman's quick association of ideas" in Flora Finching (II, xxvii, 732). Only the energies of the imagination are capable of challenging static inertia in *Little Dorrit,* and of setting the world in motion again.

EIGHT

Vanity Fair:
The Double Standard

BY ROGER M. SWANSON

A discussion of the moral stance of a novelist might well revolve about the answers to three questions relating to the standards by which characters and actions are judged. What standard is invoked to establish the degree of guilt or innocence? An act of sexual irregularity or dishonesty by a character in a Victorian novel may bring harsh condemnation, whereas the same act in an eighteenth- or twentieth-century novel may be considered praiseworthy and laudable. Second, and closely related, what degree of deviation from the standard by which the thought or deed is measured determines whether it is morally or ethically acceptable or unacceptable? In other words, where is the line drawn? Third, who is applying the standard, with what degree of rigor does he apply it, and is he consistent in applying it?

Vanity Fair seems to suggest a double standard: (1) the author, William Makepeace Thackeray, has created a world that reflects implicitly his personal standard; and (2) the narrator, a persona who is primarily "above" the performance he relates but is at times also a part of it, presents the generally accepted theory and practice of the prevailing contemporary moral standard, a standard that Thackeray attempts to show is defective. By employing the standard (explicitly, through his narrator) which he disavowed to a society he meant to criticize, and then by applying (implicitly, through irony) a more rigorous standard which he approved, Thackeray hoped to reveal both the faulty ethic by which guilt is indeterminable and his own ethic by which guilt is an ineluctable by-product when men's vanity and selfishness are set within the framework of a rigorous moral structure. His aim is moral improvement, and his method is not dissimilar from that of the eighteenth-century novelists who, by presenting social evils, hoped to promote regeneration. But instead of showing directly the ills he sought to cure, he approached them obliquely, through the eyes of one who was infected himself and who could give the most convincing account of the symptoms of the sickness. By allowing the morally unhealthy narrator to show off other people suffering from various forms of the same malady, Thackeray hoped that his readers might take precaution to prevent their own moral incapacitation.

By the mid-1840s Thackeray had come to conceive his role of novelist as that of a teacher and moralist. In a letter of February 24, 1847, he wrote,

> What I mean applies to my own case & that of all of us — who set up as Satirical-Moralists — and having such a vast multitude of readers whom we not only amuse but teach. And indeed, a solemn prayer to God Almighty was in my thoughts that we may never forget truth & Justice and kindness as the great ends of our profession. There's something of the same strain in Vanity Fair. A few years ago I should have sneered at the idea of setting up as a teacher at all ... — but I have got to believe in the business, and in many other things since then. And our profession seems to me to be as serious as the Parson's own.[1]

In *Vanity Fair* Thackeray presents his conception of human nature revealed through the interactions of a variety of characters. But the portrait he paints highlights not so much the individual and the idiosyncratic as the universal and the general. Like many of his eighteenth-century predecessors, Fielding especially, Thackeray sought to embody the common traits of man. But his vision of human nature lacked the optimistic direction of earlier novelists who sought to show man's basic goodness and the eventual triumph of the right and just over the evil and unjust, a triumph that implies the benevolent regard of the Diety and the universe for man and his fate.

Thackeray's view was more melancholic, extending into cynicism, according to some of his critics. As Thackeray states in a letter of September 3, 1848, to Robert Bell, his object in writing *Vanity Fair* was

> ... to indicate, in cheerful terms, that we are for the most part an abominably foolish and selfish people "desperately wicked" and all eager after vanities. Everybody is you see in that book. ... I want to leave everybody dissatisfied and unhappy at the end of the story — we ought all to be with our own and all other stories. Good God dont I see (in

---

[1] *The Letters and Private Papers of William Makepeace Thackeray,* ed. Gordon N. Ray, II (Cambridge, Mass., 1945), 282.

that maybe cracked and warped looking glass in which I am always looking) my own weaknesses wickednesses lusts follies shortcomings? . . . We
must lift up our voices about these and howl to a congregation of fools:
so much at least has been my endeavor.[2]

Looking at himself and at the society he knew, Thackeray set about
exhibiting those "weaknesses" and "wickednesses" in the hope that he
might convince his readers of their own follies.

The subtitle of *Vanity Fair — A Novel without a Hero* — reveals
Thackeray's conception of man as basically unheroic. In contrast to
the novels and romances to which Thackeray and the rest of the Victorian reading public were subjected, *Vanity Fair* presented a world of
people not unlike those whom one might find when he laid down the
novel and gazed out his window. The characters, with their particular
personalities, their potentials and limitations, determine to only a
limited extent the events in their lives. They can be affected by conditions external to themselves, but their reactions to such conditions are
predictable and expected. The reader comes to expect a certain pattern
of behavior from each character: from Amelia, a demand for pity and
protection accompanied by tears; from Dobbin, an avowal of selfless
loyalty to others; from George Osborne, a devotion to what offers the
most immediate pleasure and benefit to himself; from Becky, an amoral
adjustment to her economic and social environment.

Absent from the novel are characters of unblemished virtue or ir-
redeemable evil. Grotesqueries of unalloyed purity or villainy from the
French romances or the English Gothic novels had no place in the
real world that Thackeray attempted to mirror. Commenting to his
mother, Mrs. Carmichael-Smyth, on the correctness of her interpretation that Amelia was selfish, Thackeray wrote (July 2, 1847), "My
object is not to make a perfect character or anything like it. Dont you
see how odious all the people are in the book (with the exception of
Dobbin) — behind whom all there lies a dark moral I hope. What I
want is to make a set of people living without God in the world (only
that is a cant phrase) greedy pompous mean perfectly self-satisfied for
the most part and at ease about their superior virtue."[3]

The positive traits of each character all have their darker sides, and
human behavior is determined by a conglomerate of motives, often in-
scrutable, usually inseparable, always complex. An action, therefore,

[2] *Ibid.*, pp. 423-24.
[3] *Ibid.*, p. 309.

which proceeds from a Thackeray character requires careful analysis of those motives prompting it, the conditions surrounding it, and the intended effect. This interpretation of multiple causation of effects results in moral complexity and makes Thackeray's position as moralist difficult to discern.

Virtually every act in *Vanity Fair* proceeds from vanity or selfishness. Even Dobbin and Amelia, the two "purest" characters in the novel, are guilty of vanity and selfishness respectively. Dobbin's slavish devotion to George Osborne and Amelia must be seen as ridiculous rather than admirable, as some critics believe. If his kindliness, fatherliness, and subservience to the selfish Osborne are viewed as virtues, then they are virtues carried to the extreme — which in Dobbin's case become vain, fruitless, and worthless, because the object of his devotion is so undeserving. Similarly, his love for Amelia, which extends throughout the novel, becomes absurd. Even Dobbin finally realizes that she is not worthy of him, that his conception of her had been elevated far beyond her rather limited merit: "No, you are not worthy of the love which I have devoted to you. I knew all along that the prize I had set my life on was not worth the winning; that I was a fool, with fond fancies, too, bartering away my all of truth and ardour against your little feeble remnant of love. I will bargain no more: I withdraw.... [Y]ou couldn't reach up to the height of the attachment which I bore you, and which a loftier soul than yours might have been proud to share. Good-bye, Amelia! I have watched your struggle. Let it end. We are both weary of it."[4]

In spite of his appraisal, however, the ever-faithful Dobbin comes running back to his beloved when she decides that perhaps he was worthy of her affection after all. The ending, which sees them married, was evidently intended by Thackeray to be unsatisfying. In his letter of September, 1848, to Robert Bell, Thackeray noted, "... if I had made Amelia a higher order of woman there would have been no vanity in Dobbins falling in love with her, whereas the impression ... is that he is a fool for his pains that he has married a silly little thing and in fact has found out his error rather a sweet and tender one...."[5] The scene in which Dobbin finally embraces Amelia leaves a bittersweet impression on the reader.

---

[4] William Makepeace Thackeray, *Vanity Fair: A Novel without a Hero,* ed. Geoffrey and Kathleen Tillotson (Boston, 1963), p. 647; all further textual references are to this edition.

[5] *Letters,* II, 423.

The vessel is in port. He has got the prize he has been trying for all his life. The bird has come in at last. There it is with its head on his shoulder, billing and cooing close up to his heart, with soft outstretched fluttering wings. This is what he has asked for every day and hour for eighteen years. This is what he pined after. Here it is — the summit, the end — the last page of the third volume. Good-bye, Colonel — God bless you, honest William! — Farewell, dear Amelia — Grow green again, tender little parasite, round the rugged old oak to which you cling! [Pp. 660-61]

John Loofbourow points to this passage as an example of the dissonance between the fashionable finale satirized by the author ("the last page of the third volume") and the supposedly serious culmination of the Dobbin-Amelia love story.[6] Notable also is the fact that this passage is really not on "the last page" of the novel, which continues for some five more pages.

Amelia, too, reveals a selfishness and foolishness in her preoccupation with her memory of George Osborne and with her duty as a mother, which she uses as a crutch to avoid facing the undesirable realities of her world. Her treatment of Dobbin is probably the most damning. After his denunciation of her (quoted above), she comes to realize that she has manipulated him for her own selfish purposes: "Amelia stood scared and silent as William thus suddenly broke the chain by which she held him, and declared his independence and superiority. He had placed himself at her feet so long that the poor little woman had been accustomed to trample upon him. She didn't wish to marry him, but she wished to keep him. She wished to give him nothing, but that he should give her all" (p. 647).

If William Dobbin and Amelia Sedley display the most admirable character traits in *Vanity Fair,* the other people drawn by Thackeray come off less well by contrast. Not that these characters lack the potential for goodness: rather, they are controlled by their more powerful tendencies to gain self-satisfaction through power and wealth. The characters seem devoid of any real intelligence; they function as automatons seeking their own desires in the most efficient and expedient fashion, regarding highly the appearance but not the substance of morality in their pursuit.

The stratagem most often employed by the opportunists of the Fair indicates this pattern: a character determines consciously or uncon-

---

[6] John Loofbourow, *Thackeray and the Form of Fiction* (Princeton, N.J., 1964), p. 82.

sciously to advance himself (or someone for whom he is responsible) ; he selects the person occupying a position of wealth (which in Vanity Fair implies power) who can effect that advancement; he ingratiates himself to the point where the person will feel obligated to grant his wish, at the same time trying to eliminate with dispatch any competition for the prize. The outcome is determined by how well he masks his insincerity, how much of an obligation he can establish in the superior, and how long he can maintain his subterfuge in the presence of those who see through his schemes. Should the host for some reason no longer have the ability to satisfy the parasite, the latter immediately dissolves the relationship, treats the former with disdain for succumbing to his hypocrisy, and seeks a new host.

While this stratagem is employed by many of the characters in *Vanity Fair,* including George Osborne and Becky in particular, it is well illustrated in the activities of the industrious Mrs. Bute Crawley. She sees in Becky a threat to the hoped-for inheritance of old Miss Crawley's money by the Bute Crawleys, which she feels they have every right to claim. She works to ingratiate herself in the affections of Miss Crawley, Becky, and Rawdon Crawley, ". . . her husband's rival in the Old Maid's five per cents!" (p. 106). She suggests to him that Becky may be on the verge of marriage to old Sir Pitt, and this sobering thought forces the less imaginative Rawdon into action. The marriage between Becky and Rawdon takes place shortly thereafter.

Having brought about the desired marriage, Mrs. Bute attempts to secure her triumph over Rawdon and Becky by eliminating them from Miss Crawley's affections and will. Arriving opportunely at the time when the news of the clandestine marriage comes to Briggs, Miss Crawley's companion, Mrs. Bute ". . . declared it was quite providential that she should have arrived at such a time to assist poor dear Miss Crawley in supporting the shock — that Rebecca was an artful little hussy of whom she had always had her suspicions; and that as for Rawdon Crawley, she never could account for his aunt's infatuation regarding him, and had long considered him a profligate, lost, and abandoned being. And this awful conduct, Mrs. Bute said, will have at least *this* good effect, it will open poor dear Miss Crawley's eyes to the real character of this wicked man" (p. 156). As she is about to assume complete control over the hapless dowager, Mrs. Bute is forced to return unexpectedly to the rectory because of her husband's illness resulting from a broken collarbone. Her departure signals freedom for the inmates, and Mrs. Bute, thanks to Becky's recitation of Mrs. Bute's artifices, soon comes into disrepute while Becky's star ascends.

If Mrs. Bute's pattern of behavior can be accepted as common, what sort of moral world does the novel reflect? To be sure, it is not a world where virtue is unerringly rewarded, vice unquestionably punished, and justice unreservedly accorded to all. In reference to the hero of *Barry Lyndon,* the novel that immediately preceded *Vanity Fair,* Thackeray wrote,

> If the tale of his life have any moral (which I sometimes doubt), it is that honesty is *not* the best policy. That was a pettifogger's maxim, who half admits he would be a rogue if he found his profit in it, and has led astray scores of misguided people both in novels and the world, who forthwith set up the worldly prosperity or adversity of a man as standards by which his worth should be tried. Novelists especially make a most profuse, mean use of this pedlar's measure, and mete out what they call poetical justice.
>
> Justice, forsooth! Does human life exhibit justice after this fashion? Is it the good always who ride in gold coaches, and the wicked who go to the workhouse? Is a humbug never preferred before a capable man? Does the world always reward merit, never worship cant, never raise mediocrity to distinction? never crowd to hear a donkey braying from a pulpit, nor ever buy the tenth edition of a fool's book? Sometimes the contrary occurs, so that fools and wise, bad men and good, are more or less lucky in their turn, and honesty is "the best policy," or not, as the case may be.[7]

Thackeray refuses to posit a moral system of automatic and unrestricted reward for the people associated with good deeds, actions, and qualities (that is, those of whom the author approves and whom he presents as morally admirable for his readers) and defeat or punishment for those characters antithetical to his positive values. Life outside the world of the novel is far too complicated for such a simple code. George Osborne, a man of exceeding vanity and selfishness, dies midway through the story; yet his unexpected death is in no way contingent upon his character traits or morality. He might as easily have lived, as did Dobbin, Rawdon Crawley, or O'Dowd. Amelia, married in the end to Dobbin, has the protection and sympathy she has long desired, although the last the reader hears of her is a sigh. Dobbin achieves his prize, but it is an unexciting one. Rawdon, always loyal

---

[7] William Makepeace Thackeray, *The Memoirs of Barry Lyndon, Esq. and the Miscellaneous Papers Written between 1843 and 1847,* ed. George Saintsbury, VI (London, 1912), 310.

and unselfish to his wife, is separated from Becky and dies prematurely. Becky, stripped of position, wealth, and reputation, is condemned to a life of wanderlust on the Continent. And so with the other characters. Some come out better, some worse, and some about where they started. Their destinies seem to bear little relationship to their merits or deficiences. If the world of Vanity Fair is as amoral as it seems, how can the reader identify Thackeray's attitude on the morality and immorality of human behavior, and how can he determine what receives Thackeray's approbation or reproach?

Thackeray created in *Vanity Fair* not only a society that would present the character traits found in most people but also the prevailing middle-class standard by which behavior was judged in his own society. He pictures characters composed of an admixture of good and bad, who play out their dramas according to the exigencies of a middle-class world that determines morality on the basis of appearance, position, and wealth, that imposes no preordained ethic of rewards and punishments, and that permits injustice to flourish and suffering to go unrelieved. By picturing such a world, Thackeray condemns his own society and points his accusing finger at its central weakness: the lack of an adequate standard for measuring the morality of human behavior. Because that standard is lacking, because the distinctions between guilt and innocence are unclear, actions defy permanent moral classification and are judged by what might be called situational ethics. Thackeray protested such a value system by creating a world that embodied it completely and then by undercutting it through irony and satire, and he articulated that unacceptable standard through the voice of the narrator-showman, the spokesman of Vanity Fair.

Like Becky, Dobbin, and the rest, the narrator is a character in *Vanity Fair;* while usually a commentator and creator of the action, he steps into the story at points (e.g., his meeting with the English travelers at Pumpernickel, his conversations with Tom Eaves). He serves as the quintessential voice of the people whom Thackeray is criticizing. At times the ardent moralist, on occasion the detached observer, frequently prejudiced, and sometimes inconsistent, the narrator presents the reader with the voice of Vanity Fair. The opening comments of the "Manager of the Performance" in the introductory "Before the Curtain" indicate the attitude that should be taken by the visitor to Vanity Fair.

A man with a reflective turn of mind, walking through an exhibition of this sort, will not be oppressed, I take it, by his own or other people's hilarity. An episode of humour or kindness touches and amuses him here and there . . . but the general impression is one more melancholy than mirthful. When you come home, you sit down, in a sober, contemplative, not uncharitable frame of mind, and apply yourself to your books or your business.

I have no other moral than this to tag to the present story of "Vanity Fair." . . . There are scenes of all sorts; some dreadful combats, some grand and lofty horse-riding, some scenes of high life, and some of very middling indeed; some love-making for the sentimental, and some light comic business; the whole accompanied by appropriate scenery, and brilliantly illuminated with the Author's own candles. [P. 5]

Just the sort of thing, in other words, that would appeal to the upper and middle classes of bourgeois mid-Victorian society. That the show he will present has any "dark Moral," that the puppets bear any relationship to persons in the audience, that the narrator is trying to do anything more than offer an amusing program for people with little more worthwhile to do — all are denied. The performance is meant to be enjoyable, to appeal in some way to everyone, to offer a light, refreshing diversion in the midst of an otherwise busy and productive life. The narrator notifies his readers that he cannot remain detached from his performance, that he *will* make judgments on them.

And while the moralist, who is holding forth on the cover (an accurate portrait of your humble servant), professes to wear neither gown nor bands, but only the very same long-eared livery in which his congregation is arrayed: yet, look you, one is bound to speak the truth as far as one knows it, whether one mounts a cap and bells or a shovel-hat; and a deal of disagreeable matter must come out in the course of such an undertaking. [P. 80]

And, as we bring our characters forward, I will ask leave, as a man and a brother, not only to introduce them, but occasionally to step down from the platform, and talk about them: if they are good and kindly, to love them and shake them by the hand; if they are silly, to laugh at them confidentially in the reader's sleeve: if they are wicked and heartless, to abuse them in the strongest terms which politeness admits of.

Otherwise you might fancy it was I who was sneering at the practice of devotion, which Miss Sharp finds so ridiculous; that it was I who laughed good-humouredly at the reeling old Silenus of a baronet — whereas the laughter comes from one who has no reverence except for prosperity, and no eye for anything beyond success. Such people there are living and flourishing in the world — Faithless, Hopeless, Charityless: let us have at them, dear friends, with might and main. Some there are, and very successful too, mere quacks and fools: and it was to combat and expose such as those, no doubt, that Laughter was made. [P. 81]

If the central theme of the narrator is "Vanitas Vanitatum," he nonetheless accepts the fact of vanity as a partially agreeable ingredient in everyone's personality.

> It is all vanity to be sure: but who will not own to liking a little of it? I should like to know what well-constituted mind, merely because it is transitory, dislikes roast-beef? That is a vanity; but may every man who reads this, have a wholesome portion of it through life, I beg: ay, though my readers were five hundred thousand. Sit down, gentlemen, and fall to, with a good hearty appetite; the fat, the lean, the gravy, the horse-radish as you like it — don't spare it. Another glass of wine, Jones, my boy — a little bit of the Sunday side. Yes, let us eat our fill of the vain thing, and be thankful therefor. And let us make the best of Becky's aristocratic pleasures likewise — for these too, like all other mortal delights, were but transitory. [P. 485]

Although he claims to be merely a guide or showman of the Fair, the narrator is really an inhabitant. His preachments and moralizings are the stock in trade of the Fair; he cannot escape the lures of money and position. He follows Becky's ascendancy with delight and interest; he is inclined to be a bit impatient toward Amelia's simpering and Dobbin's awkwardness. The standard of morality that the narrator applies to the people he describes is qualified and inconsistent. Like Miss Crawley, who changes her opinion of Becky in an instant when she hears of her marriage to Rawdon Crawley, the narrator judges his characters according to their social and economic conditions. For example, in the earlier chapters of the novel he pointedly defends Becky's aggressive tactics to secure her advancement in the world.[8] Unlike Amelia and the other young ladies of the many families in the novel

---

[8] Thackeray has two alternatives in regard to Becky. The first, open rebellion implying rejection of the Victorian social and economic system, is unacceptable because of Thackeray's personal views, which would prohibit any outright denial of a social pattern of which he was very much a part, and because he can appeal to no supernatural or religious absolute by which to justify such an action (e.g., Charlotte Brontë in *Jane Eyre*). The second, accepting the system and determining to win by "beating the game" within its own rules, not only reveals the worst aspects of Victorian society, actually of society in general, but meshes smoothly with Thackeray's ironic-satiric view of his world.

who have interested mothers to oversee their matrimonial arrangements and rich fathers to finance them, Becky has no one.

> If Miss Rebecca Sharp had determined in her heart upon making the
> conquest of this big beau [i.e., Jos], I don't think, ladies, we have any
> right to blame her; for though the task of husband-hunting is generally,
> and with becoming modesty, entrusted by young persons to their mammas,
> recollect that Miss Sharp had no kind parent to arrange these delicate
> matters for her, and that if she did not get a husband for herself, there
> was no one else in the wide world who would take the trouble off her
> hands. [P. 27]

> ... [A]nd, if there entered some degree of selfishness into her calcula-
> tions, who can say but that her prudence was perfectly justifiable? "I
> am alone in the world," said the friendless girl. "I have nothing to look
> for but what my own labour can bring me; and while that little pink-
> faced chit Amelia, with not half my sense, has ten thousand pounds
> and an establishment secure, poor Rebecca (and my figure is far better
> than hers) has only herself and her own wits to trust to...." Of what
> else have young ladies to think, but husbands? Of what else do their
> dear mammas think? "I must be my own mamma," said Rebecca....
> [P. 88]

Let us see, implies the narrator, whether a girl of wit, beauty, and un-
scrupulousness, but destitute of family, position, and wealth, can persuade a society that respects the latter qualities to accede to the former.
But in the process of tracing her adventures, the narrator, like the
other fools and knaves of Vanity Fair, accedes as well.

Her physical charm, her wit, her accomplishments, her ability to
manipulate people, and her regard for the appearance of the morality
of her actions contribute to Becky's rapid rise to the height of society,
culminating in her presentation to the king. Her expert calculation and
good fortune came to an abrupt halt when she is discovered by her
husband having an intimate tête-à-tête with the nefarious Lord Steyne.
The implications of their presence together and the scene that follows
are immediately clear to Rawdon as well as to the reader: Becky has
arranged that Rawdon be detained at the spunging house; she has lied
to him about her efforts to free him; she has held out on him throughout their marriage, secreting love letters and money; and she has revealed her unfaithfulness to him in her intended adulterous liaison
with Steyne. Her plans, her marriage, and her reputation are clearly
ruined, despite her protestations of innocence. But the narrator asks,

"What *had* happened? Was she guilty or not? She said not; but who could tell what was truth which came from those lips; or if that corrupt heart was in this case pure? All her lies and her schemes, all her selfishness and her wiles, all her wit and genius had come to this bankruptcy" (p. 517).

While the narrator expresses genuine doubt about her guilt or innocence, he seems most interested by the consequences. He has little censure for the means she employs to achieve her end. What he is concerned with is that she misplayed a card somewhere in the game, she missed a cue somewhere in the drama, she misread a line somewhere in the play. She made a tactical error at some point that has led to her ruin; the moral issue is irrelevant. The narrator is, in fact, not only unconcerned about the ethics of his characters but apparently ignorant, himself, of the causes of their actions.[9]

The question and the uncertain answer offered by the narrator relating to Becky's guilt or innocence are intended to tell the reader more about the narrator and the many for whom he speaks than about Becky; indeed, this question of guilt or innocence lies at the heart of the novel. To the narrator, the terms "guilt" or "innocence" are really important only as they apply to those whose hypocrisy, vanity, selfishness, and social ambition and the means they use to gratify them are

[9] Critics tend to disagree on the reliability of the narrator. Harriet Blodgett, for instance, argues that the narrator is a preacher who dramatizes his message that all is vanity through his puppet show and then, as an author, writes the play out in novel form. He is, therefore, omniscient and fully in control of his performance; any fallibility in knowledge is a ploy on his part to temper his satire by showing that he, too, is subject to human limitations. See "Necessary Presence: The Rhetoric of the Narrator in *Vanity Fair,*" *Nineteenth-Century Fiction,* XXII (1967), 212-13. Both Andrew Von Hendy and Ann Y. Wilkinson come to a different conclusion. Von Hendy suggests that by not conclusively answering the question "Was she guilty or not?" and by making Becky herself uncertain of her final "bankruptcy," Thackeray reminds the reader ". . . of everyman's inability to judge accurately by the standards of Vanity Fair . . . moral judgments in Vanity Fair must always be dubious." See Von Hendy, "Misunderstanding about Becky's Characterization in *Vanity Fair,*" *ibid.,* XVIII (1963), 283. Wilkinson narrows this view: the narrator ". . . may with believability not know the ultimate motivations and outcomes of a particular situation. In fact, since we are there with him eavesdropping, we know he doesn't know any more than we do, and thus the whole problem of the novel comes home to us: the ultimate unknowability of the truth in crucial (or uncrucial) human situations. . . ." See "The Tomeavsian Way of Knowing the World: Technique and Meaning in *Vanity Fair,*" *ELH,* XXXII (1965), 386.

exposed. What is crucial is that those whom society brands guilty, whether they are in fact or not, have lessened their chances for success by allowing themselves to be discovered. Mrs. Bute's guilt and its resultant consequences derive from the general knowledge that her tactics failed. Had those tactics been successful, Miss Crawley's money would have assured Mrs. Bute's reputation as an honest and innocent woman, just as Becky's presentation to the king obliterates the smudges on her reputation. Success rather than morality provides the standard for the narrator and the society for which he is a spokesman. He may decry that such a situation exists, but he, too, sides with the winners and shows diminished respect for the losers.

If the reader were to accept at face value the observations and comments of the narrator, he would have in *Vanity Fair* a Machiavellian guidebook to the ways of achieving material success in life. Yet what the narrator presents from Vanity Fair is a photographic negative: every detail of life is shown, but the darker tones appear light and the light becomes dark. What Thackeray presents in *Vanity Fair* is a picture, developed and colored. Jonathan Swift in *A Modest Proposal* creates a narrator who believes in the values the author means to criticize severely; Thackeray in *Vanity Fair* also creates a narrator who believes in the values of a society that the author means to criticize. The consummate artistry of Thackeray's irony allowed him to speak through a somewhat confused narrator whose amoral judgment of his society implicitly revealed Thackeray's own very moral judgment. The almost complete absence of guilt attributed to a person whose actions border on criminality implies an almost wholesale condemnation of those people whose very standards of judgment were morally deficient.

The scene in which Rawdon discovers Becky with Steyne provides an illustration of how Thackeray's standard emerges. As discussed earlier, Becky holds a good deal of attraction for the narrator. He marvels at and lauds her success, which results from her elasticity, resourcefulness, and maneuverability. Thackeray's judgment of Becky is firm, however: if the narrator does not admit Becky's guilt, the author reveals it by implication. She is damned by Rawdon's simple statement: "You might have spared me a hundred pounds, Becky, out of all this — I have always shared with you" (p. 516). The reader is reminded of the night before Waterloo, when Rawdon inventories his negotiable possessions as insurance for Becky should he be killed (p. 286).

Thackeray also arranges that Becky is defeated by the two innocents she believes are least capable of exposing her, Lady Jane and little

Rawdon, people whom she cannot tolerate and whom she treats with utter contempt. Throughout the novel Becky disdains the responsibilities of motherhood and shows only disgust toward her son. Whether farming him out to country nurses or boxing his ears at home, she finds the boy bothersome and troublesome. Most damaging to Becky are the two innocent remarks little Rawdon makes in the presence of Lady Jane. Seated at the table shortly after arriving for the first time at Queens Crawley, little Rawdon comments to his aunt, "I like to dine here," and responds to her question of why with "I dine in the kitchen when I am at home ... or else with Briggs" (p. 435). Later in the visit to the family mansion, Becky,

> ... seeing that tenderness was the fashion, called Rawdon to her one evening, and stooped down and kissed him in the presence of all the ladies.
>
> He looked her full in the face after the operation, trembling and turning very red, as his wont was when moved. "You never kiss me at home, Mamma," he said; at which there was a general silence and consternation, and a by no means pleasant look in Becky's eyes.
>
> Rawdon was fond of his sister-in-law, for her regard for his son. Lady Jane and Becky did not get on *quite* so well at this visit as on occasion of the former one, when the Colonel's wife was bent upon pleasing. Those two speeches of the child struck rather a chill. [P. 439]

It is Lady Jane who provides the money that frees Rawdon from the spunging house to return to his wife and her admirer. Becky's deception of her husband and hatred of her son alienate her from Lady Jane, and Lady Jane in turn eliminates the chance of Becky's economic recovery by refusing to allow Sir Pitt to help her.

> "Upon my word, my love, I think you do Mrs. Crawley injustice," Sir Pitt said; at which speech Rebecca was vastly relieved. "Indeed I believe her to be —"
>
> "To be what?" cried out Lady Jane, her clear voice thrilling, and her heart beating violently as she spoke. "To be a wicked woman — a heartless mother, a false wife? She never loved her dear little boy, who used to fly here and tell me of her cruelty to him. She never came into a family but she strove to bring misery with her, and to weaken the most sacred affections with her wicked flattery and falsehoods. She has deceived her husband, as she has deceived everybody; her soul is black with vanity, worldliness, and all sorts of crime. I tremble when I touch her." [P. 531]

Becky's defeat at the hands of the innocent Rawdon and the previously unassuming Lady Jane contains Thackeray's implicit moral comment. It is the ambiguity of the narrator toward Becky that most clearly defines Thackeray's critical method: the narrator questions her innocence, but the author confirms her guilt, thereby condemning the narrator for judging by a false standard.

From the narrator's viewpoint and from the viewpoint of the inhabitants of Vanity Fair, Becky has much to recommend her. She is a true sportsman in life, playing on borrowed money for high stakes, enjoying her victories and laughing at her own defeats (p. 247) and discomfiture (p. 406). Any meanness in her nature comes from the conditions of life she faces, and in this light the narrator suggests that most of us, under Becky's circumstances, would compromise our virtue.

> "It isn't difficult to be a country gentleman's wife," Rebecca thought. "I think I could be a good woman if I had five thousand a year." . . . And who knows but Rebecca was right in her speculations — and that it was only a question of money and fortune which made the difference between her and an honest woman? If you take temptations into account, who is to say that he is better than his neighbour? A comfortable career of prosperity, if it does not make people honest, at least keeps them so. An alderman coming from a turtle feast will not step out of his carriage to steal a leg of mutton; but put him to starve, and see if he will not purloin a loaf. Becky consoled herself by so balancing the chances and equalising the distribution of good and evil in the world. . . . "Heigho! I wish I could exchange my position in society, and all my relations for a snug sum in the Three per Cent. Consols;" for so it was that Becky felt the Vanity of human affairs, and it was in those securities that she would have liked to cast anchor. [Pp. 409-10]

Thackeray's main purpose is to override the narrator's light treatment of Becky and to show her clearly guilty of those social crimes he saw rampant in his own society. The words used by the narrator to describe Becky are meant to be condescending but good-humoredly condemnatory, but they seem too strong not to suggest the author's irony when they are related to her actions. She is repeatedly called an "angel" along with "poor little Becky," "this modest creature," and "the gentle Rebecca." She is, at nineteen, ". . . unused to the art of deceiving, poor innocent creature!" (p. 25), as she prepares her first campaign to land Jos. Dobbin feels a continual revulsion from Becky: "He never had had the slightest liking for her; but had heartily mistrusted her from the very first moment when her green eyes had looked at, and turned away from, his own" (p. 634). She shows treachery toward her husband by denying him her help in time of need, her money, and her faithfulness. When Becky sinks into poverty, the narrator, with his high regard for what is and what is not proper to relate to his sensitive readers, finds he cannot bring himself to describe the details of Becky's period of degradation. By indicating that the narrator could not bring himself to pass on the lurid events, by the narrator's tone of high morality, condescension, and propriety, and by the implications of the imagery of the narrator's comments, Thackeray condemns both the narrator for his priggishness and hypocrisy (since the narrator devotes the rest of the chapter to exactly that chronicle of events which he claims he will not delineate) and Becky for her past actions by making happiness impossible.

> We must pass over a part of Mrs. Rebecca Crawley's biography with that lightness and delicacy which the world demands — the moral world, that has, perhaps, no particular objection to vice, but an insuperable repugnance to hearing vice called by its proper name. There are things we do and know perfectly well in Vanity Fair, though we never speak them: as the Ahrimanians worship the devil, but don't mention him: and a polite public will no more bear to read an authentic description of vice than a truly-refined English or American female will permit the word breeches to be pronounced in her chaste hearing. And yet, madam, both are walking the world before our faces every day, without much shocking us. If you were to blush every time they went by, what complexions you would have! It is only when their naughty names are called out that your modesty has any occasion to show alarm or sense or outrage, and it has been the wish of the present writer, all through this story, deferentially to submit to the fashion at present prevailing, and only to hint at the existence of wickedness in a light, easy, and agreeable manner, so that nobody's fine feelings may be offended. I defy any one to say that our Becky, who has certainly some vices, has not been presented to the public in a perfectly genteel and inoffensive manner. In describing this syren, singing and smiling, coaxing and cajoling, the author, with modest pride, asks his readers all round, has he once forgotten the laws of politeness, and showed the monster's hideous tail above water? No! Those who like may peep down under waves that are pretty transparent, and see it writhing and twirling, diabolically hideous and slimy, flapping amongst bones, or curling round corpses; but above the water line, I ask, has not everything been proper, agreeable, and decorous, and has any but the most squeamish immoralist in Vanity Fair a right to cry fie? When, however, the syren disappears and dives

below, down among the dead men, the water of course grows turbid over her, and it is labour lost to look into it ever so curiously. They look pretty enough when they sit upon a rock, twanging their harps and combing their hair, and sing, and beckon to you to come and hold the looking-glass; but when they sink into their native element, depend on it those mermaids are about no good, and we had best not examine the fiendish marine cannibals, revelling and feasting on their wretched pickled victims. And so, when Becky is out of the way, be sure that she is not particularly well employed, and that the less that is said about her doings is in fact better.

If we were to give a full account of her proceedings during a couple of years that followed after the Curzon Street catastrophe, there might be some reason for people to say this book was improper. The actions of very vain, heartless, pleasure-seeking people are very often improper (as are many of yours, my friend with the grave face and spotless reputation; — but that is merely by the way); and what are those of a woman without faith — or love — or character? [Pp. 617-18]

Respectability for Becky is impossible, for her past always catches up with her and ruins her. "Whenever Becky made a little circle for herself with incredible toils and labour, somebody came and swept it down rudely, and she had all her work to begin over again. It was very hard: very hard; lonely, and disheartening" (p. 622). She tries to maintain respectability as she did in the days ". . . when she was not innocent, but not found out" (p. 626). She adapts perfectly to her low life just as she had made perfect accommodation to the demands of high life, but she remains insecure, uncertain, frustrated. She lives out her life maintaining the respectability of an "injured woman" with whom even Dobbin and Amelia refuse to traffic (p. 666).

The rest of the characters in the puppet show are dealt fortunes only slightly better than Becky's. The narrator clearly feels an attachment to Amelia and Dobbin but no respect for them because they have not the force and energy to succeed in Vanity Fair; whatever admirable qualities they possess are not those valued in Vanity Fair. They have little social ambition, they possess no charm and radiance, they are content with their station. Such people deserve no reward in a society that places no value on virtue without cleverness and ambition. Like the other characters in the novel who respect and sympathize with Amelia and Dobbin but find them nonetheless uninteresting, the narrator cannot ultimately bestow prizes on them because they have not played the game. They have shown none of the style and aggressiveness necessary to win the trophies displayed by the purveyors of the Fair.

He wants to give Becky her deserts because she has made some brilliant moves, but cannot because she has also made damaging errors. Had she shown more finesse, more cleverness, he would undoubtedly have given her the high position she shows such alacrity in pursuing. Those who triumph do so temporarily or, if success is longer lasting (as with Lord Steyne, for instance), do so because of their superior talents and positions.

Yet Thackeray, too, limits the eventual happiness of the characters. The implicit condemnation of Becky extends also to the characters to whom Thackeray accords a higher moral valuation. The "goodness" present in Amelia and Dobbin is not strong enough to have any forceful effect on their destinies; the love of which Amelia is capable and the selflessness which Dobbin repeatedly displays are carried to excess. As the narrator withholds his rewards from them because they cannot accommodate themselves to the life of Vanity Fair, Thackeray withholds his rewards because their virtues, carried to the extreme, have become defects. The standard by which Thackeray judges Becky guilty of every crime, including murder, and makes her punishment akin to that of Tantalus, is also applied to Amelia and Dobbin, and they too are found deficient. They are awarded some degree of satisfaction, but certainly a good deal less than they might have deserved had they shown less foolishness. Their reward is merely proportional to their abilities to fulfill the ideal by which Thackeray measured them.

The standard Thackeray applies to the characters in *Vanity Fair,* to the people of Vanity Fair whom he knew and sought to expose, reflects that of the ideal world he wished to bring into existence. This ideal may be occasionally confused or unclear, yet it reflects the difficulty faced by Thackeray and his contemporaries in measuring life by a consistent and objective standard. Although the standard was imperfect and difficult to apply, it contrasted to the vanities by which all — certainly the narrator and perhaps even at times the author — were affected. By that standard, all the inhabitants of Vanity Fair are guilty to a lesser or greater degree. The mere fact that they cannot recognize their own guilt is the clearest evidence that their standard is worthless. "And for my part I believe that remorse is the least active of all a man's moral senses — the very easiest to be deadened when wakened: and in some never wakened at all. We grieve at being found out, and at the idea of shame or punishment; but the mere sense of wrong makes very few people unhappy in Vanity Fair" (p. 411).

In *Vanity Fair* Thackeray attempts to impose upon a world that fails to assign guilt (because it has no valid standard by which to measure guilt) a more ideal and therefore a much more severe standard by which that world should be evaluated. Thackeray thus uses realism as a foil for idealism. His aim, not unlike that of other nineteenth-century writers, was to impose upon the facts of the world, upon the vanities of human behavior he saw all about him, an order they could not attain. Yet to set that order upon the world of Vanity Fair explicitly would be to sermonize, to preach as a member of the clergy rather than to teach as a novelist. Thackeray preferred to let the reader distill from the novel the author's moral position rather than forcing it upon him.

NINE

Memory, Morality, and the Tragic Vision in the Early Novels of George Eliot

BY WILLIAM E. BUCKLER

The nature and function of memory fascinated nineteenth-century poets and novelists in their efforts to probe "the abysmal deeps of personality." The phrase is Tennyson's ("The Palace of Art"), and the role of memory in the fractured or integrated personality is one of the two or three major themes in Tennyson's poetry, from the beginning (e.g., "Ode to Memory") through *In Memoriam* and *Maud*. The most obvious progenitor of the concept for the century — both as subject and as theme — was Wordsworth, and indeed it may have been his most significant contribution to the search for self that the Victorians, especially, vigorously pursued. But so pervasive and functional is the topic throughout the literature of the century that one is justified in viewing it not as a formulation seeded by one major writer but as one of the omnipresent imperatives of the cultural climate out of which Victorian — and then modern — literature evolved. It was a mode of perception, of self-identification, of historical perspective, of psychological penetration and moral evaluation, even of prophecy.

For George Eliot, particularly, memory became a significant device for creating, understanding, and adjudicating characters and the value conflicts of loyalty, love, and belief in which, *in their mutual relations,* they were involved. It was for her a basic means for making the moralist relevant to the psychologist and for mediating between the classical concept of tragedy of character and the incipient naturalistic idea of tragedy of circumstance. The pattern, which emerges in the early novels with varying degrees of explicitness, is analogous to that which Tennyson develops in *In Memoriam:* "... That men may rise on stepping-stones / Of their dead selves to higher things." Like Tennyson, too, George Eliot recognized that, the present self being in significant ways a product of the "dead self," the uses of the past for fronting present crises vary dramatically with the individual personality. Hetty in *Adam Bede* has no past; Maggie's past in *The Mill on the Floss,* though real, is chaotic; only Silas Marner, if he can bridge the dwarfing intermediate years, has a "precious past" with which to enrich the future. The distinctions Eliot makes are subtly graduated, but they are clearly a part of her conception of character and of the relationship between character and survival.

In the important letter of November 31, 1858, George Eliot has given unusual information about the germ of *Adam Bede* and the significant decisions she made in the course of composing it. Two shortened sentences hit at the heart of the matter at hand: "When I began to write it, the only elements I had determined on, besides the character of Dinah, were the character of Adam, his relation to Arthur Donnithorne, and their mutual relations to Hetty . . . the scene in the prison being, of course, the climax towards which I worked. Everything else grew out of the characters and their mutual relations."[1] The tragic undertone of the novel (that is, Hetty's story) is moderated by this concept.

It is true that Hetty is self-regarding. Her vanity blinds her to the tangible, dependable, systematic values with which she is surrounded and leads her, like Emma Bovary, into a life of romantic illusion: for reality she substitutes fantasy; for love, self-adoration. She acts out pantomimes before her mirror and peoples the abbey with elegantly appointed variations on herself. She is associated with the Narcissus myth through her mirror at home and, ironically, through the dark, cold ponds of her "Journey in Despair" (V, xxxvii); during their brief period of love-making, Arthur (in a further mutation of the myth) plays Echo to her self-imaging.

But it in no way diminishes George Eliot's stern theme of the unpitying, irrevocable nature of consequences to point out that Hetty is operating within a moral/social framework to which other characters contribute. Mr. Poyser, for example, is engagingly indulgent to Hetty and tries to shield her from the verbal and moral asperity of his wife. Adam has set around her, even after he knows enough of the truth to

---

[1] *George Eliot's Life as Related in Her Letters and Journals,* arranged and edited by J. W. Cross, 3 vols. (Edinburgh and London, 1885), I, xxx.

be suspicious of the whole truth, a cluster of "ingenious probabilities" to spare disgrace to her and pain to himself. Arthur, in his most confessional mood and before matters have gone too far, is not obstructed from his "opportunity" of coming clean. But neither is he induced to do so by the perceptive but "too delicate" Mr. Irwine (II, xvi), as Irwine himself recognizes "by that terrible illumination which the present sheds back upon the past" (V, xxxix): "if he himself had been less fastidious about intruding on another man's secrets...." Hetty's character and culpability are measured within the organic tissue of this provincial world.

Hetty Sorrel's character flaw, or "sin," is clear enough: vanity, pride, self-worship. Thus she provokes a cluster of images and symbols suggestive of vanity and sexual levity: lace, earrings, mirrors, a mysterious locket, a neckerchief, peacocks, kittens, blossoms, butterflies sucking nectar, velvet peaches, leafy hiding places. In imagining herself a "great lady," she creates in the mirror an ironic image of a courtesan (I, xv):

> But Hetty seemed to have made up her mind that something was wanting, for she got up and reached an old black lace scarf out of the linen-press, and a pair of large earrings out of the sacred drawer from which she had taken her candles. It was an old scarf, full of rents, but it would make a becoming border round her shoulders, and set off the whiteness of her upper arm. And she would take out the little earrings she had in her ears — oh, how her aunt had scolded her for having her ears bored! — and put in those large ones: they were but coloured glass and gilding; but if you didn't know what they were made of, they looked just as well as what the ladies wore. And so she sat down again, with the large earrings in her ears, and the black lace scarf adjusted round her shoulders.

But Eliot's portrait of Hetty has deeper ramifications than such trappings and tableaux. For example, she lacks religion — that is, she lacks any value system sufficiently traditionalized to serve as a corrective to ego illusion, and she has no conscience. Her dislike of children, a fact reiterated in the first half of the novel and brought to bear upon her actions and reactions toward her new-born child, is of fundamental importance. Hetty does not murder her child, as had the "very ignorant girl" in the anecdote that provided the germ of the novel. She lacks the innate psychological resource for acknowledging its dependence on her and her obligation to it. She is the wholly isolated, encapsulated individual. Lacking that feeling which is "a form of knowledge," she fails to recognize the "organic filaments" (to use a phrase from Carlyle that is suggested more than once in the novel) by which society is knitted together in an interdependent whole — between the generations and between the ages. Hence Hetty's denial throughout the trial that she ever had a child is not merely the obstinacy of inverted panic: on one level of psychological credibility, it is "true." Hence, too, her confession is both a moral and a psychological necessity.

Perhaps the most tantalizing dimension of Eliot's presentation of Hetty — a dimension that knits her to one of the most pervasive thematic interests of the author — is her complete lack of memory. She is completely devoid of psychological and moral roots; her whole consciousness revolves around some recent flattery to her ego or fantastic dreams of which she is the adored center. For example, only after being aware of her pregnancy for months and having gone on her fruitless journey in search of Arthur at Windsor does her mind recur to that scene in her bedroom (I, xv) in which Dinah had, by sympathetic premonition, rehearsed the drama later to be staged "In the Prison" (V, xlv). The narrator points the matter in V, xxxvii:

> Now, for the first time she remembered without indifference the affectionate kindness Dinah had shown her, and those words of Dinah in the bed-chamber — that Hetty must think of her as a friend in trouble. Suppose she were to go to Dinah, and ask her to help her? Dinah did not think about things as other people did: she was a mystery to Hetty, but Hetty knew she was always kind. She couldn't imagine Dinah's face turning away from her in dark reproof or scorn, Dinah's voice willingly speaking ill of her, or rejoicing in her misery, as a punishment. Dinah did not seem to belong to that world of Hetty's, whose glance she dreaded like scorching fire. But even to her Hetty shrank from beseeching and confession: she could not prevail on herself to say, "I will go to Dinah;" she only thought of that as a possible alternative, if she had not courage for death.

And it is as a riddance of the awful memory of "that crying and the place in the wood" that naive Hetty hopes to get her first reward for confessing (V, xlv).

Arthur and Hetty, who are both orphans, share this defect of memory, though to differing degrees; it lies at the root of their need for a wholly affectionate environment and their susceptibility to moments of dreamy self-indulgence. But the degree of difference between them is important: Arthur is, after all, a man of structured expectations, and he has the memory of a youth spent in the strength, sun-shine, and unqualified affection between him and Adam Bede. It is this memory, more than any other single factor, that enables both Arthur and Adam to bridge the gulf of their hostility and to absorb into their value systems the positive results of their suffering. This is the central revelation of V, xlviii, especially the dozen or so paragraphs beginning "Adam could not help being moved" and ending "there was a strong rush, on both sides, of the old, boyish affection."

George Eliot's purpose in *Adam Bede,* as she says in the very first sentence, was "to reveal . . . far-reaching visions of the past." And this interior role of the individual memory knits together cultural history and the individual psyche. Like Wordsworth, whose influence upon her was steady and profound and in whose poetry she "met with so many of [her] own feelings, expressed just as [she] could like them,"[2] she was deeply and persistently aware of "a faint, indescribable something in the air" — "like those little words, 'light' and 'music,' stirring the long-winding fibres of your memory, and enriching your present with your most precious past" (VI, i).

The generic connection of *The Mill on the Floss* with *Adam Bede* is clear: although it is set in a different county and employs a new fic-tion, it is another examination of the conflict of loves, loyalties, and beliefs in a highly structured provincial society. The theme of memory as the principal and most trustworthy source of moral, psychological, and social stability, giving vital organic unity to time (past, present, future), is again examined. But there are these important differences.

(1) The "historical" time is shifted forward by three to four decades: 1829-39 instead of 1799-1805. And a "small trading town" takes the place of a squirearchy: the manipulative presence of Mr. Wakem and Guest & Co. is substituted for the personal dominance of a semi-feudal Squire Donnithorne.

(2) The "psychological" or "developmental" time is shifted *back-ward* by more than a decade (Tom and Maggie at the beginning of the novel are on the threshold of adolescence as Arthur and Hetty are on the threshold of adulthood), and the period of growth is accord-ingly doubled.

(3) A new saga element is implicitly introduced: in its various tribu-

[2] Gordon S. Haight, *George Eliot: A Biography* (New York and Oxford, 1968), p. 29.

taries, the Dodson family seems to reach out of sight and out of memory into pre-recorded "fens" or "wolds." By comparison the Tullivers — passionate, lovable, and self-destructive — seem to be more akin to a gypsy lineage, compelled to find its identity and values in a restless, unstructured self-reliance.

(4) The "real drama of Evangelicalism," which provides *Adam Bede* with much of its historical conditioning and runs deep into character, is hardly mentioned. In its place we find a motivational mentor out of the late Middle Ages, Thomas à Kempis and *The Imitation of Christ:* his practical guide to salvation through self-renunciation is set against the semipaganism of the modern acquisitive churchgoer who uses religion as a part of the emergent ritual of propriety. Dr. Kenn, who plays a smaller but more genuinely priestly part than Mr. Irwine in *Adam Bede,* reflects some of the trappings of the Oxford Movement, but social "tyranny of the majority" is shown to be an implacable force against which his doctrines of fair play and community sympathy have little or no effect.

(5) "Sister Maggie" is unchallenged as the protagonist of *The Mill on the Floss,* as Adam Bede had not been in his novel. It is a modern tragedy of individual character, and judgment of every essential aspect of the novel must be made by measuring it against Maggie.

In his introduction to *The Mill on the Floss* Professor Gordon S. Haight, with customary circumspection, quotes from a letter in which George Eliot gives her early reaction to Darwin's *Origin of Species* and tentatively applies the "struggle for existence" principle to the novel.[3] I have no particular objection to such a fanciful application, though one should remember that George Eliot had been at work on the novel for almost a year before Darwin's book appeared; that her husband was a popular but highly respected naturalist; and that the "doctrine of development" was confirmed by Darwin, not discovered by him. Further, an early enthusiast for Darwin was Samuel Butler: he later broke with Darwin, accusing him of being mechanical, of having taken "mind out of the universe." Butler developed his own psychological evolutionary hypothesis called "unconscious memory," a hypothesis that undergirds, psychologically, *Ernest Pontifex, or, The Way of All Flesh.* And perhaps it is not fanciful to suggest that George Eliot is tentatively employing an uncodified form of this hypothesis in *The Mill on the Floss.*

[3] George Eliot, *The Mill on the Floss,* ed. Gordon S. Haight, Riverside Editions (Boston, 1961), pp. v-xxi.

The thematic importance of memory to the psychological probing of the novel is incontrovertible: on almost every page we meet with the word or an analytical exposition of its significance or an implicit function of it. (A few "classic" statements can be found in II, ii; VI, vii; VI, xiii; and VII, ii. These passages make it clear that, for Maggie, morality, social structure, God, indeed her own identity, are absolutely dependent on memory.) But in some of the passages on memory the author, while she is careful to give due cognizance to "the mystery that lies under the processes,"[4] seems to reach across the generations and to suggest an evolutionary process of saga proportions. Two of these "Butlerian" passages need to be quoted:

> The same sort of traditional belief ran in the Tulliver veins, but it was carried in richer blood, having elements of generous imprudence, warm affection, and hot-tempered rashness. Mr. Tulliver's grandfather had been heard to say that he was descended from one Ralph Tulliver, a wonderfully clever fellow, who had ruined himself. It is likely enough that the clever Ralph was a high liver, rode spirited horses, and was very decidedly of his own opinion. On the other hand, nobody had ever heard of a Dodson who had ruined himself: it was not the way of that family. [IV, ii]

> I don't think any of the strongest effects our natures are susceptible of can ever be explained. We can neither detect the process by which they are arrived at, nor the mode in which they act on us. The greatest of painters only once painted a mysteriously divine child; he couldn't have told how he did it, and we can't tell why we feel it to be divine. I think there are stores laid up in our human nature that our understandings can make no complete inventory of. [V, i]

George Eliot seems to have seen Tom, especially, in this frame of reference. Although he doesn't like the Dodson clan as he is growing up, he is a Dodson through and through: he even fights the Tulliver battle with Dodson motives and Dodson doggedness. He is prosaic ("There's no lion . . ."), cruel, honorable, obedient, insensitive to pain, respectable, fair, highly competitive, patriarchal in laying down the law and in drawing the blood of the offender. Like his anal-erotic aunts and uncles, who cluck peevishly around their battlemented possessions and constantly count their apples while reciting their virtues, he has built around himself a protective armor of self-righteousness at the price of

[4] *The George Eliot Letters*, ed. Gordon S. Haight, 7 vols. (London and New Haven, Conn., 1955), III, 227.

music, imagination, tenderness, and the finer sense of justice that requires these leavening ingredients. He lacks the poetry of a recollected past: he doesn't even remember Bob Jakin, who is a foil to him and who generously, *for memory's sake,* helps him to the extent that he is susceptible of help — helps him make money. It has taken, George Eliot seems to imply, several generations of acquired characteristics to make Tom, characteristics not to be submerged by cross-breeding with the more loosely hung, loving-hearted Tullivers.

Tom plays a role second only to Maggie's in the tragic curve of *The Mill on the Floss.* It is his love for which she longs most during the decade in which we follow her; it is he who, more than anyone else, imprisons her in an environment of hate and revenge in which a free spirit like hers must wither and die; it is he who, writing in the Bible, lays the dead hand of the dead past upon her future.

At this point in the novel, between Book Third and Book Fourth, George Eliot paused, thought the matter through, and planted a midstream signpost for herself and the reader. She adapts the title of the chapter from a work of Bossuet, one of the most celebrated churchmen of seventeenth-century France, cited by Matthew Arnold in *Essays in Criticism; First Series,* as a touchstone of distinction. And she begins the chapter with an elaborate analogy that functions like an epic simile, contrasting the heroic romantic with the sordid real (somewhat suggestive of the "Prelude" with which, a decade later, she would preface *Middlemarch*). And accepting the oppressive narrowness of the world of the Dodsons and Tullivers "that will be swept into the same oblivion with the generations of ants and beavers," she yet insists on the necessity of our "feel[ing] it, if we care to understand how it acted on the lives of Tom and Maggie — how it has acted on young natures in many generations . . ." (IV, i).

Tom, of course, succumbs to it: his inherited personality structure, combined with hardship and a modicum of worldly success, makes him a partner in a metaphoric "Dodson & Co." Maggie, whose inner nature is "irradiated by sublime principles, . . . romantic visions, [and an] . . . active, self-renouncing faith," goes through a turbulent, agonizing identity crisis that ends in her destruction. This in turn poses the central critical question of the novel: its quality as tragedy.

Some commentators — for example, F. R. Leavis[5] — zero in on the

[5] F. R. Leavis, *The Great Tradition* (New York, 1948), pp. 45-46.

flood, find it wanting in true tragic dimension, and pronounce against it. Others — for example, Professor Haight[6] — try to deflect the charge by demonstrating that the flood was in fact seeded in the earliest pages of the novel.

But both lines of argument seem to me to address themselves to a secondary rather than to the primary issue. The *manner* of the death is subordinate and is essentially a matter of taste; the *inevitability* of the death reaches back through the whole fabric of the novel and challenges the author's moral and psychological authenticity: her penetration of people and the stage upon which they move.

But to take a look at the secondary issue first, one is forced by the text to accept the fact that the flood, like the prison scene in *Adam Bede,* was the dramatic climax toward which George Eliot worked from the beginning. One knows from the biography that at the beginning, too, she was copying into her commonplace book passages from the Annual Register concerning "cases of *inundation*."[7] It is also clear that the flood had resonant metaphoric implications for George Eliot: again one must recur to IV, i, "those ruined villages . . . telling how the swift river once rose, like an angry, destroying god, sweeping down the feeble generations whose breath is in their nostrils, and making their dwellings a desolation." The flood resides in the memories of the older inhabitants of St. Ogg's, as does the yet older memory of the legend of "the ghostly boatman who haunts the Floss"; both are an active part of the lore of the children. It reaches as far back as Genesis, and it provides a myth by which to read the future. Moreover, the short sequence of Maggie's self-betrayal occurs in a chapter entitled "Borne Along by the Tide" (VI, xxiii). Finally, there are recurrent stylistic passages in which the prose style itself has the swell and flow of the flood (I, i; IV, i; VII, v). Thus one may justifiably say that the flood sequence takes on the qualities of a *coda* not unlike those of Arnold's "Sohrab and Rustum" and "The Scholar-Gipsy" in which the moral theme is rewritten emblematically.

Although she alludes to Sophocles several times in *The Mill on the Floss,* George Eliot's tragic vision is not susceptible to strict Aristotelian formulation. On the other hand, the modern postnaturalistic "tragedy of circumstance" provides short measure. It is less than the one and more than the other: it is *sui generis*. There are three or four passages

[6] Haight, "Introduction," *The Mill on the Floss,* pp. xix-xx.
[7] See Haight, *George Eliot,* p. 302.

in *The Mill on the Floss* that suggest the nature of George Eliot's work-ing theory of tragedy: I, x; I, xiii; III, i; and VI, vi.

In the last citation, especially, George Eliot moderates and mutes the distinction between the thesis of classical tragedy of character and the antithesis of the modern tragedy of circumstance: "For the tragedy of our lives is not created entirely from within. 'Character,' says No-valis, in one of his questionable aphorisms — 'character is destiny.' But not the whole of our destiny." She then goes on with an analogical illustration: if Hamlet's uncle had not murdered Hamlet's father, the Prince of Denmark might have married Ophelia and lived a sane if somewhat dyspeptic life. The synthesis that George Eliot evolves, then, is based upon a perception that a character acts not in isolation but within a subtly interwoven fabric of characters — that is, "Everything ...[grows] out of the characters *and their mutual relations*." Thus it is not through an appeal to the influence of impersonal circumstance (*à la* the naturalists or the scientific positivists) that George Eliot modifies the tragedy of individual character, but through a recognition of the significant interpenetration of character upon character in the negotiation of life. It is this perception that puts the controversial chap-ter "A Variation of Protestantism Unknown to Bossuet" into perspec-tive: cultural forces of a very eclipsing kind are clearly at work in shaping the tone and expectations of a community, but they operate on the individual through the articulation of other individuals or groups of individuals. They have in this sense been socialized. This also gives compensatory thematic relevance to one of the most painfully ironic chapters in the novel (III, vii): "How a Hen Takes to Strat-agem." Mrs. Tulliver's pathetic/heroic visit to Mr. Wakem is a wholly credible illustration of how one character of a well-defined sort inter-acts on another character to press destiny forward. "Imagine," writes the author in glossing the experience, "a truly respectable and amiable hen, by some portentous anomaly, taking to reflection and inventing combinations by which she might prevail on Hodge not to wring her neck, or send her and her chicks to market: the result could hardly be other than much cackling and fluttering" — and, for the Tullivers, entry into "The Valley of Humiliation."

Books Fourth and Fifth constitute the central movement in the novel in that alternatives to tragedy are explored for the principal tragic originals — Mr. Tulliver and Maggie, the two characters most sym-pathetic to each other and the two least capable of negotiating a peaceful compromise with their community or with themselves.

Mr. Tulliver, whom the author compares with Oedipus, is a "proud and obstinate" man who goes to law in an effort, like Oedipus, to change fate and reverse his destiny. He also looks forward, in his bullish obstinacy, to Michael Henchard in *The Mayor of Casterbridge* and to Old Gourlay in *The House with the Green Shutters*. His passionate will to predominate is the law of his life, and, as the author comments in III, i, he "can only sustain humiliation so long as [he] can refuse to believe in it, and, in [his] own conception, predominate still." His ironically ill-informed efforts to educate Tom up to successful sharp-shooting are one projection of it; his altercation with Mrs. Glegg is another (I, vii). But his fatal act — an act in which Tom is co-cele-brant — is, like that of Oedipus, an act of blasphemy: he closes his heart to the possibility of ultimate justice and inscribes in the Christian Bible a pagan vow of revenge. There is, then, no alternative to a tragic outcome for the miller. The yoke of his humiliation, of working for Wakem, is made bearable only by his resolve to get the upper hand, and the slowly accumulating money, which he constantly counts and fondles, becomes the sacred instrument of his revenge. He has his Pyrrhic victory: he pays his debt and beats his enemy. But he dies fret-fully, with none of the classical serenity of self-knowledge and accep-tance: his last mumblings express at best puzzlement, and his last co-herent statement is at best ambiguous: "Does God forgive raskills? ... but if He does, He won't be hard wi' me" (V, vii). A suggestion of in-credulity over the attribute of providential magnanimity and a last as-sertion of self-righteousness: even if I'm wrong, I'm at least a lot better than the "raskills."

Maggie Tulliver, who is such a favorite of novel-readers, for whom she supplies a vehicle for vicarious escape from the barnyard world of a severely delimited existence, resists, through our romantic attachment to her, the indictment of a fallibility of tragic proportions. Certainly there is the very widest disparity of opinion on this issue, even among sympathetic readers of the novel.

But we must assume, I think, that George Eliot knew this as well as anyone — after all, she created her. And we must assume, further, that the tragic curve of Maggie's life had its peculiar kind of inevitability that the author must trace even in the face of a mountainous sympathy — ours and her own.

Some of the earliest things we learn about Maggie, though diffused through the sympathetic light of recollected childhood, are these: she is lonely, passionate with an insatiable thirst for love, utterly incapable of grounding the least flash of hostility or humiliation. She is "different" in this predominantly Dodson universe, in which the tribal chorus continuously recites her deficiences and prophesies her doom. But she is also prone to acts of irresponsibility (she lets Tom's rabbits die) and of perversity (the fetish in the attic, with its "long career of vicarious suffering"; the mannikin-like Lucy pushed into the mud; the ritual of the hair-letting). She is willful and she is ego-oriented. Her romantic pilgrimage to the gypsy camp is both an act of revenge upon her unsympathetic clan and a search for coronation: she offers herself as their benevolent queen.

Perhaps George Eliot comes closest to norming out Maggie's character in VI, vi, where she also projects her tragic destiny: "her sensibility to the supreme excitement of music was only one form of that passionate sensibility which belonged to her whole nature, and made her faults and virtues all merge in each other — made her affections sometimes an impatient [angry] demand, but also prevented her vanity from taking the form of mere feminine coquetry and device, and gave it the poetry of ambition." Maggie, then, is subject to a rather imperious form of desire and longing, both sublimated and sexual.

Maggie's search for an alternative to self-destruction is also elaborated in Books Fourth and Fifth, when she is experiencing the ill-defined turmoil of puberty: "This time of utmost need was come to Maggie, with her short span of thirteen years. To the usual precocity of the girl, she added that early experience of struggle, of conflict between the inward impulse and outward fact, which is the lot of every imaginative and passionate nature..." (IV, ii). Instead of a sympathetic, supportive family environment to help her through these trying years, the fallen Tullivers exude a universal, deadening depression. And Maggie finds her only guidance for four years in the spiritual asceticism and immolation of self practiced and taught by the medieval Thomas à Kempis, whose *Imitation of Christ* "was written down by a hand that waited for the heart's promptings ... a chronicle of a solitary, hidden anguish, struggle, trust and triumph." It is in this same time frame that Mr. Tulliver is sustained by slavery to his *idée fixe* of revenge and that Tom sacrifices himself to recovery of the family honor.

George Eliot deftly draws Maggie out of her "narrow asceticism" and back into a world in which "poetry and art and knowledge are sacred and pure"[8] through the joint influences of maturation (she turns seventeen), a gradual lightening, through expectation, of the depressing atmosphere at home, and an accidental restoration of her intercourse with the crippled Philip Wakem. It is he who hacks away at her anachronistic medievalism, who gives her a year of mutually rewarding but, to Maggie, erosively secretive companionship, and who elicits from her a sexually naive declaration of love. Though unconsciously, Maggie patronizes Philip, whose crippled body prevents her from thinking of him in sexual terms, while Philip longs for a union of body and soul: " 'Yes, Philip, I should like never to part: I should like to make your life very happy.' 'I am waiting for something else — I wonder whether it will come.' " (V, iv). That Maggie has unspoken longings that Philip cannot fully satisfy is clearly suggested by the oblique, deeply ironic last paragraph of V, v: "And yet, how was it that she was now and then conscious of a certain dim background of relief in the forced separation from Philip? Surely it was only because the sense of a deliverance from concealment was welcome at any cost."

It is the function of Stephen Guest to evoke from Maggie the flowering of sexual passion and thus to engender both her crisis and her death. Book Sixth begins with one of the most consciously stylized chapters in the novel, "A Duet in Paradise," in which Stephen and Lucy carry on light "roguish" banter and small humorous deceptions, with a touch of the drawing-room mock epic. And the author unmistakably confirms this tone: Stephen is presented as Hercules "entrapped" by sewing scissors; Tom is called "as proud as Lucifer" and is compared to Dick Turpin; Philip, who has characterized Haydn's "The Creation" as having "a sort of sugared complacency and flattering make-believe in it," is dismissed by Stephen as "the fallen Adam with a soured temper," while at the same time Stephen claims for himself and Lucy the roles of "Adam and Eve unfallen, in paradise."

Maggie, now nineteen, enters this "prelapsarian" world of innocent pleasure: like a queen in shabby clothes — or a Marie Antoinette out of the Cinderella myth — she moves like a "tall dark-eyed nymph with her jet-black coronet of hair" into an unfamiliar world orchestrated by Lucy as an innocent, twittering fairy godmother. And herein lies the deepest irony and subtlest psychological perception of the novel. The irony is that Maggie, along with Tom and Philip, has long since passed the "Golden Gates" separating the paradise of innocent childhood from the hard realities of the "postlapsarian" world. She is, as it were, an

---

[8] The judgments are spoken by Philip.

age older than Stephen and Lucy, who have not been visited by the "gift of sorrow" or suffered long years in "The Valley of Humiliation." For Maggie, the scene represents not so much a return to a lost paradise as the discovery of a paradise which she has never known and in which, now discovered, her "starved life" drinks as from an "enchanted cup" until she is "at once strong and weak: strong for all enjoyment, weak for all resistance."

Stephen Guest has from the beginning been the object of much moralistic, pseudo-psychological critical acrimony — a band box coxcomb unworthy of the attention of a spirited imaginative girl like Maggie.[9] Such criticism would rewrite *The Mill on the Floss* and deprive it of its subtlest perception. Stephen is surely not the ideal of a great-souled woman: his conscience, though sensitive, has not been finely tempered; he lacks any vision larger than his inheritance and habits and landed provincial expectations, i.e., to represent St. Ogg's in Parliament. But one measure of his undeveloped potential is his very susceptibility to the catalyzing effect of Maggie herself. He will, we may assume, be deeply altered by the shattering experience of which she is the agent.

For Maggie, Stephen momentarily completes a mythic model. She is fresh from the depressing drudgery of a third-rate schoolroom to which (or to something worse) she must soon return, and he becomes, in her imagination, an adoring prince to her hungry Cinderella. And for a fatal moment she allows the imaginative dimension of her personality to have fulfillment — a dimension which Philip cannot adequately sustain and upon which prosaic Tom, the bickering Dodsons, and the bleak future have all turned their hostile pea-shooters.

At the charity bazaar (VI, ix) Maggie confides to Dr. Kenn, in "one of those moments of implicit revelation in which her whole history is summed up, "O, *I must go*"; later at the inn at Mudport (VI, xiv) she elaborates, in a manner more attuned to Stephen's less morally intuitive understanding, the opposite thesis: "O, *I must go back*." Within this short curve Maggie forfeits the alternative to tragedy: despite all the forepangs of conscience, despite loyalty, love, and belief, Maggie yields for a few brief hours to a narcotic "high." And it is of the utmost significance to notice three aspects of this brief experience: (1) it is positively antipodal to the life style she had adopted in her puberty crisis under the guidance of Thomas à Kempis, the hedonistic

---

[9] See Leslie Stephen, "George Eliot," *Cornhill*, XLIII (1881), 152-68.

Hellenic opposite to his Hebraic self-immolation. (2) She returns to clarity of consciousness *and* conscience through the intermediate sub-conscious stage of dream, in which the legend of St. Ogg merges with her temporarily submerged value system and in which, in a frantic effort to reach out to Lucy and to Philip-Tom, she upsets the boat and begins to sink. (3) She learns at last what renunciation means — not "quiet ecstasy" but "that sad patient loving strength which holds the clue of life. . . ."

Maggie, then, has learned that Herculean secret, self-knowledge, which in the tragic tradition is worth the highest price: death. The rest is poetic justice: that the babbling world of St. Ogg's should reject her; that her stiff-necked brother should cast her out; that her weak, in-effectual mother should suddenly and unequivocally see her duty toward her; that the church should make fervid but futile efforts to succor her; that Philip should see right to the heart of the matter ("the strong attraction which drew you together proceeded only from one side of your characters, and belonged to that partial, divided action of our nature which makes half the tragedy of the human lot"); that Lucy should come to her as on a pilgrimage; that Stephen's period of recon-ciliation with the deeper truth should be painful and prolonged; that the curve of Maggie's life (with its struggles, failures, and repentances) should be short; that her death should come in the redemptive act of trying to save the life of her brother; and that "in their death they were not divided."

Silas Marner is unique in the canon. Some of George Eliot's other novelettes — those in *Scenes,* or "The Lifted Veil" and "Brother Jacob" — approach it in length; none is like it in character.

She herself referred to it as "a sort of legendary tale."[10] If we gloss her term with others — such as "emblematic narrative," "fable" or "parable," "moral allegory," "myth," "folk tale," and "fairy tale" — we are perhaps brought within a fruitful literary frame of reference for appreciating its uniqueness among her stories. It is an "emblematic narrative" in the sense that Wordsworth's "Michael" is, and it is likely that "Michael" was the model on which she rang her extensive varia-tions: she took her thematic motto from the poem, and she "felt all through as if the story would have lent itself best to metrical rather than prose fiction, especially in all that relates to the psychology of

[10] *Letters,* III, 382.

Silas. . . ."[11] That she had in mind the simple models of biblical narrative she signals, through style, in the first two chapters: "In this way it came to pass," "Thus it came to pass." It is her "fairy tale" cast of mind that hinders Mrs. Godfrey Cass from understanding why Cinderella (Eppie) doesn't leap at the chance to "come to the castle." The major motif of the gold and the golden hair obviously brush against the Midas myth. The folk tales of dwarfs, ghosts, gnomes, and brownies, perhaps in league with the devil and in command of occult powers that must be propitiated, condition the provincial response to Silas for years after his mysterious arrival in Raveloe. Dunsy's remark to Godfrey — "so you must keep me by you for your crooked sixpence" — a folk motif that Hardy uses later in *The Return of the Native,* employs a fetish for warding off evil spirits. The sequence on the pedlar after the disappearance of Silas's gold (I, viii) seems to be a lightly traced exemplification of the way myth grows in the excited provincial imagination. And Silas in his squat stone house, perpetually weaving, cursed, cut off from memory, deprived of every "breath of poetry," and trying to establish fellowship with his pots and crocks and gold, suggests a crushing inversion of the Lady of Shalott myth. But perhaps the modernized myth that is most pervasive in the story is the Christ myth: the two most crucial experiences of Silas's pilgrimage (the theft of his gold, the mysterious appearance of Eppie) occur at the Christmas season. The death-resurrection theme determines the curve of the narrative: Silas undergoes "the Lethean influence of exile"; he is "a dead man come to life again"; the agency of his resurrection from the nadir of an "insect-like existence" is the love engendered by a mysterious child; the overall time frame of the story is made up of approximately thirty-three years. But George Eliot's method in handling this element in the story is comparable to Tennyson's in his *Idylls of the King,* the first volume of which had appeared in 1859. There is an allegorical or parabolic drift in the story, but there is no incident that cannot be taken realistically. And it is this muted counterpoint between fact and fable that gives *Silas Marner* its special character.

From George Eliot's hint, we may assume that her principal concern was with "the psychology of Silas." It is in her handling not of the fable but of the lost and recovered identity of Silas that we find our most dramatic, and climactic, illustration of her perception of the nature and function of memory in her early novels.

Silas can understand only such language and customs of Raveloe

[11] *Ibid.*

as faintly stir his memory of the past. He can thus understand sickness from remembrance of his mother and the relief she got from foxglove (I, ii) ; he can understand the far-reaching effects of false accusation through the memory of his ordeal in Lantern Yard (I, vii). But the central experience that highlights this theme and makes the metamorphosis of Silas credible is his discovery of Eppie:

> In utter amazement, Silas fell on his knees and bent his head low to examine the marvel: it was a sleeping child — a round, fair thing, with soft yellow rings all over its head. Could this be his little sister come back to him in a dream — his little sister whom he had carried about in his arms for a year before she died, when he was a small boy without shoes or stockings? That was the first thought that darted across Silas's blank wonderment. *Was* it a dream? He rose to his feet again, pushed his logs together, and, throwing on some dried leaves and sticks, raised a flame; but the flame did not disperse the vision — it only lit up more distinctly the little round form of the child, and its shabby clothing. It was very much like his little sister. Silas sank into his chair powerless, under the double presence of an inexplicable surprise and a hurrying influx of memories. How and when had the child come in without his knowledge? He had never been beyond the door. But along with that question, and almost thrusting it away, there was a vision of the old home and the old streets leading to Lantern Yard — and within that vision another, of the thoughts which had been present with him in those far-off scenes. The thoughts were strange to him now, like old friendships impossible to revive; and yet he had a dreamy feeling that this child was somehow a message come to him from that far-off life: it stirred fibres that had never been moved in Raveloe — old quiverings of tenderness — old impressions of awe at the presentiment of some Power presiding over his life; for his imagination had not yet extricated itself from the sense of mystery in the child's sudden presence, and had formed no conjectures of ordinary natural means by which the event could have been brought about. [I, xii]

For the first time Silas's memory overlaps the chilling experience of his chapel days in Lantern Yard by which his trust in God and man was shattered. Instead it reaches back to the days of his early childhood, in the old home, with his mother and little sister; and it penetrates yet further, a vision within a vision, to the inner experience of love, affection, sympathy, service, reverence, awe, mystery. Thus he begins to recover the springs of his identity so long choked up by the exile and isolation of an especially "impressible, self-doubting," "deerlike," "loving nature."

Correlative to this perception is the contrast between the psychological effects of a life dominated by Mammon worship and one drawn into the mainstream of joy, discovery, and growth:

> ...and in this way, as the weeks grew to months, the child created fresh and fresh links between his life and the lives from which he had hitherto shrunk continually into narrower isolation. Unlike the gold which needed nothing, and must be worshipped in locked solitude — which was hidden away from the daylight, was deaf to the song of birds, and started to no human tones — Eppie was a creature of endless claims and ever-growing desires, seeking and loving sunshine, and living sounds, and living movements; making trial of everything, with trust in new joy, and stirring the human kindness in all eyes that looked on her. The gold had kept his thoughts in an ever-repeated circle, leading to nothing beyond itself; but Eppie was an object compacted of changes and hopes that forced his thoughts onward, and carried them far away from their old eager pacing towards the same blank limit — carried them away to the new things that would come with the coming years, when Eppie would have learned to understand how her father Silas cared for her; and make him look for images of that time in the ties and charities that bound together the families of his neighbours. The gold had asked that he should sit weaving longer and longer, deafened and blinded more and more to all things except the monotony of his loom and the repetition of his web; but Eppie called him away from his weaving, and made him think all its pauses a holiday, reawakening his senses with her fresh life, even to the old winter-flies that came crawling forth in the early spring sunshine, and warming him into joy because *she* had joy.
>
> And when the sunshine grew strong and lasting, so that the buttercups were thick in the meadows, Silas might be seen in the sunny midday, or in the late afternoon when the shadows were lengthening under the hedgerows, strolling out with uncovered head to carry Eppie beyond the Stone-pits to where the flowers grew, till they reached some favourite bank where he could sit down, while Eppie toddled to pluck the flowers, and make remarks to the winged things that murmured happily above the bright petals, calling "Dad-dad's" attention continually by bringing him the flowers. Then she would turn her ear to some sudden bird-note, and Silas learned to please her by making signs of hushed stillness, that they might listen for the note to come again: so that when it came, she set up her small back and laughed with gurgling triumph. Sitting on the banks in this way, Silas began to look for the once familiar herbs again; and as the leaves, with their unchanged outline and markings, lay on his palm, there was a sense of crowding remembrances

from which he turned away timidly, taking refuge in Eppie's little world, that lay lightly on his enfeebled spirit.

As the child's mind was growing into knowledge, his mind was growing into memory: as her life unfolded, his soul, long stupefied in a cold narrow prison, was unfolding too, and trembling gradually into full consciousness. [I, xiv]

Thus Eppie serves not as an external (and thus sentimental) symbol but as the aptest psychological and spiritual companion to the dwarfed, imprisoned identity of Silas. As she experiences her childhood, he recovers his; together their souls have a "fair seedtime," and together they grow up.

Memory, then, is a fundamental dimension of George Eliot's psychological conception of her characters *and their mutual relations.* Like such literary predecessors as Scott and Wordsworth and like many of her contemporaries — Tennyson, for example, Ruskin, and, somewhat later, Proust — she found her imagination most fruitfully stirred by the remembrance of things past. It became a means by which she could examine the capacities of her characters for love, loyalty, and belief against the dynamic process of an evolving culture. Thus her novels represent a study of the efforts of individuals and groups to negotiate their present lives with a somewhat imperious history, their society's and their own. In her first three novels this negotiation has three discrete results. In *Adam Bede,* although there is a very substantial tragic undertow, the principals achieve a significant degree of self-development and face the future with genuine, if muted, confidence. In *The Mill on the Floss* Tom and Maggie achieve at least symbolic reconciliation, but their serenity comes after a prolonged period of passionate turbulence in which temperaments and social premises are brought into violent confrontation and for which death and the acceptance of death provide the only nonsentimental resolution. *Silas Marner,* a study in dehumanization of the death-in-life variety, functions at a more fabulous level and suggests, with a fullness not discoverable in the earlier novels, how the fractured personality may recover its identity and restore to the present the lost self of a distant past.

TEN

Structure and Genre in *Daniel Deronda*

BY LEON GOTTFRIED

From the date of its publication, George Eliot's last novel, *Daniel Deronda,* has been the subject of intense critical controversy. The arguments have ranged over many issues, but the centrally recurrent question has been that of the unity of the novel's two plots and, secondarily, the effect of the double plot on the overall quality of the work. For many reasons, readers have found the novel at least weakened if not vitiated by its "Jewish" plot. Some of these — F. R. Leavis being their leading spokesman for our time — have gone so far as to propose and even to carry out a surgical operation, separating the "good" from the "bad" part, so that the story of Gwendolen Harleth could stand forth unencumbered as a distinct masterpiece of psychological, social, and ethical realism, demonstrating George Eliot's wisdom and artistry at their ripest. These critics generally denounce the Deronda plot for lacking realism in character, dialogue, moral depth, etc., and they are inclined to attribute the alleged failure to psychological soft spots in the author — vestiges of infantile fantasy-making and wishful thinking.

On the other hand, there have been sympathetic critics from the first who not only have considered *Daniel Deronda* highly artistic in its interweaving of two plots and many worlds but have even believed it to be its author's masterpiece. Starting with George Eliot's contemporaries Edward Dowden and David Kaufmann, such critics have attempted, sometimes with great sensitivity and ingenuity, to prove the essential unity of the novel by analysis of its time scheme, plot interpenetrations, patterns of analogical and contrasting actions and characters, patterns of imagery, symbolism, allusion, and other technical elements. Such close reading tends to bear out the author's claim that everything in the book is related to everything else, and it is true that any attentive reader may rediscover for himself that technically, at least, *Daniel Deronda* is a highly artful, meticulously planned piece of work. Yet, with all respect to those sympathetic readers who admire the novel as a whole, the opinion of the common reader still seems to be the correct one — *Daniel Deronda* does not, as a whole, cohere organically, in spite of its rich texture and careful organization.

But it is not critically satisfactory to fall back upon psychological or other extrinsic explanations of what we find inadequate, nor do I believe that it is relevant to criticize the Daniel Deronda plot simply on the ground that it lacks "realism." For the fact is that George Eliot has attempted, with a high degree of artistic consciousness and for very specific reasons, to join into a single work a novel and a romance, and we can make little progress toward understanding this work if we merely criticize the romance as though it were a novel.[1] Furthermore, I believe that her purpose was justifiable and was not in itself responsible for her failure. It was a purpose shared in various ways and degrees, not only by such masters of romance as Scott, Dickens, Dostoyevsky, Hawthorne, and Melville but also by such "realists" as Fielding, Henry James, and James Joyce — namely, to poeticize the novel. By that I mean precisely to develop in the novel an art form fully answerable to all the demands of mythic expression and fully equal to poetry, the traditional vehicle for myth, thereby to assist in making the world of the higher imagination available to modern man.

Given her intention, we may look upon George Eliot's entire career as a preparation for the writing of *Daniel Deronda,* and it will not be surprising to find that she, and some of her more sympathetic readers, believed that in her final novel she had composed her masterpiece. In most of her fiction through *Middlemarch* she had explored the possibilities of realism, and enlarged them in her way, as fully as any of the great realists of the century. She had also developed superb resources

---

[1] Such criticism, for example, perhaps forgetful of Sir Walter Scott's Covenanters, queries the credibility of Mordecai's manner of speaking on the ground that no one whose native tongue was English could "really" so adapt his speech to the language of biblical poetry and prophecy. George Eliot herself compares the effect she seeks with that of Scott's Balfour of Burley; see George Eliot to John Blackwood, Feb. 25, 1876, in *The George Eliot Letters,* ed. Gordon S. Haight, 7 vols. (London and New Haven, Conn., 1955), VI, 223. In my use of the terms "novel" and "romance" I am generally following Northrop Frye, *Anatomy of Criticism,* 2nd ed. (New York, 1967), pp. 186-92, 303-6.

— Shakespearean, they have been called — of control of imagery and symbolism, in addition to her mastery of scene, dialogue, and psychological and social observation and notation. She had also, in her verse, attempted more or less pure mytho-romantic projections, even if not very successfully. In *Romola* she had deliberately sought to interweave romance and symbolism with history,[2] and in *Silas Marner* she had succeeded very well in uniting social realism with fable. Finally, in *Middlemarch* she had pushed her possibilities as a realistic novelist to new heights of perception and realization. She was now ready for something different. In her quest for enlargement of the novel's capabilities she was not alone in the nineteenth century. In Russia Tolstoy, a greater realist even than George Eliot, was using something he called "history" to give mythic dimension to his *War and Peace,* while Dostoyevsky (like Dickens in England) was searching in the dark corners of the psyche's projective processes for new fictive modes and images. In America Melville and Hawthorne, like Poe, had composed tales of pure imagination and had also struggled to bring the world of fact, of history, into significant relationship with myth and romance. Hawthorne had helped especially to bring the more ancient genre back into light by so usefully reminding us of the generic distinction between the novel and the romance.

A central modern literary problem has been that of evolving vital literary forms acceptable to our empirical and skeptical age, forms that could win assent as "serious" or "credible" but that could yet stir us in the deepest roots of our humanity, "where all the ladders start." Since *Don Quixote,* novelists have been uneasily eying the world of romance, with its capacity for giving expression to an inner world of dreams, wishes, and secret fears. But with the "rise of the novel" in the eighteenth-century world of Locke and Defoe, the romance was compelled to go into hiding or to appear carefully disguised in the dress of everyday reality, like the gods of ancient Greece in Heine's fable. To be sure, the romance has maintained a continuous life in popular literature, and even during the eighteenth century it did not utterly disappear even from the higher literature, as we can see from the underlying structure of *Tom Jones.* In the Romantic period, as might be expected, the mode of high romance was revived by Scott and others, but for the most part during the eighteenth and much of the nineteenth centuries, the elements of romance, as far as prose literature was

---

[2] George Eliot to Sara Sophia Hennell, Aug. 23, 1863, *Letters,* IV, 103-4.

concerned, had to be absorbed into the form most acceptable to the modern, empirically minded audience: that is, into the novel.

But the romance set a high price on its services to the novel. It required incorporation into the basic structure in order to work at all. It could freely yield the surface to realism, for romantic devices used obtrusively or superficially are almost certain to appear as serious if not fatal defects in a novel. Invisibly assimilated into the substructure of the younger form, however, the romance can be a deep source of strength for the novel. A novelist, then, who feels the power of romance to reach those depths of psychic response touched by myth might follow Hawthorne's course of locating romance in a recognizable world. Hawthorne's interesting failure in *The Marble Faun* attests to some of the difficulties in placing too obvious a romance in a modern setting. A more promising means of wedding the world of the senses to the world of romance was that of Henry James. Essentially, it consists of keeping the reader engrossed and "believing" in the credibility of the events he consciously perceives, while the mythic elements of the underplot do their work unobserved — the work, that is, of kindling and modifying our responses at the deeper and perhaps unconscious levels of imaginative intuition. In one of the places where he discusses the matter, his preface to the New York edition of *The American,* James uses the figure of a balloon. As romancer, his task is to lure the reader into the gondola of the moored craft, and then to cut the hawser so gently, so deftly, that the reader is borne aloft from earth without ever quite realizing when the rope was cut, or even perhaps that it has been cut.

Now turning back to *Daniel Deronda,* we see that George Eliot's use of her favorite device of double plotting presents a special problem, for while one of her plots is pre-eminently novelistic, the other is radically romantic. Hence, apart from the quality of either in itself and in spite of the artful means employed to connect them, the two plots do not inhabit the same universe. Gwendolen Harleth is at the center of one of these fictional worlds, Mordecai at the center of the other, and Daniel Deronda is the mediator between them. That there should be a gulf between these worlds is, to be sure, a significant part of the author's intention, underscored by her use of contrasting images of pettiness, narrowness, and agoraphobia in Gwendolen's world, and of broad horizons, open vistas, and long views in the world of Daniel and Mordecai. Indeed, the theme of the novel, taken as a whole, requires some such difference, for just as windows must be opened in the stuffy and frightened enclosures of Gwendolen's mind before she can be born as a moral being, so Daniel's amorphous moral yearnings must be channeled into a definite vocation before he can leave his prolonged adolescence and become a man. But as far as this moral theme goes, we can also find in such a character as Klesmer the embodiment of depth, breadth, and commitment, and yet he belongs completely to the "realistic" plot and world. The problem confronting the reader is that the gulf between the worlds of Gwendolen Harleth and Mordecai is more than social, psychological, or moral. It is ontological, like that which separates, for example, Emma Woodhouse from Heathcliff.

Double plotting in itself can be a valuable technique, and George Eliot herself has handled it beautifully, for example, in *Middlemarch.* But if we compare *Daniel Deronda* with *Middlemarch,* or with *Anna Karenina,* we can readily see that in these double-plotted novels, both plots move within the same universe and share the same assumptions about reality. In *Daniel Deronda,* however, Gwendolen has her being in a world of mixed motives, moral choices, and psychological causation where the laws of consequence (almost of Nemesis) hold merciless power. But in his life apart from Gwendolen Daniel exists, like most heroes of romance, in a world governed by a prefigurative pattern of muffled birth secrets, omens, mystic talismans, clairvoyant recognitions, mysterious heralds, typological recurrence, ritual deaths, rebirths, initiations, and apotheoses. Certainly Gwendolen's story also makes use of some unlikely coincidences and melodramatic elements, but its ambience remains that of Dr. Leavis's "Great Tradition," the tradition of what Lionel Trilling has called "moral realism." In the "Jewish" plot, however, not only some details but the essential structure of the story is of another order, and this structure, when examined, reveals a carefully planned mythic organization that takes on, literarily, the form of romance.

Let us look at some of the elements of the Daniel Deronda plot, apart from Daniel's involvement with Gwendolen. Daniel, a foundling of mysterious, faintly alien, but presumably high-born parentage, is reared in a foster home. He is endowed with all the unmistakable attributes of the hero, at least *de nos jours:* intelligence, good looks, physical vigor, magnanimity, artistic talent, moral sensitivity, unimpeachable virtue, and intrinsic aristocracy enhanced by aristocratic training. At the age of thirteen (a Jewish boy's confirmation age) he suffers a shock in respect to the secret of his birth that starts him on his quest for identity. He is attracted to water, especially rivers; one day, later in his life, he rescues from drowning a mysterious damsel, herself of alien extraction but also a creature of perfect virtue, talent, beauty, natural aristocracy, and reverent humility. He promptly falls in love with her but assumes that they must be forever separated by their different ancestries. In his peregrinations he is "recognized" twice by mysterious strangers (Mordecai and Joseph Kalonymos) as the awaited leader or savior of their (his) people, but he rejects both "recognitions." At last he is compelled to a recognition of his true identity by a third mysterious stranger who turns out to be his own mother. This regal woman had once, as she asserts, reigned as a queen (of the stage) for nine years before disappearing to become mother of the hero. She had attempted to deny the fate marked out for him by ancient prophecy but finally had to succumb to it. She presents him with three gifts: the secret of his identity, the prophecy concerning his fate, and a talisman (her miniature portrait). The hero, now triumphantly armed, goes to a foreign city to claim his birthright (a trunkful of strange old documents, with its "curious key") and to fulfill his aborted recognition by one of the strangers, his father's old friend. He then returns to his home (foster) country to be united in the bond of brotherhood with the first mysterious stranger, Mordecai, and of marriage with the maiden to whom he can now claim the right. He dedicates himself to a life of heroic leadership in the quest to redeem his people and finally disappears into the East.

This tale reflects a variety of typical hero myths, but it most particularly resembles that of Moses in the Old Testament, a resemblance underscored by explicit reference in several places in the text. Like his prototype, Daniel has been abandoned in infancy by his mother to save him from real or imagined slavery. He is taken across the water to a land where he is reared as a princeling in the wealthy house of the ruling family (class) and given all the advantages of that position. Ultimately he is called upon to use his gifts, both natural and acquired, to raise his fallen people from their bondage — not only to alien governors but also to their own servile attitudes, which are the result of long oppression and degradation. The story of Moses and the bulrushes undergoes reversal and displacement, but otherwise the pattern is remarkably straightforward.

The modern Moses, however, must be appropriate for the later age. He cannot be merely a tribal chieftain; he must be both man of the world and spiritual emancipator. That he will be a man of the world is assured by his training as an English gentleman (just as Moses was an Egyptian aristocrat), but for his role as spiritual emancipator, he needs a second or spiritual education. This will be provided by a mentor. Here Daniel's story also borrows from that of Jesus, for Daniel's mentor is also a herald and a forerunner, a martyr and prophet who prepares the way by preaching the message of the coming of one greater than himself and by initiating (baptizing) his successor when he appears. (It goes without saying, perhaps, that these motifs are all within the Hebrew messianic tradition.) Like Moses and Christ, Daniel emerges reborn from a river, the man of the East coming in a glory from the West, in his epiphany to Mordecai at Blackfriars Bridge. Unlike Moses, but in keeping with the teachings of the later prophets, the Christ-like Daniel is to be a savior not only of the Jews but, through them, of the Gentiles as well, for his values (and, it should be emphasized, those of Mordecai also) are universalistic, not tribal. He is to lead in the great reconciliation of "separateness and communication" under the mystic Unity in the Jews' profession of faith (the Sh'ma). It is Daniel who, by being what he is and by leading the revival of the Jews, is to be a bridge between past and future, East and West, England and Europe, Europe and Asia, Christianity and Judaism, and (why not?) art and life.[3]

If the skeptical reader thinks that I may be overstating the case, let me assure him that quite the reverse is true. For George Eliot has taken almost no end of pains to direct the reader's attention to the mythic and heroic possibilities of real life in the here and now. She overtly compares Daniel not only to Moses and, more guardedly, to Christ but also to Orestes, Rinaldo, the prophet Ezra, and, through imagery or allusion,[4] to still other heroic figures. Indeed, I have omitted mention of many of the omens, portents, signs, and symbols employed by the author, selecting only the most obvious points required to illustrate the structure of heroic romance in the Daniel Deronda story.

If the task of subtly merging romance and novel as described by Henry James is a difficult one, how much more difficult is that which George Eliot set for herself in *Daniel Deronda*. For here she has attempted to create an unbroken continuum while linking together one plot almost devoid of mythic dimension, almost painful in its intensely

---

[3] See the epigraph from Heine at the head of VIII, lxiii.

[4] George Eliot can be enormously persuasive in her use of allusion. See, for example, her skillful introduction of Leopardi's *Ode to Italy* (V, xxxix; VI, xlv), with its clearly implied but unexpressed relevance to the Daniel Deronda plot.

imagined realism (in spite of a few mythological allusions and melo-dramatic incidents), with another that is almost purely romantic and mythic in both form and texture. To be sure, she had a purpose in doing so, that of attempting to express the interaction and possibility of a continuum between the narrow world of daily life and that of possible heroic fulfillment. But perhaps the very purity of her means defeated her. For the novel of Gwendolen Harleth, in itself a major achieve-ment of realism, cannot cohere with the world of Daniel Deronda, which is so essentially romantic. Gwendolen's story is rich in social and psychological realism, and it centers on the theme of growing moral awareness. Daniel's, on the other hand, contains neither society nor psychology, and in place of developing moral consciousness there is predestination and recognition.

George Eliot's delineation of the Cohen family, as an attempt to add social dimension to the "Jewish" plot, is something of a *tour de force*. But plainly the Cohens' honored boarder, Mordecai, moves and has his being in a world not dreamed of in their philosophy. They provide a background, not a society, for the visionary heroes, as do the Meyricks, another attempt, less successful and more sentimental, to give the Daniel Deronda plot some social density. But these two families exist only within the stage settings of their respective homes. It is significant that only these two families are admitted as guests to the wedding of the hero, but they still do not provide a real social ambience for the wedded pair. At most they are a circle of admiring but uncomprehend-ing observers, a chorus, turned with reverence and some pride toward the charmed inner circle within which dwells only the community of saints — Mordecai, the prophet; Daniel, the bride of Mordecai's soul (the imagery is the author's); and the ethereal Mirah, sister of Mor-decai and earthly bride of Daniel.

The absence or thinness of social texture, not uncommon in romance but so different from George Eliot's characteristic mode of social real-ism, is matched in the Daniel Deronda plot by the lack of that psycho-logical richness for which George Eliot as novelist is so notable. It is true that she offers many long and sometimes tedious pages of at-tempted psychological explanation of her hero, but such explanations are no substitute for the quickness and penetration with which she handles, often with a minimum of explanation, such characters as Klesmer or Sir Hugo Mallinger, not to mention Gwendolen Harleth. In any case, psychology seems almost irrelevant here, for we are deal-ing with characters whose actual being is in a world of myth and magic rather than of cause and effect. Admittedly Daniel has some moments of ordinary humanness, such as are never allowed to Mirah or Mordecai, but they are fleeting and insignificant in the general consistency of his self-possession and the ease with which he copes with moral problems, including that of his evident attraction to Gwendolen. In truly mythic fashion, Daniel *is;* he never really *becomes.* His selfhood is more a matter of discovery than of achievement. What is true for Daniel is even more fully the case for the other two inhabitants of his heroic world, and all attempts to provide the brother and sister with a past fail really to explain them at all. George Eliot did not, then, ease us into her balloon of romance and then deftly cut the rope without our full awareness. She has instead actually forced our attention to the vast gulf between the balloon and the ground of the empirical world by attaching her romance to one of the most powerfully conceived and finely articulated pieces of realistic fiction we have in English.

If the major problem of unity in *Daniel Deronda* derives from the severe discontinuity of the genres of the two plots, the problem is enhanced by differences in the fullness of vision embodied in them. In his early review of the novel Edward Dowden grasped with full sympathy the author's intention of uniting what he called her "poetic" gifts with her novelistic genius.[5] But if she expressed her "poetry" in the Daniel Deronda plot, we must ask whether it is sufficiently rich and full to balance the realism in the other. It is not a serious objection that the characters in the romantic plot are too "flat" or lack social and psychological complexity; that is quite permissible in romance. What is more serious is the absence, in her "poetic" vision, of a sense of the demonic or the inexplicably destructive, of darkness as a necessary setting for the light. The great romancers from Spenser to Hawthorne have sensed, consciously or intuitively, the profound connections between our wishes (the "good") and the fears that are their shadows, and they have been compelled to take account in their work of these darker powers. Indeed, modern romancers have sometimes been accused of imbalance in their obsession with the power of darkness.

In popular, sentimental romance, "evil" is always displaced; it is "other" — the yellow peril, the sinister Jew, the diabolical Communist agent, etc. — but nevertheless it is a necessary part of the scheme. In

[5] Edward Dowden, "Middlemarch and Daniel Deronda," in *Studies in Literature 1789-1877* (London, 1909), pp. 275-76. Essay reprinted from *Contemporary Review* for Feb. 9, 1877.

high romance, on the other hand, the relationship between good and evil is far more intimate, mysterious, and compelling. Now certainly George Eliot was not deficient in moral perception; as much as any other English novelist she understood moral complexity and possessed a sense of the reality of evil in the phenomenal world. But in application it was only in that world that she could deal — and how masterfully! — with it. For whatever combination of temperamental and philosophical reasons, "evil" seems to have had no metaphysical reality for her. She could understand it only in relation to the intricate network of minute causes and effects that govern our daily lives. "Evil" was a problem to be analyzed and, if not solved, then at least understood; it was not a transcendent mystery. In the character of Grandcourt, Gwendolen's draconian possessor, George Eliot has created what may be a triumphant exception to these strictures — a monstrous and unredeemed yet highly believable and vital compound of egoism, satiety, and lust for power. But even allowing that he is an exception, it remains true that Grandcourt exists only in her "real" world. She permits no such wickedness to invade her "poetic" universe; hence there can be no such character in her romance.

While George Eliot excluded from her "poetry" the "mystery of iniquity" (to use a Pauline phrase much admired by Melville), she did possess a strong sense of the ultimate inexplicability of goodness. The latter appears to be the source of her romantic imagination, and it accounts for such characters as Mordecai, Mirah, and Daniel as well as for such sentimental aberrations as the Meyrick ladies. The forces of darkness, which are real enough in her last novel, are almost entirely contained within the realistic Gwendolen Harleth plot. Mirah's father, a genuine villain, is the only possible exception. But he is really only a petty criminal and a weakling, not a potent threat to the order of virtue. He is "bad," not "evil," and he may do harm, but he cannot undermine (unlike Grandcourt, for example). He exists in the story principally to provide an opportunity for the purely good to exercise their virtue. Great novelist though she was, George Eliot did not have the comprehensive imagination that could populate one single microcosm with three such figures as Billy Budd, Claggart, and Captain Vere, and that could set in motion the sequence of events in which Billy, a saint, becomes a guiltless murderer whose own death is required to balance some awesome cosmic scale.

Yet in spite of the disparities of genre and of ethical assumptions in the two plots of *Daniel Deronda,* the Siamese twins are too intimately joined to sustain surgical separation. Not only is Daniel personally indispensable to the Gwendolen plot, but his whole story of self-discovery is vital to the thematic structure of the book. The author's plan required a double perspective so that her modern hero could be seen simultaneously against a background of ordinary reality and heroic myth. If we allow that double plotting in such a case may have been desirable and even necessary to give full scope to the ideas and feelings George Eliot wished to embody, what could she have done? That is difficult to answer. To rewrite *Daniel Deronda* in such a way as to realize all its potential while eliminating its incoherence, one would have to be an even better novelist than George Eliot. Many critics would be satisfied by a move toward total realism. Daniel could be cast in a more "human" mold; he might have doubts, mixed motives, even occasionally lose his temper, say or do something hasty or frivolous, or fail at least momentarily to have the right answer in some moral crisis. Most if not all of the mystery of his identity and the plot linked to it would have to be eliminated or much altered. More conflict could be allowed to enter into his situation or, rather, the conflicts latent in it could be allowed to surface and affect the course of events. Mirah could be drastically altered or eliminated and Mordecai considerably revamped. The resulting novel could be a masterpiece of realism, perhaps even a greater work than *Middlemarch* — but it would be of the same kind. If the mythic, romantic elements are thematically essential, then such a revision would change the novel so radically that it would be quite apart from the direction of the author's intention.

Another method might be to use the elements of romance less obtrusively, more subtly, as hints and shadows, and to disperse them carefully through both plots. They should be imperceptible at first to most readers, and perceptible ultimately only to the particularly discerning. Something like this might be the method of Henry James; indeed, it is the method of most of his major novels. But then we should have something else again — a fine Jamesian novel, perhaps, but not what George Eliot seemed to be trying for. Her aim, as Dowden perceived, was to create a work of fiction that would stretch the form to its outermost boundaries, from a realism as uncompromising as that of Flaubert and as rich in texture as that of Tolstoy, to a spiritualized romance as elevated as, let's say, Spenser's *Faerie Queene.* Thus another possible way of preserving both plots and both genres might be to give the romance enough weight of moral complexity to balance that of the Gwendolen Harleth story. The shadow of evil might enter it seriously, and the most serious place would be in the soul of the hero himself. One might imagine, for example, a conflict between altruism and the ugly realities of power in the political story — fit theme for Conrad, perhaps. But this would require far more elaboration of the Zionist element and would seriously unbalance the novel in another way.

Or perhaps the problem is insoluble. In any case, we can never know what George Eliot would have written had she been able to read the later James, Joyce, Proust, Conrad, and Mann before composing it. She did read and freely allude to Dante, but I find no sign that she made any structural use of him. On the basis of what we have, we can say that, like some other major novelists of her time (and some minor ones as well, such as Walter Pater and Oscar Wilde), she found the realistic mode inadequate to express the full extent of her vision of the possibilities of life or art. To extend her range of meanings, she had to extend the range of her art by finding new artistic modes, or by going back to more ancient ones. Had she succeeded, we should be hailing her as a great innovator and pioneer of the modern novel instead of deploring, as so many of her critics do, how she let us down by not giving us another and perhaps even better *Middlemarch*. But if she failed, or partially failed, I should like to see her failure recorded as a noble one, charged not only with high intention but with keen awareness of the state and necessary direction of her art. As a part of the respect we owe to a great novelist, we should judge her art as art even when it does not altogether succeed, and not as a slow leak in her subconscious mind.

ELEVEN

Coming to Terms
with George Meredith's Fiction

BY MARGARET CONROW

Although George Meredith is a major writer of the nineteenth century, academic criticism has not reached a consensus or even a majority opinion about his works. Scholars and critics, like mountain climbers with their mountains, study literature mainly because it is there, and Meredith's originality and historical prominence have challenged some climbers recently. However, we are still side-tracked from the best route through his brambles by the many pitfalls as well as the sudden unexpected vistas that his fiction affords. One of the few points of agreement about him is that his works seem to be made up of (or sometimes patched together with) a great many elements: comedy, romance, psychological analysis, satire, philosophy, lyricism, symbolism, tragedy, tragicomedy. Lately it has even been argued that the element of fact is a salient characteristic of his fiction.[1] Aside from the subject of ingredients, widely varying opinions have been held on his place, importance, value, style, technique, and philosophy. It would be tedious to document the array of attitudes that have been expressed on these subjects by even the major commentators on Meredith. On the other hand, it is very interesting to examine some of the reasons for the difficulty readers have had in coming to terms with George Meredith's fiction.

Several hazards in Meredith's fiction have been partially explored. Some of these, the problems of genre, of unity and authorial intrusion, of the place of intellectual content and philosophy, are common to all criticism. It is not coincidental that novel criticism and Meredithian criticism are both in an unsettled state. Some unresolved problems par-

---

[1] Thornton Y. Booth, *Mastering the Event: Commitment to Fact in George Meredith's Fiction*, Utah State University Monograph Series, vol. XIV, no. 2 (Logan, 1967).

ticular to Meredithian criticism are problems of the comic spirit, of the reception of *Richard Feverel,* of Meredith's biography and reputation, and of the Meredithian style.

Since the one work of criticism that Meredith wrote is *The Essay on Comedy and the Uses of the Comic Spirit* (1877, originally delivered as a lecture), it might seem common sense to consider the comic spirit as central to his own work, but in practice this approach has led critics astray. For instance, interest in the comic spirit partly accounts for the attention paid to *The Egoist* at the expense of the other works of his middle period, the more somber *Beauchamp's Career* and *One of Our Conquerors* and the more romantic *Diana of the Crossways.* Interest in the comic spirit and the comic character of Countess Louisa is responsible for the overrating of *Evan Harrington.* It governs most critics' attitude toward Meredith in spite of some observation that comedy and the *Essay* are not completely reliable guides to either Meredith's practice or his point of view.[2] Because *The Egoist* best illustrates Meredith's theory of comedy, its noncomic elements are glossed over, and it is referred to in limiting terms as a "novel of high comedy," even though this gives a wrong impression of the work.[3] The most recent book on Meredith, V. S. Pritchett's *George Meredith and English Comedy,* has a somewhat misleading title, drawn perhaps from the first chapter. Pritchett actually stresses the romantic and psychological aspects of Meredith's fiction. Yet he also recognizes a combination of modes and tries to unify them by the notion of comedy, falling prey to the idea that this must be the key to Meredith: "He is a poet, a symbolist who must be lyrical; lyrical, he must also be comic: moving from the comedy of manners to the grotesque; there is the social satirist; there is the man of fantasy; there is the realist. And there is the man who has ideas about the state of England; there is the wit and artist who feeling deeply for Nature as a headlong force yet identifies it with the sanity Comedy teaches us."[4]

[2] Gillian Beer, "Meredith's Idea of Comedy, 1876-1880," *Nineteenth-Century Fiction,* XX (1965), 165-76; Frank C. Curtin, "Adrian Harley: The Limits of Meredith's Comedy," *ibid.,* VII (1953), 272-82.

[3] Phyllis Bartlett, *George Meredith: Writers and Their Work,* Supplement 161 to *British Book News* (London, 1963), p. 33; Norman Kelvin, *A Troubled Eden: Nature and Society in the Works of George Meredith* (Stanford, Calif., 1961), p. 104.

[4] V. S. Pritchett, *George Meredith and English Comedy,* Clark Lectures for 1969 (London, 1970), pp. 66-67.

If Meredith's works are not ill-assorted combinations and are not primarily comedies, what are they? Another difficulty in reading Meredith is the problem of genre. We do not know what it is we are reading. Virginia Woolf said that Meredith "has been, it is plain, at great pains to destroy the conventional form of the novel."[5] Should we call him a novelist, or was he something else, a poet writing prose perhaps, or a romancer? Or, as a novelist, did he write the romantic novel, the novel of ideas, the comic novel, the autobiographical novel? His work seems to fall into all categories: *The Amazing Marriage* is his lyric romance,[6] *Vittoria* his historical novel, *Beauchamp's Career* his novel of ideas, *Harry Richmond* his *Bildungsroman,* etc. Since the problem of genre and particularly genre of the novel is of current interest, Meredith may benefit from further investigations into the subject. At present, insofar as the distinction between a novel and a romance is clear, Meredith is a romancer. (Most unclear are the distinctions among the romances: are the American romance of Chase, the symbolic novel of William Tyndall, the prophetic novel of E. M. Forster, the lyric novel of Ralph Freedman, the fictional romantic mode of Scholes and Kellogg, and the modern novel of Maurice Shroder all the same genre or sub-genre?)[7] Reading his books as romances, we should put less emphasis on his satire and comedy, more on his symbolism and imagery, and not expect realism, accommodation to the social scene, historic verisimilitude, or clear and expository prose.[8]

Another recurring subject in Meredithian criticism is complaint about the lack of unity in his fiction.[9] Such complaints are the con-

[5] Virginia Woolf, *The Common Reader; Second Series* (London, 1932), p. 228.

[6] Floyd Lawrence, "Lyric and Romance: Meredith's Poetic Fiction," in *Victorian Essays: A Symposium* ... (Oberlin, Ohio, 1967).

[7] Richard Chase, *The American Novel and Its Tradition* (New York, 1957); William York Tyndall, *The Literary Symbol* (New York, 1955); E. M. Forster, *Aspects of the Novel* (New York, 1927); Ralph Freedman, *The Lyrical Novel: Studies in Herman Hesse, André Gide, and Virginia Woolf* (Princeton, N.J., 1963); Robert Scholes and Robert Kellogg, *The Nature of Narrative* (New York, 1966); Maurice Z. Shroder, "The Novel as Genre," *Massachusetts Review,* IV (1963), 291-308. Essays by Freedman, Scholes and Kellogg, and Shroder are reprinted in Robert Murray Davis, ed., *The Novel: Modern Essays in Criticism* (Englewood Cliffs, N.J., 1969).

[8] The most famous, but not the only, critic of Meredith's social scenes is E. M. Forster in *Aspects of the Novel,* pp. 135-36.

[9] Donald Fanger, "George Meredith as a Novelist," *Nineteenth-Century Fiction,* XVI (1962), 217-328; Henry James to Edmund Gosse, Oct. 11, 1912, in

verse of the more positive emphasis on his richness and variety. Actually the idea of unity is subordinate to the question of genre: both are related to the reader's emotional response to the problem of what attitude he shoud take toward what he is reading. When he has not been able to decide by the end of the work, he says "This is not a novel" or "This work has no unity." An abstract theory of the unity of a work is something very open to logical discussion and analysis, but the psychological appreciation of unity is more complicated. Such a situation gives critics and analytical readers many difficulties. A famous example is the critical problem of the authorial intrusion, which was once most logically and sensibly derided as destroying the unity of a novel as an illusion of life, a critical viewpoint that unfortunately, in spite of its logic, did not fit with the reader's intuitive suspicion that he was possibly more aware of James and Joyce as narrators than he was of Thackeray or Trollope. The recognized importance of Wayne Booth's book *The Rhetoric of Fiction* (1961) is due to the fact that instead of merely opposing intuition to analysis, he sufficiently analyzed the complexity of the problem to better accord with our actual responses. When the authors gave up their position on the sidelines, they did not retreat into the audience but, rather, took over the direction and the acting. This is why Booth gives such importance to the "implied narrator." Pritchett says that "several critics in the '20s . . . saw in Meredith a link with contemporary novelists. . . . The personal conversational voice is clearly the mark of Meredith's immediate successors."[10] Yet sometimes Pritchett also objects to Meredith's personal note. It is not, however, the fact or the degree or the kind of presence that is the problem. Rather, it is that the reader does not know how to "take" Meredith; the problem of the narrator is the same as the problem of the book as a whole. In Meredith's case the reader's uncertainty can be alleviated by approaching him as a romancer rather than as a comic or satiric or social novelist. Gillian Beer's recent book, *Meredith: A Change of Masks*, attempts to settle the genre problem and the unity problem by limiting the major modes to two, the comic and the tragic, and by showing that Meredith's books constantly shift and change throughout between a comic and tragic view of their subjects.[11] Her book is the best sympathetic study so far of Meredith's peculiar gifts,

The Letters of Henry James, selected and edited by Percy Lubbock, 2 vols. (New York, 1920), II, 250-52.

   [10] Pritchett, *Meredith and English Comedy,* pp. 39-41.

   [11] Gillian Beer, *Meredith: A Change of Masks* (London, 1970).

so her approach has its merits. However, the qualities of romances suggested in the studies mentioned above seem a better and clearer description of Meredith's effects.

At one time what seemed most important about Meredith was his philosophy and his ethical ideas. These were highly regarded if not overrated at the turn of the century, and the inflation of his reputation at that time was partly responsible for his following eclipse. He suffered not only from the general reaction against Victorianism but from the reaction in New Criticism against content as opposed to form. With the reintroduction of ideas as a permissible subject of criticism, Meredith is again in a curious position. In many ways less didactic than his great contemporaries Thackeray, Eliot, and Dickens, he nevertheless partly qualifies for his position somewhere near them by the very ambition and largeness of his ultimately ethical purpose. Beer, who emphasizes the artistry of the novels, observes that "Meredith's intensely experimental approach to the novel is always a part of his moral concern with human personality."[12] It is even possible that he will be revived once again mainly for his ideas rather than for his artistic achievements. The view of Meredith as a philosopher and sage is not absent from the two studies of Meredith published prior to Pritchett's and Beer's, Walter Wright's *Art and Substance in George Meredith* and Norman Kelvin's *A Troubled Eden*.[13] It is hoped that the suggestion that he be revived for his difficulties, as a "teachable author," will not catch hold.[14]

On the question of the relationship of an author's ideas to his fictional creations, Gerald Bullett has made this provocative comment on George Eliot: "If you are a character in a George Eliot novel, the chief thing you have to fear is your author's unqualified moral approval."[15] All readers of Eliot must feel the truth of this remark. Yet a character owes his quality to his author's ideas and moral opinions as well as to his author's powers of observation and sympathy. Whether the characters or the ideas are going to dominate depends on whether

---

[12] *Ibid.*, p. 2.

[13] Walter Wright, *Art and Substance in George Meredith* (Lincoln, Nebr., 1953), p. 4; Kelvin, *A Troubled Eden*, p. 104.

[14] Thornton Y. Booth, "Consider George Meredith," *English Journal*, LV (1966), 690-95.

[15] Gerald Bullett, *George Eliot: Her Life and Books* (New Haven, Conn., 1948), p. 182; recalled in Louis Auchincloss, "Is George Eliot Salvageable?" in *Reflections of a Jacobite* (New York, 1961), p. 59.

or not the author's opinion of them is indeed unqualified, or whether it is sufficiently objective for the reader to feel some independence in them and toward them. Phyllis Bartlett says that the "power of Meredith's heroes and heroines to recover their mental health and vitality after damaging experiences" is one reason for reading Meredith, and she speaks of "the spirit of having 'come through' [which] pervades most of Meredith's novels."[16] His characters do illustrate his ideas and attitudes — for instance, he was optimistic about the possibilities for personal freedom — but in his best works they also have an independent quality that comes from a flexibility in his own attitude toward them, even though the reader is aware that he has a personal opinion about them. An interesting example of this living quality coexisting with the author's moral judgments is found in *Diana of the Crossways*, which we shall discuss later.

The reception of Meredith's first major work, *The Ordeal of Richard Feverel*, published in 1859, is an important subject in Meredithian criticism. The book was thought to be immoral by several reviewers and by readers of Mudie's Circulating Library, who caused it to be withdrawn from that list.[17] The importance of this reception and its effect on Meredith personally and on his subsequent fiction are matters still unsettled. They have been taken up recently by L. T. Hergenhan, who has extensively studied the early reviews of Meredith. Hergenhan seems to think that a misreading of the book, caused by its confusions and ambiguities, was more important than the morality issue, at least among the reviewers.[18] He argues that the morality question was ignored in subsequent reviews of Meredith's work, except by R. H. Hutton in the *Spectator*'s review of *Vittoria*.[19] However, although it is worthwhile to keep separate the complaints by the reviewers and the complaints by Mudie's readers, it is clearly not quite true that the subject had no continuing life. It surfaced again with the appearance of *Modern Love*,[20] and in connection with his fiction it appeared in Justin Mc-

[16] Phyllis Bartlett, "The Novels of George Meredith," *Review of English Literature*, III (1962), 43.

[17] Lionel Stevenson, *The Ordeal of George Meredith* (New York, 1953), pp. 72-73.

[18] L. T. Hergenhan, "The Reception of George Meredith's Early Novels," *Nineteenth-Century Fiction*, XIX (1964), 213-35.

[19] L. T. Hergenhan, "George Meredith and 'The Snuffling Moralist': Moral Disapproval of His Early Works and Its Effects," *Balcony*, no. 5 (1966), 3-12.

[20] Stevenson, *The Ordeal*, p. 110.

Carthy's significant article in the *Westminster Review*.[21] Another very
interesting feature of this article is that McCarthy also discusses the
novels of Mrs. Caroline Norton, the model for *Diana of the Crossways*.
The article is in some ways favorable to Meredith, but it is not likely
that he appreciated the revival of his troubles with *Richard Feverel*
by such praises as the following: "We are so thoroughly impressed with
the conviction that art and morals alike suffer by the prudish conven-
tionalities of our present English style, that we are inclined to welcome
rebellion against it merely because it is rebellion. We are disposed to
give a friendly reception to George Meredith and Mrs. Norton were
it for nothing but the mere fact that conventionality might be inclined
to shriek out against them." In spite of his rebellious spirit, McCarthy
wrote that "we do not feel we are brought any nearer by the experience
of Richard Feverel to the solution of that great social question about
the sowing of wild oats." In *Diana of the Crossways* Meredith clearly
not only sympathizes with Diana but in some ways identifies with her
— Gillian Beer speaks of his "romance with his heroine."[22] Certainly
one reason for his feelings of kinship with her stems from this early
linking of his name with that of her historical counterpart in the same
article on the same basis.

It is well known that one of Meredith's constant themes was the
relationship between the sexes. Less observed is the way this subject
was given direction by the surprising public reaction to *Richard Feverel* and *Modern Love*. Meredith did not just become petulant or
crotchety, or turn inward to commune with himself, or ignore the
public, as suggested for instance by G. M. Trevelyan.[23] Nor did he
turn away, except in *Evan Harrington*, from direct treatment of the
subjects that had brought him notoriety. Rather, he began to look at
society and women more closely for an explanation that might relate
his private and public failures. (*The Ordeal of Richard Feverel* is a
more personal and autobiographical book than it at first appears: it
reflects the troubles of Meredith's first marriage.)[24] One of the differences between *Richard Feverel* and all the work which followed is
that organized society, the social scene, and women became much more
important, and certainly much more closely and realistically observed.

[21] Justin McCarthy, "Novels with a Purpose," *Westminster Review,* Amer.
ed., XXVI (1864), 11-22.

[22] Beer, *Meredith*, p. 167.

[23] G. M. Trevelyan, *A Layman's Love of Letters* (Cambridge, 1953).

[24] See Stevenson, *The Ordeal,* and Kelvin, *A Troubled Eden.*

However, this is not to say they are more realistically *described*. It is the continuing subordination of increased social observation and excellent psychological understanding to a romantic style and point of view that makes Meredith's work unique. Meredith's first response in fiction after *Richard Feverel* was *Evan Harrington* (1861), a deliberate evasion of any serious theme. This book was designed to win him a reading public and offend no one; the high place accorded it in many valuations of Meredith is unjustifiable.[25] Of course, none of Meredith's books is uninteresting, but the whole provincial issue of "Can Evan Harrington be both a tailor and a gentleman?" is successfully avoided in the best magazine style. Meredith's creative energies at the time of writing this second novel were more engaged with the sonnets of *Modern Love,* with which he allowed few considerations for convention or expediency to interfere. He seems to have been surprised and hurt once again by the discovery that some subjects were taboo whether treated in prose or poetry. During the next ten years he continued to write fiction that he thought would appeal to the wide and powerful public. Those works are imitations and compromises, although they contain many suggestive elements. *The Adventures of Harry Richmond* (1871) is a transitional work, a turning point in his popular reputation and also in his artistic growth. The change in the novel from the projected story of "Contrivance Jack" to the published form through the intervention of his conception of Richmond Roy is a signal of the change.[26]

The development of his ideas bore fruit in the romances from *Beauchamp's Career* (1874) to *One of Our Conquerors* (1891), in which with symbolic fiction and elaborate style he turned to the more psychological aspects of aristocratic manners and a feminine ideal. But while he pursued his own course, the actual social scene changed more radically than he ever understood and in a different direction than he had anticipated. Woman moved rapidly toward positions of true social, personal, and political equality with men; aristocratic habits of thinking and living, instead of spreading to the masses, ceased for many to be an ideal or a concern. The painful didacticism of Meredith's latest works seems a belated protest against facts. The truth seems to be that Meredith outlived his times. This originally ostracized radical became the idol of conservative critics of the nineties who wished to be as

[25] For a recent instance, see Pritchett, *Meredith and English Comedy.*
[26] See Stevenson, *The Ordeal,* p. 176.

broad-minded as possible. A revealing comment on Meredith's late popularity is this one by G. S. Street on the upper-class atmosphere in his fiction: "Surely there is more to be said for the blatant snobbery of an earlier time, than for this [present] proletarian exclusiveness. The accident of Mr. Meredith's choice of material is a consolation."[27]

A study of Meredith's biography apparently has not helped critics to form a coherent view of his artistic achievements. A certain elusive quality is present in his life story as it is in his books.

Meredith once said to Robertson Nicoll, "I was one man in youth and another man in middle age. . . . I have never felt the unity of personality running through my life. I have been six different men, six at least." He was explaining that one reason he could not believe in a future life was that he could not imagine "which personality . . . endures."[28] His biography as we know it seems to underline the truth of this reflection, since, although the stages in his life are clearly marked, the transitions between them are clouded. It is exactly at the most crucial periods of his life that we most lack information: his activities on his return to England from school in Germany, when he was sixteen and seventeen and finished with his formal education; his courtship of Mary Nicolls and his separation from her; his courtship of his second wife and his relationship with her. The very serenity of his second married life, his lack of intimate corresponding friends, and the fact that few of the memoirs and letters that refer to Meredith are concerned with the 1870s are all factors concealing the naturally subtle transition between his expansive younger middle age and that time when, in Stevenson's view, Meredith "had completely molded himself in a dramatic personality. . . . It was a flawless structure which had become his second nature . . . none of his more recent friends (in the eighteen-eighties and nineties) felt any genuine intimacy."[29]

In spite of the barriers between us and an understanding of Meredith's personal life, we ought to have some idea of the general relationship between the stages of his life and the stages of his work. His personal life from 1864 to 1885 (the years of his second marriage) was quiet and relatively undisturbing; he was more free than he had been up to this time to concentrate his creative powers on his literary work. His mature works gained depth from the successful surmounting of his personal difficulties. In this middle period (*Harry Richmond*, 1871, or

---

[27] G. S. Street in *The Yellow Book,* V (1895), 178.
[28] Quoted in Stevenson, *The Ordeal,* p. 350.
[29] *Ibid.,* p. 237.

Beauchamp's Career, 1874, to *One of Our Conquerors,* 1891) his novels came more slowly and show the good effects of sustained attention. It was also at this time that he attempted some short stories. Although mentally intoxicating to his visitors up until his death in 1909, his physical energy had begun to decline as early as the 1880s, and his creative energy was diminished after the publication of *One of Our Conquerors* in 1891 and *Poems: The Empty Purse* in 1892. He had a long old age. After the death of his wife, the increase in his paralysis, and the loss of his earlier intimates, he began to live almost wholly in the philosophy and personality that he had made up to do him worldly service. It was at this time (the 1890s and after) that he became celebrated as a Grand Old Writer and the Last Great Victorian, was sought after for his opinions on literature, society, women, and politics, and was revered by many as the light of the age.[30] So it is understandable that his character and ideas became increasingly exaggerated and theatrical. This last period has contributed greatly to a view of Meredith as a brilliant but hard and impenetrable writer and person, without subtlety or real depth, and thus incapable of development and change. It should be remembered, for instance, that it was in this period that Henry James knew him. Lionel Stevenson quotes this autobiographical reflection: "It is a misfortune to live to be eighty. A man's life ought to finish when he is five and sixty. He must stop working then, or else do work that is inferior. People will praise it at the time and write articles about it, but posterity will know better and see its weakness."[31] Meredith was sixty-five in 1893, before the publication of *Lord Ormont* (1894) and *The Amazing Marriage* (1895). Of course, since publication date is not the same as composition date, there is no way to be sure that Meredith was definitely referring to these two novels as "inferior" or to know how exactly he was using the age sixty-five as a dividing line. But I agree with his comment.

Gillian Beer's choice of novels implies a view of Meredith's development that is the closest of any critic's to the pattern I have outlined. For instance, she does not see *Evan Harrington* as an exception to the comment that "in the novels of the eighteen-sixties (in many ways the least successful of his career) we see him trying out a series of technical experiments which crystallise into the achievement of *Harry*

---

[30] Lionel Stevenson, "Meredith and the Interviewers," *Modern Philology,* LI (1953), 50-63; G. M. Young, "The New Cortegiano," in W. D. Handcock, ed., *Victorian Essays* (London, 1962), p. 214.

[31] Stevenson, "Meredith and the Interviewers," p. 63.

Richmond."[32] However, she seems to consider *Harry Richmond* one of his major accomplishments and suggests a steady development after it, with *The Amazing Marriage* a production of interest and merit equal to his best work.

A closer look at the novels is needed to support some of the suggestions made in this essay. Meredith was always a romantic and symbolic writer, but a comparison of the symbolism of his last two novels with that of *The Egoist* will show the decline of his creative powers and will incidentally emphasize the importance of the noncomic element in *The Egoist*. A defense of *Diana of the Crossways* will support the view that Meredith's middle period showed a consistent creativeness. A brief look at the prose style will suggest that, although certainly an artificial and sometimes an awkward medium, it is appropriate to the substance and character of Meredith's vision.

Meredith's late works are didactic because they reveal in plot, in conception, and in comment the desire to impose by force of statement his ideas and "reading of life" in order to prove it to himself. Then appears the symbol without the substance, the disappearance of the necessary flexibility in his attitude which creates independence in the characters. The symbolism, instead of being an integral part of the characters or the action, is part of the author's didacticism, imposed from above. The symbols are taken seriously by Meredith as truth, not as suggestive mysteries, and for the reader nothing is left but intellectual appreciation of them. In *Lord Ormont* the earl's troubles with his country and his troubles with his wife are not merely related or analogous: they are equal to the problem of existence, because Lord Ormont stands for England, England stands for men and history, Aminta stands for women, and women are symbolic of life:

> She had ... the self-collected and self-cancelled look. ... One would be near the meaning in declaring it to bewilder men with the riddle of openhandedness. We read it — all may read it — as we read inexplicable plain life; in which let us have a confiding mind, despite the blows at our heart, and some understanding will enter us. [iv, 65]

> He said of his country: *That Lout comes to a knowledge of his wants too late.* True. ... But what if his words were flung at him in turn! ... it rang correctly ... a fair example of the creatures men are; the greatest of men; who have to learn from the loss of the woman — or a fear of the loss — how much they really do love her. [xxx, 342]

---

[32] Beer, *Meredith,* p. 37.

Lord Ormont represents England's present state and present faults; Matthew Weyburn represents the future. Lord Ormont writes an essay giving a detailed plan for the safety and defense of England, but he throws it into the fire: his ideas are no longer relevant. Matthew Weyburn instead founds an international school that will represent and foster the best traits of each nation. Matey and Aminta take great care not to offend the public and the society they renounce — they are simply above and beyond it. The book is short, light, insubstantial, visionary. Some of the gentleness of a utopian atmosphere is conveyed through the use of metaphors of water.[33] As in Meredith's other works, water symbolism reflects the religious mystery of life (in contrast to earth, the symbol of life force, nature, or passion). The book has had therefore a certain appeal, in spite of its faults. In form it is a return to the allegorical fictions of *Farina* and *Shagpat,* published before *Richard Feverel.* Comparing it with these books gives an excellent idea of the emotional and artistic distance between Meredith's early and late years.

The Amazing Marriage includes the more novelistic character of Fleetwood, who struggles to develop and has several interesting sides to his character, but the novel is nevertheless like *Lord Ormont* in that the rest of the characters are symbols first and characters second. The book brings up some interesting problems about the totality of an author's work. Of course those who desire to know as much as possible about Meredith will want to read *The Amazing Marriage.* If it were all we had of Meredith, he would be historically less important, but we would be more interested in this particular book because it has the mark of an artistic personality. It is "Meredithian," an adjective with a distinctive meaning. But since it is not all we have, we are able to recognize that Carinthia is not the individual and independent personality that is Clara, Diana, or Cecilia. She is an extreme and reduced illustration of two qualities that Meredith saw in women — natural force and stubborn single-mindedness. So is Aminta — she exemplifies passive sexuality and limited common sense. Aminta does not need the latter because she is to be saved by her complement, Matthew, also a mere example of the characteristics of such Meredithian heroes as Vernon and Redburn, without their personalities. Both Carinthia and Aminta show a decrease in Meredith's social observation, or perhaps

[33] See Bernard Brunner, "Meredith's Symbolism: Lord Ormont and His Aminta," *Nineteenth-Century Fiction,* VIII (1953), 124-33.

in their symbolic role of the Natural Character of Woman, they show
Meredith's reaction against his previous social observations. Similarly,
Fleetwood's character is diminished rather than augmented by knowledge of the Meredithian symbolism of his name. This diminution is a
measure of the thinness of the book, which cannot survive the force
of suggestiveness that is carried elsewhere by Meredith's woods (as in
the "The Woods of Westermain" or the forest in Germany in *Richard
Feverel*).

Actually the most interesting feature of *The Amazing Marriage* is
the satire on fictional devices. His flexibility and ambiguity are certainly in play here. The first assumption, that he identifies his own
superior methods with those of the analytical narrator and that he
portrays the critics of his novels in Dame Gossip as supporting romance
in the pejorative sense of childish escape literature, does not accord
either with the effect of the text and story or with some of the comments by the opponent narrators. Gillian Beer and Joseph Kruppa
emphasize Meredith's sympathy with the Dame Gossip narrator.[34] The
life of the book is primarily in its attack on the assumption that facts
and romance are distinguishable characteristics in one's view of stories,
whether fictional or "real-life." It is interesting that Maurice Shroder
in a discussion of fictional technique finds that satirization of traditional devices is a common technique in twentieth-century novels.[35]
But in spite of this intriguing and forward-looking experiment, the book
is hard to read, and neither the characters nor the theme justifies its
difficulties and improbabilities.

In contrast with the symbolism of the two late novels, that of the
major romances does contribute several levels of meaning. The difference can be recognized even in the names: unlike "Fleetwood" and
"Woodseer," "Willoughby Patterne" and "Clara Middleton" have references that enhance rather than exhaust their characters. What is
Willoughby a pattern of and what is Clara in the middle of? The
complicated answers to these questions do not overwhelm the significance of the personalities, plot, or action, whereas once it is seen
that Fleetwood is fleeing from nature, his character and confusions
are fairly well summarized. The richness of *The Egoist* is shown by

---

[34] Beer, *Meredith*; Beer, "*The Amazing Marriage*: A Study in Contraries,"
Review of English Literature, VII (1966), 92-105; Joseph Kruppa, "Meredith's
Late Novels: Suggestions for a Critical Approach," *Nineteenth-Century Fiction*,
XIX (1964), 271-86.
[35] Shroder, "The Novel as Genre."

the fact that in spite of several close studies of it, two familiar symbols may still support further elucidation. These are the porcelain vase and the cherry tree.

Charles Hill and Robert Mayo both have called attention to the way the comparison of woman with sacred vessels is satirized throughout the book.[36] Daniel Schwartz says that "the breaking of the porcelain symbolically anticipates the rupture of the engagement" and that "porcelain with its association with Patterne not only represents Willoughby's attempts to impose psychic stasis on the people of Patterne Hall, but it comes to symbolize mutability. Its fragility implies the very lack of perfection that Willoughby refuses to admit into his conception of love."[37] Willoughby's neurotic desire for perfection, which leads ultimately to a rejection of sex and life itself, is well explained by Irving Buchen. Although he does not mention the porcelain vase, Buchen refers to a symbol from one of Meredith's poems in which "the urn" is the funereal urn and represents the principle of death. Clara's rejection of Willoughby's caresses (which actually pleases Willoughby, who found Constantia too responsive for perfection), Buchen interprets strangely. He says that "her virginal aspirations represent her fear of the urn" and that "Meredith clearly implies that if she breaks her engagement to Willoughby, she will never marry . . . what Clara really wants is to leave Society altogether and to exist merely as a noble savage."[38] But it is Willoughby who constantly wants to withdraw from society and preaches against the world to Clara, who simply desires to withdraw from Willoughby and not from life, society, or sex. Far from implying that if Clara breaks her engagement to Willoughby, she will never marry, Meredith implies that if she marries Willoughby, she will be unfaithful to him. This is the real meaning of the breaking of the porcelain vase.

Gillian Beer says that "Meredith may be invoking echoes from Restoration and Augustan comedy: the famous double-entendre scene of

[36] Charles Hill, "Theme and Image in *The Egoist,*" *University Review,* XX (Summer, 1954), 281-85; Robert D. Mayo, "Sir Willoughby's Pattern," *ELH,* IX (1942), 71-78.

[37] Daniel Schwartz, "The Porcelain Pattern Leitmotif in Meredith's *The Egoist,*" *Victorian Newsletter,* no. 33 (Spring, 1968), 26-28; see especially p. 27.

[38] Irving Buchen, "The Egoists in *The Egoist:* The Sensualists and the Ascetics," *Nineteenth-Century Fiction,* XIX (1964), 255-69; see especially pp. 260, 261.

'viewing the china' in Wycherley's *The Country Wife*. . . ." Certainly the
sexual associations are important to Meredith's meaning, but the links
with comic tradition limit the reader's view of this theme, making it
appear merely clever or even distasteful. Beer goes on to say that the
"willow-pattern story and the images from the porcelain . . . are an
additional emotional restraint on us as readers because they give us
controlling knowledge, but the nagging repetition of the porcelain
imagery grates after a time. . . ."[39] One can say that the reader's dis-
traction is due to Meredith's habit of putting too many ingredients into
one novel; one can also recognize that approaching the book from a
more ideal and romantic angle can illuminate its meaning and our
understanding. The breaking of the vase is more than a clever allusion
if it is related to Meredith's conception of virginity as a psychological —
or perhaps moral — but not a physical condition. His ideal was a romantic monogamy of the spirit, which he allowed to his heroes and
heroines. Horace brings a porcelain vase as a wedding present because
he is just the man to shatter the conventional propriety of a pattern
marriage based on false premises. He does Clara a good turn by smash-
ing the vase, not just because he breaks up her engagement/marriage
but because he helps her to know herself. She loses the innocence that
made her accept Willoughby in the first place. But as the heroine of
a romance, rather than of a comedy, social novel, or tragedy, she does
not have to pay the price by a predictable marriage with De Craye;
she can have an ideal relationship with Vernon. Michael Sundell calls
attention to a remark by Flitch when he returns Clara's purse to Patterne Hall: "As Flitch says, the purse is 'intact' (xxxiv, 279), and in
effect Flitch has also returned Clara 'intact,' unflawed by dishonesty
or by the compromising protection which Horace threatens to force
upon her."[40] Those who do not like romances will say that Meredith is
trying to have Clara both experienced and innocent, a virgin and not a
virgin, but others will feel he does indeed give us the best of two worlds.

The cherry tree in *The Egoist* is another example of the subtlety and
consistency of Meredith's mature handling of symbols. It has been noted
that the tree is a hybrid, unable to bear fruit, but only Michael Sundell
has suggested what the point of this might be. "Clara comes upon him
(Vernon) asleep under the tree he worships, the beautiful but unpro-

[39] Beer, *Meredith*, pp. 131-32.

[40] Michael Sundell, "The Functions of Flitch in *The Egoist*," *Nineteenth-Century Fiction*, XXIV (1969), 227-35; see especially p. 232.

ductive double blossom wild cherry, symbolic of nature tamed by artifice to a lovely sterility. In having Clara awaken him, Meredith suggests that she must awaken his manhood so that he may escape the graceful sterility of life at Patterne."[41] The cherry tree is a symbol of Clara's situation as well as of Vernon's. Its white, virginal blossoms will fade, and must fade, just as porcelain vases get broken. Clara regrets it but must accept it. When Clara leaves for the station, she and Cross-jay "were in time for a circuit in the park to the wild double cherry blossom, no longer all white. Clara gazed up from under it, where she had imagined a fairer visible heavenliness than any other sight of earth had ever given her. That was when Vernon lay beneath. But she had certainly looked above, not at him. The tree seemed sorrowful in its withering flowers of the colour of trodden snow" (xxv, 7). Meredith's understanding of the relationships among nature, man's nature, and society was very subtle. Man cannot imitate nature directly, but his attempts to refine or improve upon nature may be very costly or even self-destructive. Willoughby's refinement in the extended passage on his leg (Chapter ii) is shown to be ridiculous and ultimately vulgar. On the other hand, Cecilia in *Beauchamp's Career,* product of aristocratic English society, is an example of the loveliness of refinement; she is society's virginal double-blossom tree. In some ways she is more virginal, unproductive, and lovely after her happy and successful marriage than before, when she was involved in a vital, complicated, interesting, and unsatisfying relationship with Nevil Beauchamp.

Like all of Meredith's novels, *Diana of the Crossways* has had its defenders and its attackers, but in this case the majority opinion seems to be clear. The book has not been liked,[42] yet it cannot be dismissed as an unimportant production. Some of the complaints are that it appears to be an evasion of its own issue, the liberated woman, or that it is only another version of Victorian prejudices on the subject. Another is that it contains a major technical mistake in totally avoiding a sensible explanation of the motive for Diana's action in betraying her friend Dacier, although this betrayal is the turning point of the plot. Dacier returns one evening after a dinner party to tell Diana an ex-

---

[41] *Ibid.,* p. 230.

[42] J. B. Priestley, *George Meredith* (London, 1926), p. 42; E. A. Baker, "George Meredith," in *History of the English Novel,* VIII (London, 1937), 375; Wright, *Art and Substance,* p. 15; Kelvin, *A Troubled Eden,* p. 112; Robert W. Watson, review of *A Troubled Eden* in *Victorian Studies,* VI (1961), 364-65; Pritchett, *Meredith and English Comedy,* p. 120.

citing political secret. Their friendship, though romantic, has not included physical contact, but this evening Dacier embraces her, and she
resists. After he leaves, she immediately takes the secret to sell to the
newspaper editor, thereby seriously compromising Dacier's political
future and, of course, losing his friendship. Both Jack Lindsay and
Gillian Beer have understood that Diana's betrayal of Dacier is not
due simply to sexual revulsion at the kiss he takes from her before he
leaves, nor to Victorian shock on discovering that his friendship is not
entirely cerebral. Diana has said to Dacier by her act, "Since you have
used our friendship and political sympathies to gain a personal advantage with me, I will use them likewise — to gain money and prestige
to make me independent of you." Of course, this is a neurotic, exaggerated overreaction, and she betrays herself as well as Dacier by it,
but in the realm of personal revenge, against the background of the
failure of her independent life, her action seems to her at the time
to be poetically just.

Diana and Dacier once planned to elope. Diana has wrongly thought
that she and Dacier have had a new kind of relationship since their
elopement was thwarted. Dacier is not usually impulsive. On second
thought, he was quite happy not to have thrown away his career and
antagonized his family. "But then it had been so splendid an insanity
when he urged Diana to fly with him. Anyone but a woman would
have appreciated the sacrifice" (xxvi, 290). When they meet again,
Diana is playing the part of the "New Woman," but she is not successful. Her writing is not popular, her financial speculations are failing,
her husband will not disappear, and she cannot hold Dacier's friendship without continuing her expensive dinners to which she invites
friends influential to him, or without a closer physical intimacy that
she does not want. Here is an example of the author's ideas being
responsible for the situation but not being substituted for the story.
Meredith did not, it is true, believe in the independent woman or in
a deeply abiding nonsexual friendship between the sexes. In this book
he does dramatically present an intelligent, sympathetic, intellectual
woman who is personally incapable of gaining spiritual freedom as an
emancipated feminist. Her failure is due to both private and public
pressures. She is not overwhelmed by Meredith's ideas as much as by
the reader's preconceived idea that she must be capable of independence. It is perhaps limited and Victorian of Meredith to believe that
Diana and Dacier have no future together without marriage or

that their friendship must include living together. But he was also realistic in assuming that Dacier could not have continued his prominent political career if he lived openly with a married woman, and he does think it is a limitation in Dacier that his friendship is not sexually disinterested. The idea that Meredith somehow undermined his whole presentation and revealed his Victorianism by making Diana conventionally unyielding or ultimately irresponsible comes from reading the book as a kind of purpose novel instead of as a portrait of times and personalities. Diana's sexual repression is not very deep. In fact, Meredith presents it as a protective reaction against cultural and social pressures (which also explains why she married the cold and uninteresting Warwick; she made the mistake then of thinking she could marry socially to be free personally). The book is basically a romance: although the heroine cannot reform the society, she escapes its pressures and achieves personal happiness anyway. It also suggests a romantic view of society by intimating in the last paragraph that things may be better for the next generation.

No doubt the chief, and certainly the first, difficulty that Meredith's work presents to his readers is his idiosyncratic style. Response to Meredith's style has been as varied as response to his work as a whole, and it shows as little consensus about its development or its relative strengths and weaknesses. Judgments of Meredith's style are common, for it is obtrusive, but descriptions of it are limited by the general inadequacy of all stylistic criticism.[43] Gillian Beer has an excellent analysis of the way in which his style expresses his shifting point of view, which she sees in turn as essential for his unusual achievements as well as for his uncertainties and tensions. The importance of images in Meredith's prose cannot be missed, and several studies have looked closely at the image patterns. Roger Wilkenfeld has noted that generally there is a lack of consistency in these patterns, and Joseph Kruppa forthrightly states, "Those who have searched for coherent image patterns in Meredith's work have come away with empty hands."[44] Meredith's works do have a static quality in spite of changes within the characters and surprises in the plot; they are romances, they emphasize

[43] Richard Ohmann, "Generative Grammars and the Concept of Literary Style," *Word,* XX (1964), 423-39; "Methods in the Study of Victorian Style," *Victorian Newsletter,* no. 27 (Spring, 1965), 1-4.

[44] Roger B. Wilkenfeld, "Hands Around: Image and Theme in *The Egoist,*" *ELH,* XXXIV (1967), 369, n. 2; Kruppa, "Meredith's Late Novels," p. 272.

the cyclical and the ideal, and they are permeated by an outside force. The Meredithian manner is developed in the novels following *Harry Richmond* and is most expressive and successful in his major works. It is generally nonperiodic and deliberately abrupt in rhythm, made complex by isolated and sometimes incompatible images, by a lack of connectives and an emphasis on abstract and startling nouns. It is more particularly characterized by a peculiar use of articles, either omitted where one would expect to find them or substituted for the personal pronoun; by a great fondness for prepositions, either in an adverbial function or in a prepositional phrase, often used in preference to a verbal noun or verbal adjective, and particularly in strings of prepositional phrases; and by a tendency to use adjectives as nouns and occasionally to use transitive verbs intransitively.[45]

These characteristics are naturally related to one another and, furthermore, show a romantic origin. A romantic concern with the difficulties of definition and identification is emphasized by the experiments with the definite article; a similar romantic preference for incompleteness appears in the refusal to supply objects for the transitive verbs, and in the use of an adjective where a noun would be more standard. The use of prepositional phrases contributes to the jerkiness of the rhythm; the lack of developed rhythm or structure throws the emphasis onto the isolated and independent parts, and the exaggeration of the substantives contributes to their static symbolic function. Seen at short range, the world is a disconnected, unreasonable, comic conglomeration; from a distance, it appears to be animated by some mysterious,

---

[45] Some examples: "His imperceptible sensible playing of the part, on a substratum of sincereness, induces fascinatingly to the like performance on our side" (transitive verb used intransitively, from *One of Our Conquerors*, vi, 55). "The primitive is born again, the elemental reconstituted." "It is the palpable and material of them still which they are tempted to flourish . . ." (adjectives used as nouns, from *The Egoist*, xxxix, 182; xi, 131). "She shone for him like the sunny breeze on water." "The rising from table left her to Sir Willoughby." ". . . then, as a hawk with feathers on his beak of the bird in his claw lifts head" (omission of an article, before "water," "table," and "head," from *The Egoist*, xxiii, 269; xv, 172; xxvi, p. 20; also note the succession of prepositional phrases in the last example). An extreme example of the use of prepositions is this one from *The Amazing Marriage* ". . . the downy drop to ground and muted scurry up the bark of long-brush squirrels, cocktail on the wary watch, were noticed by him as well as by her; even the rotting timber drift, bark and cones on the yellow pine needles, and the tortuous dwarf chestnut pushing level out, with a strain of the head up, from a crevice of mossed rock, among ivy and ferns . . ." (xi, 120).

romantic, constant principle of "Change in Recurrence," "Youth in Age," "Union in Disseverence," "Song in the Songless," "Outer and Inner."

It is interesting that Meredith's mature novels are thought to exhibit the worst features of his style, instead of simply its most pronounced character, and that his other novels are sometimes praised for their comparatively simple prose. This relative judgment naturally has given the reader (of Meredithian criticism or of Meredithian prose) a rather schizophrenic feeling. It is not a value judgment so much as an expression of dislike of Meredith when he is most like himself. The relationship among the styles of his different periods can, of course, only be demonstrated by quotations of some length. Good examples for comparison purposes are three passages of similar subject, Meredith on his readers and his methods, from *Richard Feverel* (xxv, 225-26), *Beauchamp's Career* (xlviii, 236-37), and *The Amazing Marriage* (xlv, 474). In the first the rhythm as well as the images are more conventional; in the last petulance and crabbiness are reflected by the exaggeration of his stylistic methods, so that this might deservedly be called Meredithese. In the middle period we have a fine example of Meredithian romantic images combined with a wry and humorous tone; originality and even idiosyncrasy are balanced by confidence and objectivity.

The tendency for all essays on English writers to relate their subjects at some point to Shakespeare was begun for Meredith by Virginia Woolf. Of course Meredith had anticipated his critics by the titles of his chapters in *Richard Feverel*. But a mentor much closer to Meredith whom he himself acknowledged was Byron. The combination of the romance and the satire is comparable, and even Lucy and Richard resemble Juan and Haidée much more than they do Ferdinand and Miranda. The similarity even suggests a direct influence: after an impassioned and secret young love in a beautiful natural setting, Haidée and Lucy both die from brain fever brought on by the erroneous belief that their lovers have been killed (*Don Juan*, Cantos II-IV). But if Meredith in his first important novel shows affinities with the earlier romantic satirist, one of the many differences between them was the brevity of Byron's life. Meredith was able to, and did, make use of his long life to show a maturity and development not always attributed to him. Rather than being a careless, erratic, superficially brilliant writer, he was a writer with a coherent pattern of growth, whose mature works show a sustained control.

TWELVE

Hardy's Scholar-Gipsy

BY WARD HELLSTROM

Matthew Arnold has received great critical attention in recent years, attention that has often centered on his indebtedness to or influence upon the work of others. And Hardy's allusions to Arnold have long been duly noted by biographers and critics, but it has not been until recently that the profound effect of Arnold on Hardy has been systematically analyzed in a fine essay by David DeLaura, " 'The Ache of Modernism' in Hardy's Later Novels." Professor DeLaura is quite right in his contention that "much of Hardy's anatomy of the modern condition — and of its personal correlatives — centers in his complex response to Matthew Arnold."[1] It is both the breadth and the nature of that response which I wish to trace in this essay.

My emphasis here is different from DeLaura's, though not, I think, contrary. My attention will be addressed to only one novel — *Jude the Obscure* — where DeLaura more ambitiously confronted not only the three "modern" novels — *Return of the Native, Tess,* and *Jude* — but *The Woodlanders* and *The Laodicean* as well. Nor am I so directly concerned with Hardy's response to Arnoldian "Neo-Christianity," which at any rate is perhaps more evident in *Tess* than in *Jude*. What I am interested in is the pervasive effect of Arnold's thought on the novel. It seems to me that Hardy may have originally intended to dramatize in his novel certain Arnoldian precepts, adhering to some and rejecting others. Indeed, I suspect that the germ of *Jude* may well have been generated in Hardy by his reading of Arnold.

My purpose in this essay, however, is not to establish a source for *Jude* but to illuminate the thought of both Hardy and Arnold by examining the points at which their thinking converges and those at which it diverges, in the hope that such an exercise may prove useful to students of Hardy and Arnold alike.

[1] David DeLaura, " 'The Ache of Modernism' in Hardy's Later Novels," *ELH,* XXXIV (1967), 380.

On April 16, 1888, Hardy recorded in his notebook, "News of Matthew Arnold's death, which occurred yesterday. . . . The *Times* speaks quite truly of his 'enthusiasm for the nobler and detestation of the meaner elements in humanity.'" For April 26 the following entry appears: "Thought in bed last night that Byron's *Childe Harold* will live in the history of English poetry not so much because of the beauty of parts of it, which is great, but because of its good fortune in being the accretion of descriptive poems by the most fascinating personality in the world — for the English — not a common plebian, but a romantically wicked noble lord. It affects even Arnold's judgment." The entry for April 28 is: "A short story of a young man — 'who could not go to Oxford' — His struggles and ultimate failure. Suicide. [Probably the germ of *Jude the Obscure*.] There is something [in this] the world ought to be shown, and I am the one to show it to them — though I was not altogether hindered going, at least to Cambridge, and could have gone up easily at five-and-twenty."[2]

There can be little doubt that the final entry is indeed the germ of *Jude*, but critics have not connected that germ with Arnold. Such a connection is given credence at least by the reference to Arnold's death on April 16 and the allusion to Arnold's critical judgment of Byron on April 26 (a judgment suggested by Arnold in a number of places but made specifically in his essay on Byron).[3] Hardy seems clearly to have had Arnold in mind when he conceived of *Jude*, and it is possible at least to associate the story of Jude with a similar story in Arnold — "The Scholar-Gipsy."

To suggest that *Jude the Obscure* may have had its source in Arnold's "The Scholar-Gipsy" will perhaps seem pointless, but a comparison of the two works allows a comparison of the thinking of the two men as they confront similar problems. "The Scholar-Gipsy" has a "subject" remarkably similar to that of *Jude*. The scholar-gipsy of Glanvil's book is, like Jude, a "scholar poor, / Of pregnant parts and quick inventive brain," who tires "of knocking at preferment's door."[4] And he wanders

---

[2] Florence Emily Hardy, *The Life of Thomas Hardy: 1840-1928* (New York, 1962), pp. 207-8 (hereafter cited as *Life*). Bracketed material appears in the text and is probably Hardy's, as he is known to have written much of the *Life*.

[3] Arnold's "Byron" can be found in *Essays in Criticism: Second Series,* published posthumously in 1888, but it had appeared originally as an introduction to the Golden Treasury volume of Byron's poetry and had been reprinted in *MacMillan's Magazine* (Mar., 1881).

[4] Ll. 34-35. All citations (hereafter in the text by line) to Arnold's poetry will refer to Kenneth Allott's edition of the *Poems* (New York, 1965).

round and round Oxford, as Jude wanders round Christminster. But
where Arnold's scholar gains immortality because he has what the
speaker of the poem has not — apparently hope — Hardy's scholar
proves all too mortal when, hope gone, he commits suicide. Such details
in "The Scholar-Gipsy" as the "boys who in lone wheatfields scare the
rooks" (l. 64) may have suggested to Hardy the young Jude's occupation in Farmer Troutham's fields, but more significant, I think, are the
similarities between the two worlds of Arnold's poem and those of *Jude*.

The scholar-gipsy's world is rural and intuitive, possessed with the
magic of folklore; the gipsy wanders the Berkshire moors and Cumner
hills in search, Kenneth Allott tells us, "for the truth that can be received by the poetic imagination."[5] Whatever the exact nature of the
"spark from heaven" (ll. 120, 171) and the "heaven-sent moments"
(l. 50) for which the scholar-gipsy waits, it is clear that the rural, non-
intellectual, healthy, and individual world of the gipsies is contrasted
sharply to the urban, hyperconscious, diseased, and collective world of
the speaker of the poem. The speaker and his world are afflicted with
"sick fatigue" and "languid doubt" (l. 164); modern life is itself a disease in which one suffers the "strong ... infection of our mental strife"
(l. 222) and in which "each half-lives a hundred different lives"
(l. 169). The speaker's world is without the hope that the scholar-gipsy
has and is therefore without his promise of immortality.

Hardy in *Jude*, it seems to me, addresses himself to essentially the
same problems. Over the course of his novels he had moved from the
more or less idyllic rural world of *Under the Greenwood Tree* to
the destructive urban world of *Jude*. In *Jude* there are only remnants
of that natural world before the disease of modern consciousness, and
they appear in the persons of Aunt Drusilla and Widow Edlin, the last
of the rustics, whose response to the world is at once natural and uncomplicated, unlike the hypersensitive responses of Jude or Sue or Phillotson.[6] But Hardy in *Jude* is, I think, both less romantic and more consistent than Arnold in "The Scholar-Gipsy." Arnold's gipsy wanders a
world that never existed in search of a vaguely conceived spark from
heaven, and in his wandering he is granted immortality. I would agree
with Lionel Trilling that " 'The Scholar-Gipsy' is a passionate indictment
of the new dictatorship of the never-resting intellect over the soul of

---

[5] Arnold, *Poems*, ed. Allott, p. 334n.

[6] The scholar-gipsy, unlike Hardy's rustics, is highly conscious. Hardy's rustics
are at ease because they are unconscious, not because they are rural or have
hope or are immortal.

modern man,"[7] but the vehicle for that indictment is the contrast of modern man with a palpably false romantic notion of a scholar-gipsy. The nostalgic tone of the poem seems to me artificial, since the object of that nostalgia is a world of no more substance than that of *Ivanhoe* or *Gone with the Wind*. And while it is possible to be nostalgic about both those worlds which never existed, such nostalgia would not be possible either for the dramatically realized speaker of the poem or for Matthew Arnold himself, whose accurate perceptions of the modern dilemma make quite improbable such a false perception of the past.

In Hardy the case is quite different. There is a yearning for a natural, agrarian, and uncomplicated world that is dying, but there is no conscious falsification of that world. If the natural world is beautiful, it is also terrible and ruthless; if it contains Dick Dewy, Gabriel Oak, and Giles Winterborne, it also contains Arabella Donn and Sergeant Troy and is intruded upon by Dr. Fitzpiers, Alec D'Urberville, and Angel Clare. If Egdon Heath is beautiful, that beauty is qualified by the destructive potential of the weir, for example, which claims Eustacia's life, or the adder, which kills Mrs. Yoebright. Hardy knows and admits the equal potential for good and evil of the natural world and contrasts it with the painful destructiveness of a social world that has the terror of nature but not its beauty.

Rather than contrasting modern man with a romanticized and imaginary figure of a legendary past, Hardy faces the problem of modern man's consciousness — if you will, "the new dictatorship of the never-resting intellect over the soul of modern man" — more directly and realistically. In the novel, which Hardy described as all contrasts,[8] he places the confrontation of the past with the present, of nature with society, of rural life with urban life, inside the soul of a single man. Jude is the natural man who becomes the modern conscious man, the rural man who becomes urban, the workman who seeks to become the scholar. We are not asked by Hardy to believe that a man who is so acutely aware of the modern dilemma as the speaker of "The Scholar-

[7] Lionel Trilling, *Matthew Arnold* (Cleveland and New York, 1968), p. 105.

[8] "Of course the book is all contrasts — or was meant to be in its original conception. Alas, what a miserable accomplishment it is, when I compare it with what I meant to make it! — e.g. Sue and her heathen gods set against Jude's reading the Greek Testament; Christminster academical, Christminster in the slums; Jude the saint, Jude the sinner; Sue the Pagan, Sue the saint; marriage, no marriage; &c., &c." (*Life*, pp. 272-73).

Gipsy" can at the same time be so blissfully unaware of the falsity of his reading of the past. Jude, of course, begins the novel as one who romanticizes, not the past, to be sure, but the future. He is both idealistic and a visionary. But though he remains idealistic throughout, his vision is continually transformed as he becomes increasingly aware of himself and of his world. Unlike Arnold's speaker, he does not simultaneously hold two quite contrary visions of the world.

Jude begins the novel subject to what Hardy calls in the preface "the strongest passion known to humanity." A detailed examination of the nature of that passion will have to be deferred till later, but something should be said of it here. At first glance the strongest passion may seem to refer to the sex drive, but both Arabella and Sue associate Jude's passion with Christminster, not with sex. When Arabella sees Sue in her bakery booth at the Kennetbridge Fair, she remarks on the cakes, shaped like Christminster Colleges: " 'Still harping on Christminster — even in his cakes!' laughed Arabella. 'Just like Jude. A ruling passion. ...' [Sue responds:] 'Of course Christminster is a sort of fixed vision with him, which I suppose he'll never be cured of believing in. He still thinks it a great centre of high and fearless thought, instead of what it is, a nest of commonplace schoolmasters whose characteristic is timid obsequiousness to tradition' " (V, vii).[9]

Later, when Jude leaves Sue and the children at Christminster, Sue "thought of the strange operation of a simple-minded man's ruling passion, that it should have led Jude, who loved her and the children so tenderly, to place them here in this depressing purlieu, because he was still haunted by his dream" (VI, ii). It is Christminster that is the object of Jude's idealistic vision, a vision similar in its romantic inclination to the nostalgia of Arnold's speaker. The city is for Jude "the new Jerusalem" and "a city of light"; "the tree of knowledge grows there" (I, iii). He embodies his ideal in Christminster; it becomes for him the concrete goal toward which his dream pushes him. Later he substitutes Sue Bridehead for Christminster. As Hardy tells us, "Hers became the City phantom, while those of the intellectual and devotional worthies who had once moved him to emotion were no longer able to assert their presence here" (III, viii).[10] And later yet, Jude rejects Sue as the em-

[9] I have used the Harper edition (New York, 1957). Because of the many editions available, I have cited within the text part and chapter numbers.

[10] That Sue is to embody the ideal is foreshadowed when, before Jude meets her, Hardy describes her as "almost an ideality" (II, iv).

bodiment of his ideal when he tells her in her final hysterical return to Phillotson, "Sue, Sue, you are not worth a man's love!" (VI, viii). Though Jude maintains his idealism, as we shall see, he does not embody that ideal in anything of so little substance as the scholar-gipsy; at least he does not continue to do so after he gains the knowledge of himself and of his world that he has at the end of the novel.

Whether "The Scholar-Gipsy" was the actual source for *Jude the Obscure* is not of great importance. But a comparison of the two works does demonstrate that Hardy and Arnold addressed themselves to the same problem and arrived at strikingly similar perceptions of "the modern condition." While it is not perhaps surprising that Hardy's approach is more realistic than Arnold's, and gloomier, it can be demonstrated, I think, that his conclusion is also more heroic and affirmative. But such a demonstration must be postponed until I have examined some other Arnoldian influences and their relation to Jude's aspirations.

Early in the novel, as we have seen, Jude embodies his idealism in Christminster, which is certainly more than the symbol of a college education. Exactly what Christminster does represent is not very clear to young Jude, but it is apparently clear to Hardy. On the night that Jude first enters the city, he dreams that specters speak to him. One of the specters, though not named, is Matthew Arnold: "One of the spectres (who afterwards mourned Christminster as 'the home of lost causes,' though Jude did not remember this) was now apostrophizing her thus: 'Beautiful city! so venerable, so lovely, so unravaged by the fierce intellectual life of our century, so serene! . . . Her ineffable charm keeps ever calling us to the true goal of all of us, to the ideal, to perfection' " (II, i). The passage Hardy quotes is from Arnold's "Preface" to *Essays in Criticism: First Series* (1865). And it is a very important passage because it is a key to one of the roles that Christminster plays in the novel.[11] Christminster is that which calls Jude to his true goal, to the ideal, to perfection, as Hardy suggests. Arnold makes clear, and surely Hardy was familiar with, the meanings of both the *ideal* and *perfection* in the "Sweetness and Light" chapter of *Culture and Anarchy* (1869). Of the *ideal* Arnold says, " 'It is in making endless additions to itself, in the endless expansion of its powers, in endless growth in wisdom and

[11] Christminster also functions, of course, as setting. For my analysis of its use as setting, see "Hardy's Use of Setting and *Jude the Obscure*," *Victorian Newsletter*, no. 25 (Spring, 1964), 11-13.

beauty, that the spirit of the human race finds its ideal. To reach this ideal, culture is an indispensable aid, and that is the true value of culture.' "[12] Somewhat later he says of *perfection:* "But above all in our own country has culture a weighty part to perform, because here that mechanical character, which civilisation tends to take everywhere, is shown in the most eminent degree. Indeed nearly all the characters of perfection, as culture teaches us to fix them, meet in this country with some powerful tendency which thwarts them and sets them at defiance. The idea of perfection as an *inward* condition of the mind and spirit is at variance with the mechanical and material civilisation in esteem with us, and nowhere, as I have said, so much in esteem as with us" (V, 95).

These passages seem to me extremely relevant to our understanding of the novel. Christminster is not itself so much the goal as it is a magnet drawing Jude to his goal, to his ideal, to perfection. But that perfection for Jude, as for Arnold, is not an external object, not Christminster itself, but an inward condition in which the spirit seeks an "endless expansion of its powers" and "endless growth in wisdom and beauty." By associating the idea of perfection with Christminster in Jude's mind, Hardy closely parallels Arnold's association of perfection with Oxford. In *Culture and Anarchy* Arnold says, "Oxford, the Oxford of the past, has many faults; and she has heavily paid for them in defeat, in isolation, in want of hold upon the modern world. Yet we in Oxford, brought up amidst the beauty and sweetness of that beautiful place, have not failed to seize one truth, — the truth that beauty and sweetness are essential characters of a complete human perfection. When I insist on this, I am all in the faith and tradition of Oxford" (V, 105-6). Because Jude's impulse is intellectual, because it is toward the cultivation of his own best self, he naturally idealizes the city he associates with culture, with light. But even as early in the novel as Jude's first arrival in the city, the impossibility of externalizing the ideal is vaguely sensed by him when he becomes aware of "the isolation of his own personality" (II, i). Hardy foreshadows just such an awareness, it seems to me, in his motto from Swinburne for Part II, "At Christminster": "Save his own soul he hath no star." Jude must depend on Jude.

Hardy's quotation from Arnold's "Preface" is apparently, then, in-

[12] *The Prose Works of Matthew Arnold,* ed. R. H. Super, V (Ann Arbor, Mich., 1960), 94. Arnold quotes himself from "A French Eton" (1863). All further citations to Arnold's prose are to the Super edition, with volume and page given in the text.

tended to indicate to the reader the nature of Jude's pursuit of the ideal. But the passage, of which Hardy quotes only a part, may have suggested to him further possibilities for the novel. The passage reads:

> . . . who will deny that Oxford, by her ineffable charm, keeps ever calling us nearer to the true goal of all of us, to the ideal, to perfection, — to beauty, in a word, which is only truth seen from another side? — nearer, perhaps, than all the science of Tübingen. Adorable dreamer, whose heart has been so romantic! who hast given thyself so prodigally, given thyself to sides and to heroes not mine, only never to the Philistines! home of lost causes, and forsaken beliefs, and unpopular names, and impossible loyalties! what example could ever so inspire us to keep down the Philistine in ourselves, what teacher could ever so save us from that bondage to which we are all prone. . . . [III, 290]

If Jude shares Arnold's highly romanticized vision of Oxford-Christminster, at least early in his life, clearly Hardy does not. Surrounded by a wall that gives a freezing negative to his aspirations, Christminster not only draws Jude to his goal but is the means for thwarting his attainment of that goal. Christminster even seems to celebrate Jude's death, as Hardy introduces the cheers of the Remembrance Day games in the midst of Jude's deathbed recitation of passages from Job. The Christminster of Hardy is, then, radically different from the Oxford of Arnold; rather than being the opponent of Philistinism, Christminster seems to be the preserver of it.

The idea of Philistinism brings us to another area for discussion: the further effect of *Culture and Anarchy* and particularly the Hebraic-Hellenic controversy that informs *Jude the Obscure.*

In an essay entitled " 'Jude the Obscure': Hardy's Symbolic Indictment of Christianity" Norman Holland, Jr., reminds us that "Jude" in German means "Jew," and he suggests that "Phillotson's name echoes 'Philistine,' which can be taken in the Biblical sense of the non-Jewish, that is, nonaspiring people who destroyed Samson. . . . 'Philistine' may also be taken in Arnold's sense, as the conventional middle-class person who oppresses the artist — Sue."[13] Holland's purpose was quite different from mine; I therefore wish to develop his suggestions in a different direction.

Jude, the Jew, is the Hebraic man both figuratively in the biblical

[13] Norman Holland, Jr., " 'Jude the Obscure': Hardy's Symbolic Indictment of Christianity," *Nineteenth-Century Fiction,* IX (1954), 51-52.

sense and literally in the Arnoldian sense, and Phillotson is the Philistine in both senses. Though both senses are not absolutely separable, it is possible to examine separately the biblical overtones of the relation between Jude and Phillotson. That is, one can examine the biblical sense in which Jude is the Hebraic man and Phillotson the Philistine. I shall then return to the discussion of Jude as Hebraic man in the Arnoldian sense.

In the novel Jude is likened to St. Stephen, to Joseph, to Samson, and to Paul; he paraphrases Mark, alludes to Kings, and quotes from Ecclesiastes, Job, Deuteronomy, I and II Corinthians, and Judges. Early in the novel, when Sue chooses a classical allusion, it is appropriate that Jude should choose a Hebraic one.[14] Clearly Jude is identified with Hebraism and twice most specifically with Samson. The first time, he and Arabella at the tavern at Alfredston sit looking "at the picture of Samson and Delilah" (I, vii). The suggestion that Jude plays Samson to Arabella's Delilah is then reinforced toward the end of the novel when Jude, asleep in the pork-shop after his drunken revel, is described as Arabella's "shorn Samson" (VI, vii). He is further like Samson in that he figuratively defeats the Philistines (in the person of Phillotson), as we shall see, and, like Samson, his victory necessitates his own death.

Jude is also literally the Hebraic man in the Arnoldian sense. He begins the novel as a nominal Christian whose apparent concern is with conduct, whose apparent desire is for ordination and service; he thinks he is governed by a moral impulse that Arnold associates with Hebraism. We may also attribute to his Hebraism "that devout energy in embracing [the] ideal," which Arnold defines as Hebraic in the "Preface" to *Culture and Anarchy* (V, 255). But from the beginning Jude's true unconscious desire is for light; his real impulse is not moral but intellectual. Christminster's appeal to him is that it promises light, and even his interest in Sue is determined in part by his "wish for intellectual sympathy" (II, iv). Jude, the Hebraic man, has the impulse toward Hellenism that Arnold describes in *Culture and Anarchy:* "Essential in Hellenism is the impulse to the development of the whole man, to connecting and harmonising all parts of him, perfecting all, leaving none to take their chance" (V, 184). It is really self-development which Jude seeks. His ideal is the ideal Arnold describes as Hellenic: "To get rid

---

[14] On the morning that Sue and Jude set off to the magistrate's office to get married, she remarks that she feels "as if a tragic doom overhung our family, as it did the house of Atreus." Jude answers, "Or the house of Jeroboam" (V, iv).

of one's ignorance, to see things as they are, and by seeing them as they are to see them in their beauty, is the simple and attractive ideal which Hellenism holds out before human nature; and from the simplicity and charm of this ideal, Hellenism, and human life in the hands of Hellenism, is invested with a kind of aërial ease, clearness, and radiancy; they are full of what we call sweetness and light" (V, 167). It is really the Hellenic in the idealized Christminster and in the idealized Sue that appeals to Jude: it is the intellectual, not the moral, side of Christminster and the aerial, radiant, and theoretical paganism of Sue that attract him. Indeed, Jude develops in the novel through his gradual process of "Hellenisation." It is such a process that Arnold saw as necessary for England: "Now," says Arnold, "and for us, it is a time to Hellenise, and praise knowing; for we have Hebraised too much, and have over-valued doing" (V, 255). When one remembers that Jude Fawley was in an early version called Jude England,[15] the suggestion that Hardy originally intended to dramatize the Arnoldian prescription for England seems at least credible.

Sue, of course, is the antithesis of Jude. She begins as Hellenic — she purchases statues of Venus and Apollo and prefers Athens, Rome, and Alexandria to Jerusalem, as well as Corinthian to Gothic architecture. Sue is likened to Ganymedes and alludes to Venus Urania. Her regression from Hellenism to Hebraism is the direct opposite of Jude's progression from Hebraism to Hellenism.[16] She begins as apparently Hellenic, though her real affinity is all along with Hebraism, which manifests itself fully in her final enslavement to the forms of Christianity. And that enslavement takes a specifically Arnoldian form: Arnold says in his chapter "Hebraism and Hellenism," "The Greek quarrel with the body and its desires is, that they hinder right thinking; the Hebrew quarrel with them is, that they hinder right acting" (V, 165). The fundamentally Hellenic Jude is interrupted in his pursuit of the intellectual by his physical attraction to Arabella; he leaves his study of Griesbach's text of the Greek Testament, for example, to court her (I, vii). His body, in other words, hinders right thinking. Sue, on the other hand,

---

[15] See Robert C. Slack, "A Variorum Edition of Thomas Hardy's *Jude the Obscure*" (Dissertation, University of Pittsburgh, 1953), I, xliii.

[16] Jude clearly recognizes the reversal of their original positions. When they are at Aldbrickham, Hardy says of Jude, "He was mentally approaching the position which Sue had occupied when he first met her" (V, viii). Sue's "conversion" to Christianity at the end of the novel of course puts her where Jude began.

who is fundamentally Hebraic, must bring her body into subjection to allow her right acting. She tells Jude after her return to Phillotson, "He is a kind husband to me — And I — I've wrestled and struggled, and fasted, and prayed. I have nearly brought my body into complete subjection" (VI, viii). The essentially Hebraic nature of her capitulation is underscored by the motto, which is taken from the Apocryphal Esther, for this final part of the novel: ". . . And she humbled her body greatly, and all the places of her joy she filled with her torn hair." Her hysterical surrender to Christianity is evidence that she has succumbed to what Arnold calls the dangers of the tendency to Hebraize: "we have seen that it leads to a narrow and twisted growth of our religious side itself, and to a failure of perfection" (V, 238).

Hardy is indebted to *Culture and Anarchy* for more than the Hebraic-Hellenic motif that informs the novel. As Holland suggests, Phillotson is the Arnoldian Philistine, but not simply, I think, because he "oppresses the artist — Sue," though that may be one of his functions. He is the representative of, as well as the victim of, those enslaving middle-class values that constitute Philistinism. Thwarted by society in his attempt to cultivate his best self, he accepts those values that violate his humane instincts and produce not his *best self* but his *ordinary self*, to use Arnold's terms. Arnold distinguishes the two kinds of self clearly in his chapter "Barbarians, Philistines and Populace": "In almost all who have it, it [the humane spirit] is mixed with some infusion of the spirit of an ordinary self, some quantity of class-instinct, and even, as has been shown, of more than one class-instinct at the same time; so that, in general, the extrication of the best self, the predominance of the *humane* instinct, will very much depend upon its meeting, or not, with what is fitted to help and elicit it" (V, 146). Now Sue has the humane instinct, but she is also the "product of civilization" (III, ii) and is "easily repressed" (II, v); she therefore capitulates. Phillotson, too, has the humane instinct, which expresses itself in his initial liberation of Sue. He tells his friend Gillingham, "I have come to a conclusion: that it is wrong to so torture a fellow-creature any longer; and I won't be the inhuman wretch to do it, cost what it may!" though Gillingham warns him that "there's the question of neighbors and society." Indeed, Gillingham is the voice of society as he warns Phillotson that his action will "upset received opinion" and lead to "general domestic disintegration" (IV, iv). Phillotson, however, obeying his humane instinct, the expression of his best self, releases her anyway.

But Phillotson cannot maintain his position and cultivate his humane instinct in a society that not only does nothing to help and elicit it but actually does everything to repress it. Phillotson capitulates to society and develops his ordinary self, his Philistine self, as he had previously capitulated in forgoing his dream of a Christminster education and his dream of ordination. He is unable to persevere in his humane response of liberating Sue from a cruel social bondage to him when society brings the forces of repression to bear upon him. It is clear that when he takes her back, he is motivated in part by fleshly desire, but Gillingham recognizes that his action is the result also of a "reactionary spirit induced by the world's sneers" (VI, v). Society in its Hebraic emphasis on moral conduct continually pushes toward the re-establishment of the degrading marriages between Jude and Arabella and between Sue and Phillotson, and its success is sanctioned and applauded by the church in the persons of a vicar (VI, v) and a parson (VI, vii).

Jude, of course, is the antithesis of Phillotson. As a matter of fact, it is because Phillotson is used by Hardy as a foil for Jude that we can understand fully what Jude is. That is, we can see more clearly where Jude succeeds by seeing where Phillotson, who is identically motivated, fails. For example, Jude and Phillotson share the same desires, which are to be fulfilled in the same ways. The novel opens with the departure of the schoolmaster for Christminster, where he tells us, "My scheme, or dream, is to be a university graduate, and then to be ordained." Jude, of course, has the same dream. We are also told that Phillotson "thought of learning instrumental music. But the enthusiasm having waned he had never acquired any skill in playing" (I, i). Jude, on the other hand, cultivates his slight skill in music (III, x) and even learns to play the harmonium (III, i). Both men covet the same woman. They have the same desires, but where Phillotson continually submits, Jude continues to strive. Phillotson relinquishes his aspirations for a university degree and ordination and fills the socially acceptable role of schoolmaster, while Jude, cruelly thwarted by society, never gives up his "ruling passion" for culture. Phillotson also remarries Sue because his remarriage will provide social sanction for his renascent desire and further, as he says, because "it will set me right in the eyes of the clergy and orthodox laity, who have never forgiven me for letting her go. So I may get back in some degree into my old track" (VI, v). Jude, on the other hand, recognizes that a degraded Sue is not a fit object for his love, though he pities her. Phillotson, in other words, chooses his ordinary self rather than his best self; he chooses slavery rather than freedom. By the end of the novel he is simply the Philistine and has no life beyond the em-

bodiment of middle-class values. He has not cultivated his own personality but has accepted the roles required of him by society. He has,
like the speaker of "The Scholar-Gipsy," allowed society to determine
that he "half[-live] a hundred different lives." He has fitted himself for
the role among the mass of men that is described by Arnold in "The
Buried Life" (ll. 16-22) :

> I knew the mass of men concealed
> Their thoughts, for fear that if revealed
> They would by other men be met
> With blank indifference, or with blame reproved;
> I knew they lived and moved
> Tricked in disguises, alien to the rest
> Of men, and alien to themselves.

A man disguised, a man who becomes the roles he plays, Phillotson is
indeed alien to himself and alien to the rest of men.[17]

Jude is quite the reverse: equally thwarted by an indifferent and
sometimes hostile society, he never capitulates, never becomes enslaved
to the society that seeks to change his identity. Though he is denied a
university degree and ordination and finally Sue, he remains free to
cultivate his best self, what Arnold calls in "The Buried Life" his
"genuine self" (l. 36). He remains constant to his search after knowledge of his buried life, constant to his attempt to expand his powers and
add to his growth in wisdom. Unlike Phillotson, Jude refuses to give
in to society and accept what it will allow him to have, because to
accept only those goals that society allows is to become a slave. To compromise one's ideals is at once to deny one's idealism and to deny one's
"genuine self." Jude's choice is death rather than denial. In a world

---

[17] Hardy plays ironically on Phillotson's alienation. When Phillotson is most
free and most himself — after his liberation of Sue — he is defended by those
most alien to society: "It has been stated that Shaston was the anchorage of a
curious and interesting group of itinerants, who frequented the numerous fairs
and markets held up and down Wessex during the summer and autumn months.
Although Phillotson had never spoken to one of these gentlemen they now
nobly led the forlorn hope in his defence. The body included two cheapjacks,
a shooting-gallery proprietor and the ladies who loaded the guns, a pair of
boxing-masters, a steam-roundabout manager, two travelling broom-makers, who
called themselves widows, a gingerbread-stall keeper, a swing-boat owner, and
a 'test-your-strength' man" (IV, vi). They even do battle for him, a battle in
which the church warden is struck on the head with a map of Palestine, indicating perhaps that they are the least "Hebraised" members of the community.

that seeks to suppress the idealist and destroy idealism, a world that seeks to substitute the "ordinary self" for the "best self," the choice of death is a legitimate and affirmative one. Society is defeated by Jude's choice of freedom, by his choice of the "genuine self." Like Samson, Jude overcomes the Philistines in his death.

Earlier in this essay I suggested that Hardy's conclusion in *Jude* was both more affirmative and more heroic than Arnold's conclusion in "The Scholar-Gipsy." Here I hope to demonstrate more fully, and thereby clarify, the affirmative and heroic nature of Hardy's vision by comparing it to that in another Arnold poem — "Empedocles on Etna."

If Hardy and Arnold can be said to anatomize the modern condition in *Jude* and "Empedocles," those anatomies are strikingly similar. There is a similar contrast between country and city, and in both works the protagonist is a wanderer. There is the same restlessness, the same recognition of the debilitating effects of consciousness, the same sense of alienation. Though the modern condition is essentially the same in each, however, the responses of Jude and Empedocles to that condition differ.

Empedocles tells us that he has lived ever "Far from my own soul, far from warmth and light" (II, 396), and he fears a reincarnation that will force his unwilling return

> Back to this meadow of calamity,
> This uncongenial place, this human life;
> And in our individual human state
> Go through the sad probation all again,
> To see if we will poise our life at last,
> To see if we will now at last be true
> To our own only true, deep-buried selves,
> Being one with which we are one with the whole world....
> [II, 365-72]

Empedocles has obviously not been true to his deep-buried self. Though he has not enslaved himself to society, to be sure, he has enslaved himself nevertheless. He tells us,

> Slave of sense
> I have in no wise been; but slave of thought? ...
> And who can say: I have been always free,
> Lived ever in the light of my own soul? —
> I cannot.
> [II, 390-94]

Empedocles seeks the solution to his enslaved condition in suicide, which will set him free:

> And therefore, O ye elements! I know —
> Ye know it too — it hath been granted me
> Not to die wholly, not to be all enslaved.
> I feel it in this hour. The numbing cloud
> Mounts off my soul; I feel it, I breathe free.
>
> [II, 404-9]

Empedocles is apparently confused. Earlier, as we saw, he recognized that the way to become one with the whole world was to be "true / To our own only true, deep-buried selves." Now, only a few lines later, he seeks to become one with the universe by denying self. The confusion here about the character and motives of Empedocles is not clarified by Arnold's comment in the Yale manuscript of the poem: "Before he becomes the victim of depression and overtension of mind, to the utter deadness to joy, grandeur, spirit, and animated life, he desires to die; to be reunited with the universe, before by exaggerating his human side he has become utterly estranged from it"[18] I assume that "it" refers to "universe" rather than to "human side," that is, that Empedocles is concerned about becoming estranged from the universe, not about becoming estranged from his human side, and therefore chooses death. But earlier, freedom and oneness with the world were identified by Empedocles as the result of being true to our deep-buried self. Here that self is apparently denied in favor of oblivion.

In Jude's case there is not, I think, the same confusion. Jude's final choice is, like Empedocles', a choice of freedom over slavery, and that choice also necessitates his suicide.[19] But Jude, unlike Empedocles, has all along been free, as he has always chosen to be true to his best self rather than to his ordinary self. He has always chosen to be Jude rather

---

[18] Quoted in Arnold, *Poems*, ed. Allott, p. 191n.

[19] There can be little doubt that Jude's death is actually suicide. Hardy's early note about a young man who could not go to Oxford prescribed suicide, and in the novel Jude admits that he committed suicide. When he returns from having seen Sue for the last time, the following dialogue between Arabella and Jude takes place:

"You've done for yourself by this, young man," said she.

"I don't know whether you know it."

"Of course I do. I meant to do for myself."

"What — to commit suicide?"

"Certainly."

"Well, I'm blest! Kill yourself for a woman." [VI, ix]

than to be a Phillotson. Admittedly the slavery of Empedocles and the slavery that threatens Jude are not precisely the same: Empedocles is enslaved by thought, and Jude is threatened by Philistinism. And neither is the final freedom that Empedocles achieves the same as Jude's, as we shall see. But admitting the differences, one is still confronted in poem and novel by essentially similar assessments of the modern condition and its consequent dilemma — the choice of freedom or slavery in existential terms.

Both Jude and Empedocles choose freedom. But the freedom they choose and the death that choice requires are essentially different. Empedocles clearly chooses death as an escape. As we saw, the prospect of death for Empedocles lifts from his soul "the numbing cloud" and allows him to breathe free. But he is attracted to death because it promises him a kind of immortality: as he tells the elements, "it hath been granted me / Not to die wholly, not to be all enslaved" (II, 405-6). He appeals then to the vapors and fire of Etna, "Receive me, save me!" (II, 416). Empedocles chooses death to be free; that is, freedom is the consequence of his choice of death. Jude, on the other hand, chooses freedom and dies; that is, death is the consequence of his choice of freedom. Moreover, Empedocles chooses something outside himself. He predicates his salvation on something external. Jude, on the contrary, is concerned only with his choice of self, to which all other considerations are subsidiary and consequential. Jude does not choose immortality or salvation, as Empedocles does; he chooses only to be Jude. Empedocles really chooses the finite, the something else, and his choice, predicated on fear, is finally not free. Jude, in the choice of self, chooses freedom.[20]

Both Hardy and Arnold clearly understand the dilemma: they recognize the necessity to seek the buried life and to choose the best self. They recognize the necessity of the choice of freedom rather than slavery. And yet Arnold apparently cannot bring himself to follow his own argument to its logical extreme. In "The Scholar-Gipsy" he offers in place of a

[20] Cf. Kierkegaard's rather prolix assertion that the choice of self is the choice of freedom: "the only way I can manage to choose absolutely is by not choosing this or that. I choose the absolute. And what is the absolute? It is myself in my eternal worth. Nothing else but myself can I ever choose absolutely, for if I choose something else, I choose it as something finite, and so I do not choose it absolutely. . . . But what is this self of mine? At first sight, and as the first expression for it, I would answer: It is the most abstract thing of all, and yet in itself it is at the same time the most concrete thing — it is freedom." See Walter Lowrie, *Kierkegaard* (New York, 1962), I, 90.

heroic existential choice of despair, of self, and of freedom a pitiable longing for a vague and falsely romanticized past. In "Empedocles on Etna" the protagonist is brought to the point of choice only to choose a nebulous immortality or salvation, and even here his quasi-heroic choice is undermined by the poem itself, which ends with Callicles' song in praise of Apollo and his muses nine, who hymn "the Father / Of all things" (II, 461-62). Even in "Dover Beach," it seems to me, Arnold backs off from facing things squarely. In a world which he recognizes "Hath really neither joy, nor love, nor light, / Nor certitude, nor peace, nor help for pain," the speaker still requires solace from without. After denying the existence of love, he requires of his beloved, "Ah, love, let us be true / To one another!"[21] There seems to me in all these examples a reluctance on Arnold's part to withdraw from man all external support. And his reluctance seems to be the result of a lack of faith in man. The affirmation of palpably false external ideals strikes me as no affirmation at all but, rather, the consequence of an inability finally to affirm the validity of that very self which Arnold tells us so often we should seek. Though it may seem that I quarrel with Arnold for not doing what I wish he had done, I think my objection is really that he retreated from the conclusions to which the poems themselves lead. It is perhaps Arnold's unwillingness to face squarely and affirmatively what he sees that causes him so often to wander away from such a confrontation, for example, in what many consider the confused conclusions of "The Scholar-Gipsy" and "Stanzas from the Grand Chartreuse."[22] At any rate, Arnold's conclusions are significantly different from Hardy's.

Hardy, it seems to me, invariably carries his argument to its inevitable conclusion. There is no false hope held out at the end of *Jude,* and yet I think *Jude* ends more affirmatively than "Empedocles on Etna." There

---

[21] Sidney Feshbach admits the contradiction here but justifies the inclusion of love by reference to Empedocles, Arnold's apparent source: "But how to account for the poet's assertion of Love if Strife is everywhere present? Sadness, human misery, and spiritual emptiness have been presented so convincingly throughout the poem that a declaration of love in the last stanza appears sentimental, and only sentimental because without support of poetic or rational argument. But again in Empedocles can be found the justification, the philosophical argument that is not given in the poem, for discovering love in the present strife-torn age." See "Empedocles at Dover Beach," *Victorian Poetry,* IV (1966), 274.

[22] I refer here to the elaborate "Tyrian trader" simile at the end of "The Scholar-Gipsy" and a similarly elaborate simile about "children reared in shade" at the end of "Stanzas."

is no affirmation through the hope of salvation, no affirmation of or allusion to "the Father / Of all things." Jude simply and powerfully affirms himself in the face of the overwhelming rejection of him by the elements of life — by Arabella, by Sue, and by Christminster. Jude is left at the end of the novel without external support of any kind, finally thwarted in the attainment of any of his ideals, and yet he continues to affirm his idealism as the actions of his whole life have affirmed it in the face of an indifferent universe. In a novel that is "all contrasts" Hardy renders and underscores the affirmative nature of Jude's response by juxtaposing it to the antithetically negative responses of Phillotson and Sue. Phillotson capitulates, and Sue capitulates, but Jude remains constant in his defiance and is in stark contrast to them. They are defeated by a society that seeks to repress them. Jude alone remains free and to him is the victory.

My analysis of *Jude* I hope suggests the depth of Hardy's indebtedness to Arnold. Perhaps it also clarifies to some extent why Hardy's reaction to Arnold was often negative. In the year of Arnold's death Hardy recorded in his notebook the following entry: "The besetting sin of modern literature is its insincerity. Half its utterances are qualified, even contradicted, by an aside, and this particularly in morals and religion. When dogma has to be balanced on its feet by such hair-splitting as the late Mr. M. Arnold's it must be in a very bad way."[23] In *Jude* Hardy seems to have been at pains to reintroduce the sincerity he found lacking in modern literature, and in that process he reveals the complexity of his response to Matthew Arnold.

[23] *Life,* p. 215.

THIRTEEN

Conrad and Dostoyevsky

BY LEONARD ZELLAR

In Conrad's correspondence there are only two references to Dostoyevsky, both in letters to Edward Garnett and both emphatically negative. The most frequently cited is the one in which he calls Dostoyevsky "the grimacing, haunted creature." The context in which this judgment appears makes it all the more emphatic, for Conrad is contrasting Dostoyevsky to that most European of Russian novelists, Turgenev, who has "absolute sanity and the deepest sensibility, the clearest vision and the most exquisite responsiveness, penetrating insight and unfailing generosity of judgment, an unerring instinct for the significant, for the essential in human life and in the visible world, the clearest mind, the warmest heart, the largest sympathy — and all that in perfect measure!"[1] This estimate of Turgenev, with its emphasis on the sanity and measure of his artistry, stands in sharp contrast to Conrad's estimate, in the other letter to Garnett, of Dostoyevsky's most considerable creation, *The Brothers Karamazov*. "But it's an impossible lump of valuable matter. It's terrifically bad and impressive and exasperating. Moreover, I don't know what D[ostoyevsky] stands for or reveals, but I do know that he is too Russian for me. It sounds to me like some fierce mouthings from prehistoric ages."[2]

Another letter to Garnett has frequently been cited as evidence of Conrad's hatred not only of Dostoyevsky but of everything Russian. This one is in response to a letter from Garnett in which he warns Conrad that in a review of *Under Western Eyes* about to appear in *The Nation,* he accuses Conrad of prejudice against things Russian. Although the letter has been most usually cited in terms of Conrad's attack on Garnett (who had afforded him his entrée to literature and had been a close friend of years' standing) as the "Russian Embassador

[1] G. Jean-Aubry, ed., *Joseph Conrad: Life and Letters* (New York, 1927), II, 192.

[2] *Ibid.,* p. 140.

to the Republic of Letters," the crux of the letter, from another point of view, is his defense of the artistic objectivity of his treatment of his Russian subject matter, a defense that is amply supported by any sensitive and unbiased reading of the novel.

> But it is hard after lavishing a "wealth of tenderness" on Tekla and Sophia to be charged with the rather low trick of putting one's hate into a novel. If you seriously think that I have done that then my dear fellow let me tell you that you don't know what the accent of hate is. Is it possible that you haven't seen that in this book I am concerned with nothing but ideas, to the exclusion of everything else, with no arrière pensée of any kind. Or are you like the Italians (and most women) incapable of conceiving that anybody ever can speak without some subtle hidden purpose, for the sake of the thing said, with no desire of gratifying some small personal spite — or vanity.[3]

It would seem fair to say that although the public Conrad most certainly evidenced hatred of Russia and something less than admiration for Dostoyevsky, and that although there is ample evidence of his commitment to the Anglo-French movement in the art of fiction, there are, nevertheless, equally ample grounds for serious, even fundamental, qualifications. Conrad the artist possessed the capacity for objectivity inseparable from the practice of great art. Conrad the tragic artist had that dangerous understanding of, even attraction toward, the abyss that is the *sine qua non* of a successful pursuit of the tragic vision. He, like his tragic heroes, was not one of those disdained by destiny; he was by experience and by imaginative vision mindful of all that life "may contain of perfidy, of violence, of terror."[4]

Now the vast majority of references to Dostoyevsky in Conrad criticism and scholarship have to do with the unavoidable similarities between *Under Western Eyes* and *Crime and Punishment*. As Frederick Karl has observed, "It is difficult to believe that Conrad could have written *Under Western Eyes* without Dostoyevsky's *Crime and Punishment* before him as a model."[5] But such associations are usually limited to parallels between characters and situations and to some important verbal echoes. The possibility that beneath these surface similarities

---

[3] Edward Garnett, ed., *Letters from Joseph Conrad — 1895-1924* (Indianapolis, 1928), pp. 232-33.

[4] Joseph Conrad, *The Nigger of the "Narcissus" and Typhoon and Other Stories* (London, 1950), p. 19.

[5] Frederick Karl, *A Reader's Guide to Joseph Conrad* (New York, 1960), p. 212.

there may lie more fundamental similarities of vision is rarely admitted;
in fact, the emphasis is usually on the irreconcilable dissimilarities.
Karl, for instance, punctuates his enumeration of the parallels by indicating that the two authors differed "obviously in ideology and political ideas."[6] Jocelyn Baines's summary of parallels is repeatedly qualified in terms of the fundamental differences between the two authors.[7]

This prevailing notion of the conflict between the two visions seems
to be based upon three factors: (1) the testimony of the correspondence, which we have already looked at; (2) the identification of Conrad's literary precedents primarily in terms of the art novel — his preoccupation with technical concerns, which would align him with the
Flaubert-Turgenev-James tradition; and (3) the biographical background that provides a basis for his Russophobia.

Although there is no question of Conrad's concern for the *mot juste,*
for strategies of point of view, and for the rendering of character and
theme through concrete incident and imagery, there is, of course, no
necessary opposition between such technical concerns and the exploration of the tragic vision. And it is Conrad's tragic vision that assigns
him to the line extending from Melville (whom he also abominated)
and Dostoyevsky through Faulkner. Still in the area of technique, the
use of mythopoeic devices such as the night sea journey and of character doubling is *at least* as important as his cultivation of those technical
devices more closely associated with the Flaubert-Turgenev-James tradition. More important, these devices serve as vehicles to explore the
demonic and human duality, which in turn are inextricably bound to
the tragic vision. It is also worth noting — despite Conrad critics' usual
assumption of Dostoyevsky's formlessness — that the testimony of the
recently published Dostoyevsky notebooks and of such studies as Robert
Louis Jackson's *Dostoyevsky's Quest for Form* seem to indicate that
Dostoyevsky's concern for the art of the novel was hardly less intense
or less subtle than that of his western compeers.[8]

The biographical evidence would seem at first glance to establish a
firm, even adamant, foundation for Conrad's hatred of things Russian.
The Russian oppression of his native Poland and Conrad's tendency
toward a mystic nationalism in themselves provide obvious and ade-

[6] *Ibid.*

[7] Jocelyn Baines, *Joseph Conrad: A Critical Biography* (New York, 1960),
pp. 369ff.

[8] Robert Louis Jackson, *Dostoyevsky's Quest for Form* (New Haven, Conn.,
1966).

quate sources of his Russophobia. Add to this his parents' martyrdom to the Polish cause against Russia, and the case becomes more intense. Finally, his own Russian citizenship constituted a barrier to almost any career he might have set out upon in his young manhood. To exacerbate the situation almost beyond the possibility of any tolerance Conrad might have been able to summon up for Dostoyevsky, there is the fact that in his fiction Dostoyevsky's contempt for the Poles is both strong and consistent.

Conrad's presumed western bias, on the other hand, is at least equivocal. As we shall see below, his criticism of western individualistic, rational, technical, material values is powerful and persists throughout the effective portion of his career. There is evidence, furthermore, that his rejection of Panslavism — even the Russian variety — may have been more superficial than substantial. Referring to Conrad's letter to Galsworthy in which he averred that in the composition of *Under Western Eyes* he was "trying to capture the very soul of things Russian,"[9] Albert Guerard remarks, "But he was at least briefly captured by that soul, and on the devil's side without knowing it."[10] On the same topic Bernard Meyer observes:

> This remarkable capacity to steep himself deeply in the atmosphere and feelings of a supposedly hated nation is indeed arresting, and causes one to wonder whether in the more obscure reaches of his mind there may not have lurked a hidden sense of identification with that nation as an expression of fundamental Slavic affiliation. Hay brings forward evidence in support of such a view, pointing out that while throughout his later writing life Conrad repeatedly insisted that Poland was a Western nation, during his sea-faring days he had apparently advanced the idea that Poland might one day become the leading *Slavic* nation in the Panslavonic movement. "What interests us here," she adds, "is that Conrad had obviously embraced for a certain time certain aspects of the Russian mystique."[11]

As for the loyalty to the memory of his martyred father, here we encounter perhaps the richest of the biographical ambiguities. The ambivalence of his attitude toward his father can most fruitfully be approached in terms of the Korzeniowski-Bobrowski dualism. This dual-

---

[9] Jean-Aubry, ed., *Joseph Conrad*, II, 64.
[10] Albert Guerard, *Conrad the Novelist* (Cambridge, Mass., 1958), p. 244.
[11] Bernard Meyer, *Joseph Conrad: A Psychoanalytic Biography* (Princeton, N.J., 1967), p. 213. The reference within the quotation is to Eloise Knapp Hay, *The Political Novels of Joseph Conrad* (Chicago, 1963), p. 298.

ism is, in turn, closely related — probably profoundly related — to the central conflicts out of which he forged his tragic vision.[12] It is certainly a factor in the Razumov-Haldin relationship in *Under Western Eyes* and is the thematic justification for the technical device of character doubling.

Those critics who have perceived the fundamental similarity of the visions of these two great novelists have been led to that perception out of a sense of the tragic vision which they share. Gustav Morf, for instance, in a single passage underlines the combined Slavonic-tragic vision of the two authors:

> This ever-present sense of the unreality of existence, the perpetual wonder at existence, has, in Joseph Conrad, an intensity which I would not hesitate to call Slavonic. We Westerners have not introspection enough to wonder eternally at the same problems, and to pass and re-pass in our minds the same questions. When we recognize them as in-soluble, we lay them aside, sometimes after having made a theory of them. Conrad was racially incapable of this. He was brooding over them throughout his life. At heart, he was a mystic like Dostoevsky.[13]

And Douglas Hewitt asserts, "His relationship to Dostoevsky seems to me, indeed, to be a close one and most significant where there is least question of 'influence.' The more we compare them the more do we see certain of Conrad's limitations, but the more, also, his achievements."[14] Finally, Albert Guerard offers perhaps the most telling statement of Conrad's position in modern fiction: "By artistic intention [Conrad] may belong, as he wished, to the race of Turgenev, and Flaubert, or even to that of Marryat. But as a writer and creative temperament he evokes rather Dostoevsky . . . and Faulkner, the most distinguished of his direct successors."[15]

In the light of the foregoing, then, it is perhaps not mere perversity to insist that despite Conrad's clear and intense dislike for Dostoyevsky, there are remarkable and significant similarities in their fiction. There is, as we have seen, no avoiding the likenesses between Razumov and

---

[12] On this subject see especially Meyer, *Joseph Conrad,* and Robert R. Hodges, *The Dual Heritage of Joseph Conrad* (The Hague, 1967).

[13] Gustav Morf, *The Polish Heritage of Joseph Conrad* (London, 1930), p. 85.

[14] Douglas Hewitt, *Joseph Conrad: A Reassessment* (Cambridge, 1952), p. 129.

[15] Guerard, *Conrad the Novelist,* p. 2.

Raskolnikov, both of whom have separated themselves from their fellow men in keeping with a belief in their superiority based upon a morality of intellect. Without pushing this point, it is safe to generalize that both Dostoyevsky and Conrad repeatedly dramatized the inevitable justice that life deals out to intellectual audacity. Conrad's Decoud, Razumov, and Heyst and Dostoyevsky's Ivan Karamazov, Raskolnikov, and Stavrogin fall into the pattern. This justice is, furthermore, not meted out by society but is a matter of the relationships between the character, his deepest self, and certain fundamental aspects of reality.

Now I wish to argue here a rather more fundamental correspondence between the two writers than has heretofore been advanced. I believe that it goes close to but just short of the heart of the vision of each author — at which point they become radically separate. For Dostoyevsky surrendered himself to a supreme and comprehensive illusion that Conrad found anathema. They share, nevertheless, a sense of the existential quality of life; a belief in the ultimate efficacy of simple, earned value; a number of political and social aversions, almost always on the same grounds; and a sacramental vision of life. But Conrad's vision is finally humanistically oriented, Dostoyevsky's theistically. The leap of faith separates them. But up to the point of that leap, in the vast area of Dostoyevsky where the liberal humanist can marvel and admire, there is more of the essential Conrad than in all the Flauberts, Turgenevs, and Jameses put together.

The germs that Raskolnikov dreams of at the end of *Crime and Punishment* cause men to go mad with pride and self-will. This is the disease of modern, western, secular civilization, and that civilization, in Dostoyevsky's fiction, is like a plague out of Europe. It appears frequently, as with Raskolnikov, Stavrogin, and Ivan Karamazov, as a fever that either purifies or kills. Similarly in Conrad it appears as a physical condition of rot or sterility. In both Dostoyevsky's and Conrad's worlds it comes between men and those elements in life that are the sources of primal energies.

The phenomenon of secular religion is, in a sense, the starting point of Dostoyevsky's criticism of the modern world. Pride of intellect, individualism, democracy, materialism, science — in general, those qualities associated with middle-class dominance, and the qualities that Conrad reacted so deeply against — are all parts of what Dostoyevsky would call the religion of humanity. This religion is the creation of a secular, middle-class world that has turned its back on the traditional sources of value, both religious and social. The middle class comes off consistently badly in Dostoyevsky, and ultimately for the same reasons as in Conrad: its values and activities are cheap and banal because they lack firm foundation, because they are founded on expediency.

Looked at rationally, the world and the life of man are indeed chaotic. From this point of view that which is secular, individual, and scientific is indeed preferable. Furthermore, from this point of view man's condition is amenable, perhaps perfectable, and man's pride in his science, technology, and political and social institutions is justified. Such a view is not, however, consistent with perhaps the most important view that Dostoyevsky and Conrad share — that life is a larger unity than the merely rational point of view can comprehend, that there is a dimension to the personality which is of equal validity and probably more force than the rational. Both writers also defer more to tradition than is the wont of modern western man. Different as the two traditions are, the accumulated experience of life at its most fundamental level — among peasants and among the men who go down to the sea in ships (and, for that matter, among Faulkner's Negroes) — yields simple, tested, enduring values, vastly different from and inaccessible to modern man's intellectual formulations.

When Ivan's Grand Inquisitor asks Christ, "Didst Thou forget that man prefers peace and even death, to freedom of choice in the knowledge of good and evil?"[16] he speaks as the exemplar of secular religion. For such an attitude, considering man only from the rational and material points of view, robs him of not only his spiritual dignity but also his moral dignity — which means also his tragic dignity. By invoking the "true lie" on a grand scale, the Grand Inquisitor lulls men into that stupor in which they cease to exert pressure against the destructive element and are absorbed into it. This becomes clearer through the parody in a book like *Brave New World*, where Henry Ford has been elevated to deity, where men live like little children with all their physical and emotional needs attended to, where tragedy is impossible because men no longer have the responsibility, or privilege, of decision, where the moral fiber is as flimsy and shoddy as the acetate garments the characters wear.

Also like Conrad, Dostoyevsky prefers his colorfully and impressively damned characters to his smug, satisfied, middle-class characters. There are not many characters in fiction more despicable than the Luzhin of

---

[16] Feodor Dostoyevsky, *The Brothers Karamazov*, tr. Constance Garnett (New York, 1950), p. 302.

Crime and Punishment and the Rakitin of *The Brothers*. Theirs is indeed a bourgeois world where everything is for sale from body to soul. He also ridicules such comfortable and sham rebels and revolutionaries as Miusov of *The Brothers* and Stepan Trofimovitch of *The Possessed*. Conrad's comfortable, ridiculous, and essentially bourgeois anarchists have their equivalents in Dostoyevsky. And they are also morally equivalent, for the real anarchists in both Dostoyevsky and Conrad are moral anarchists.

Without getting into the more philosophical and theological aspects of Dostoyevsky's vision, he, like Conrad, saw secular religion, paradoxically, as a belittlement of man. Based on a sense of human superiority, it makes man god over a cheap and shoddy world. Furthermore, by ignoring spiritual and imaginative possibilities in man's nature, it fashions man after a distinctly burger model. Most important, it reduces man morally by narrowing the range of his moral responsibility. The psychologically oriented defense attorney of *The Brothers* attempts to prove that it is not Dmitri but society that is responsible for the crime. This is, of course, moral anarchy with a vengeance; it is also, according to Dostoyevsky and Conrad, the drift of our world. But Dmitri, who, unlike the defense attorney, knows that he is technically innocent, enlarges his freedom and his dignity in realizing and accepting his moral responsibility.

If there is a larger justice, then, what is it? What is that justice which life deals out to the intellectual audacity of the Ivans and Raskolnikovs and Decouds and Razumovs? What is its source?

For both authors that larger justice inheres in a sacramental view of life. Life as a whole; it must be accepted and loved for its totality; it must be lived existentially. Analysis and abstraction have the taint of death upon them. Just as deadly are rebellion and its pale cousin resignation, for life requires commitment by the very reason of its unity and wholeness. Life is also existential in the sense that it is immediate, here and now. You cannot divide people into classes as Raskolnikov does without abstracting and killing life, as he does kill his own soul. You cannot love man in the mass as Ivan and his Grand Inquisitor would; you have, like Swift, to love Tom, Dick, and Harry. Only the individual carries life and deserves love. Ivan and Decoud murder life by abstracting it, by giving only a part — and that a minor part — of themselves. Charles Gould and Nostromo also murder life by giving themselves to abstractions while Mrs. Gould and Giselle stand by.

After Siberia had disillusioned Dostoyevsky of his Schillerian idealism and his dream of a secular utopia, after he had had his initiation to the abyss in the Siberian house of the dead, he could never free himself from the knowledge of his underground self. Yet he yearned toward the lofty ideal of man embodied in characters like Prince Mishkin and Father Zossima. If this dualism tortured him in his personal life and drove him into the arms of the church and autocracy in search for external order, it provided Dostoyevsky the artist with the breadth and intensity of vision out of which tragedy is fashioned. That vision relates the abyss to the loftiest ideal; it embraces the totality of life and culminates in an affirmation that transcends simpler personal and temporal solutions.

Although Conrad had most certainly seen his share of perfidy, violence, and terror before he went to the Congo in 1890, that experience seems to have confirmed his vision of the abyss. "Before the Congo I was just a mere animal," he once remarked to Garnett.[17] For Conrad, as for Marlow, "It was the farthest point of navigation and the culminating point of my experience. It seemed to throw a kind of light on everything about me — and into my thoughts."[18] Like Dostoyevsky's Siberian experience, it opened up to him the awesome grandeur of the depth and breadth of human experience. "The mind of man is capable of anything — because everything is in it, all the past as well as all the future. What was there after all? Joy, fear, sorrow, devotion, valour, rage — who can tell? but truth — truth stripped of its cloak of time. Let the fool gape and shudder — the man knows, and can look on without a wink."[19] As Lord Jim confronts his dark double, Brown — as Ivan had confronted Smerdyakov, Raskolnikov Svidrigailov, Mishkin Rogozhin — all that separates them is a narrow, muddy stream. Marlow tells how Brown related to him "the opening of this strange conversation between these two men, separated only by the muddy bed of a creek, but standing on the opposite poles of that conception of life that includes all mankind — . . . ."[20]

During Marlow's conversation with Jewel, he had "for a moment . . . a view of a world that seemed to wear a vast and dismal aspect of disorder." But "it was only a moment! I went back into my shell directly.

[17] Baines, *Joseph Conrad*, p. 119.
[18] Joseph Conrad, *Youth, Heart of Darkness, and The End of the Tether* (London, 1946), p. 51.
[19] *Ibid.*, pp. 96-97.
[20] Joseph Conrad, *Lord Jim* (London, 1946), pp. 380-81.

One *must* — don't you know? — though I seemed to have lost all my words in the chaos of dark thoughts I had contemplated for a second or two beyond the pale."[21] And indeed one *must*. To sustain oneself indefinitely in a tension between heaven and hell is to court insanity. One needs only to read through some of the letters Conrad wrote at the conclusion of his creative efforts — especially *Nostromo* — to realize how badly he needed to return to a more or less normal world. It would seem only decent that in return for the unrestricted view of life he has given us in his fiction, we grant his right to return to his shell. A conservative country gentleman with more than his share of petty financial, medical, and family problems might very well resent the intrusion of the "grimacing, haunted creature," who was in a very real sense his own dark double.

[21] *Ibid.*, p. 313.

Notes on Contributors

LEE T. LEMON is professor of English at the University of Nebraska. His main area of interest has been in literary theory, on which he has written *The Partial Critics* and many other works.

GEORGE GOODIN, associate professor of English at Southern Illinois University in Carbondale, has been working on politics and the novel. The present essay was read at the Walter Scott Bicentenary Conference at the University of Edinburgh.

MARY ALICE BURGAN, associate professor of English at Indiana University, has published several essays on teaching the short story and is currently working on a book about money in the English novel.

DONALD RACKIN, associate professor of English at Temple University, is working on the flux-stasis motif in Victorian literature. His article on *Alice in Wonderland* was the 1966 *PMLA* Prize Essay.

CHARLES I. PATTERSON, JR., professor of English at the University of Georgia, has written several studies of nineteenth-century literary criticism and has recently published *The Daemonic in the Poetry of John Keats*.

GEORGE J. WORTH is chairman of the Department of English at the University of Kansas. Among his studies of Victorian literature is *James Hannay: His Life and Works*.

MIKE HOLLINGTON is lecturer in comparative literature at the University of East Anglia. For the Cambridge edition of Milton he has recently written the introduction to Books XI and XII of *Paradise Lost*.

ROGER M. SWANSON is assistant professor of English at Arizona State University. He has been working on moral problems in Victorian fiction.

WILLIAM E. BUCKLER, professor of English at New York University, was formerly Dean of the College and Vice-Chancellor for Academic Planning. For many years he has edited the *Victorian Newsletter* and has just completed his fifth Riverside edition: *Selections from the Victorian Poets.*

LEON GOTTFRIED, professor of English at Washington University in St. Louis, wrote the present essay while teaching at the University of Malaya, Kuala Lumpur. He is the author of *Matthew Arnold and the Romantics* and is currently at work on Walter Pater.

MARGARET CONROW is assistant professor of English at Kansas State University. Her major interest has been in the Victorian novel and in the interrelationships among literature and the other arts.

WARD HELLSTROM, professor of English at the University of Florida, has written widely on Victorian literature and is the author of *On the Poems of Tennyson.*

LEONARD ZELLAR, professor of English at Sam Houston State University, is now in the process of completing his work on Joseph Conrad.

Index